中國事物
THINGS CHINESE

THINGS CHINESE

RITA AERO

DOLPHIN BOOKS
DOUBLEDAY & COMPANY, INC.
GARDEN CITY, NEW YORK 1980

The text in this book was set in 10 point Palatino. The typography was done by Good Times Graphics in San Francisco. The Chinese typography was set by China Cultural Printing Co. in San Francisco's Chinatown. The book and cover were designed and executed by the author.

The cover art is from the Metropolitan Museum of Art in New York. It is a five-clawed dragon, one of a set of four, probably used to decorate the robe of an emperor during the eighteenth century. The red impression on the cover is from an ivory seal. The fine-patterned characters are a poem which translates: "Two men are close friends, one living in the north, the other in the south. The one in the north sees the trees budding, the other watches the golden cloud against the twilight; both are thinking of each other...when can they have a drink together and discuss their literature?"

LIBRARY OF CONGRESS CATALOG CARD NUMBER: 79-6852
ISBN: 0-385-15673-1

FIRST EDITION

Acknowledgments

It's possible I might not have attempted a project of this scope were it not for the superior research facility and staff at the Asian Art Museum in San Francisco. I am especially indebted to the head of the Asian Art Library, Fred Cline, who encouraged this book from its very start and then went on to make certain that I had all the information and help that I could possibly need. After the manuscript was completed, the Senior Curator at the Museum, Clarence Shangraw, took the time to read, edit, and clarify certain points. His contributions, both visual and editorial, are an important part of the finished book.

Perhaps the most rewarding part of this project came in working with an excellent research, writing, and editing team. I am grateful to Alexander Besher, Richard Brzustowicz, George Csicsery, Philip Hood, Kathy Ingley, Laura Israel, Daphne Lucke, and Walter Schaefer for their contributions to this book. I am indebted to Cheryl Haynes who dealt with the manuscript on a day-to-day basis and made thoughtful suggestions that were invaluable to this work; to Stephanie Rick and Jim Webb for their editorial help; to Tan Chang and Sharon Deveaux for their contributions to the illustrations; and to Scott Bartlett and Judy Maas for their assistance with the book's design.

Special thanks go to Susan Schwartz, my editor, whose enthusiasm and encouragement created that rare momentum so important to good beginnings; and to Sheldon Fogelman, my agent and adviser, who always makes sure that everything turns out fine in the end.

And, finally, a number of my friends, family, and associates were particularly supportive while I abandoned myself to this work. They know who they are. I thank them.

SOURCES OF ILLUSTRATIONS

The People's Republic of China is making an effort to introduce a standard romanization (which most approximates Mandarin pronunciation). The *pinyin* system was recently adopted by the United Nations Conference on Standardization of Geographical Names. The spelling of most Chinese cities and provinces throughout the text of this book are in *pinyin* resulting in Beijing instead of Peking and Guangzhou rather than Canton. Other Chinese names and words are spelled using a modified Wade-Giles system. The actual Chinese ideograms for the major topics in the book are shown in the right hand margins in the order that they appear.

中國事物
THINGS CHINESE

中國事物

INTRODUCTION

In planning this work I had to adjust constantly to the immense scope of China's history and achievements. We are dealing with a culture that possesses the oldest continuously spoken language on earth, an ingenious culture that invented—and discarded—moveable type more than four centuries before the idea struck Gutenberg. As a people long familiar with abrupt social change, the Chinese have seen, for example, prohibition enacted and repealed more than 41 times in the past 2,400 years. Perhaps because the Chinese have survived almost every possible adversity, they have an inherent sense of destiny that extends well beyond the life of any individual, any ruling government. With a cultural vision that was sustained through many successive generations, and consumed countless individual lives, they managed to erect the only man-made structure on earth visible from the moon: the Great Wall.

The view of China presented in this book provides a multifaceted impression. No final conclusions are drawn, no real plot unfolds, no continuous viewpoint is established. The book might be opened at random, a page read here and there, and the original intention would remain intact: to present China in a geometric form rather than in the traditional linear form. When one experiences China for the first time, one experiences on diverse levels: the smells, the faces, the tiny alleys winding away from the main street, that certain feeling of vast numbers, the shops and arguing and money changing hands, laughter and curious looks, the taste of strange foods and stranger sounding words, bright, unreadable signs and posters, the upward tilt of a tiled roof, and people in all directions on their way everywhere.

To portray China visually I used some of the earliest photographs taken there—the first views of China brought to America. Although recent photographs are now available, I was touched by the innocence captured in these older relics and the almost clinical approach of the turn-of-the-century photographers experimenting with their new technology. Most of the graphic illustrations come from Ch'ing Dynasty Chinese compendia, a form of text historically favored by this practical culture.

I started in my research looking for the differences between the Chinese and the Americans—and they were not difficult fo find. Most fundamentally, as societies we *think* differently. We seem to perceive nature and relate to our cultural realities from opposite ends of the philosophical spectrum. The Chinese viewpoint begins in the singular man and expands to his relationship with all of society and all of nature. Responsibility in China always rests within the individual—society becomes a mass of individual relationships, while individual relationships become the structural units of government. In America we perceive ourselves first as a social ideal, and our potential individuality filters down from this ideal. Responsibility rests within the central government, which in turn is more an ideal structure than a mass of individuals. Consequently there are aspects of nature, of society, and of our own selves that often do not "fit" the ideal. In most Western religions we start with a weak, flawed man attempting to appease a perfect, all-powerful God. The Chinese begin with a good man trying to harmonize with an ever-changing deity or "principle." In government, the man in the West may evade the central lawmaking body, whereas in China one's fellow individuals embody the law and are in fact responsible for one another. Co-operation and self-government come a little easier in China; individual achievement and philanthropy are more common in the West.

And yet it is from the midst of these great differences in thought that so sharply emerged the similarities between the Americans and the Chinese. I was struck by the emotional congruence of our cultures. Both Americans and Chinese are exceptionally self-sufficient and courageous. Furthermore, the Chinese and the Americans share a warm sense of humor. We are both fond of jokes, easily amused, and are both quite sentimental. Temperamentally, we are possessed of a drive to learn quickly, while each of our cultures tends to apply our sciences in the most pragmatic manner.

An important and often overlooked reason for our emotional similarities is that our two nations, on opposite sides of the planet, are geographically alike. We have virtually the same land masses and very similar climates. There is little difference climatically between Canton and Miami, Wuhan and New Orleans, or Peking and Philadelphia. The influence of such a large, varied, and rich geographical environment shapes the evolution of our cultures and defines our instincts for survival. Underneath our differences we are reflexively parallel in our feelings of pride, unity, and confidence.

As we move together into the twenty-first century I think it's important for us to realize that the Chinese are thoroughly fascinated by Americans. The Chinese are endlessly enthralled by our way of life, our technologies, even our passing fashions. Furthermore, they are preoccupied with the question, "What do the Americans think of us?" They have, just in the past few years, thrown their doors open to America, that they might get a closer look at us and that we may experience them. It is a tender, vulnerable time in history and one that historians and philosophers have long anticipated: the true meeting of East and West—the meeting of the youngest, most vital, and the oldest, most durable civilizations on earth. Such an event, in a world this size, could only happen in this technological age, an age when instant communications, satellite realities, and effortless travel make us one.

Rita Acro
San Francisco 1980

中國事物

ABACUS

The standard Chinese abacus looks simple: a rectangular frame holding between twelve and thirty rods or wires, each of which has strung on it seven flattened beads. The frame and its rods are separated into upper and lower areas by a space bar: Two beads on each rod are above the bar, and five are below it. Each of the rods or columns is like a "place" in our decimal notation, but the values given to the places can be changed as needed.

The earliest reference to the abacus is probably in *Shu Shu Chi I*, or *Memoir on Some Traditions of the Mathematical Art*, which traditionally dates from the end of the second century A.D. The early references do not seem to describe the modern abacus, however, which is first illustrated in a book dated 1436, and first described in detail in 1593. The Chinese abacus is useful not just for addition, subtraction, multiplication, and division, but also for more complex procedures such as extracting square roots and cube roots. It is still widely used for commercial purposes throughout the Far East. In the spring of 1980 the Chinese produced the first electronic abacus. The calculator-abacus combines features of both digital mathematics and the ancient abacus.

ACUPUNCTURE

Acupuncture is a uniquely Chinese medical practice. In acupuncture therapy, special needles are inserted into various points on the surface of the body, depending on the desired effects, with the intention of altering the flow and distribution of a certain kind of energy called *ch'i*, along a set of channels usually called "meridians."

Acupuncture has been used as a therapeutic technique for perhaps 2½ millen-

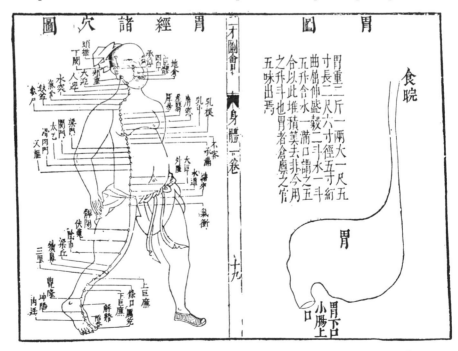

ACUPUNCTURE CHART FROM THE *Wei Ching* OR *Treatise on the Stomach*. FROM THE *San Ts'ai T'u Hui*, A CHINESE ENCYCLOPEDIA OF THE EARLY SEVENTEENTH CENTURY.

nia. It is treated in some detail in one of the oldest Chinese medical texts, the *Nei Ching (Book of Medicine)*, where some 360 points are described. Although over 650 different points have been recognized and described, only about 450 of these are currently used, and of those only about 100 are commonly employed.

Western studies of acupuncture treat it primarily, if not completely, as a method of anesthetizing patients before surgery, or for relieving chronic pain. This is far from the traditional Chinese understanding of the technique, since in China acupuncture has always been regarded not just as a way of alleviating symptoms, but also as a way of curing or preventing illness.

The anatomy or physiology on which acupuncture is based make little sense from the viewpoint of Western anatomical and physiological investigations. Western anatomy is concerned with the parts of the body and their connections; Chinese anatomy is concerned with the interplay of a number of functional systems that are adjusted through acupuncture.

Acupuncture, in New China, is becoming an important therapy in mental-health care as well as in physical applications. Electro-acupuncture has recently been introduced, where a slight current of five to eight volts is sent through the needles in order to stimulate a particular acupuncture point. All modern hospitals in China have acupuncture facilities.

[See DOCTORS.]

AGRICULTURE

It is almost certain that Chinese civilization was founded in the practice of agriculture. The plethora of Chinese religious practices and nature gods, and the organization of China's writing as well as its social structure are all indebted to a primeval agricultural society. The Chinese claim that the art of agriculture was taught to them by the legendary Emperor Shen Nung (2838-2698 B.C.). An ancient ceremony in which the Emperor plowed a "sacred field with a highly decorated plow" was performed annually until as late as 1900.

Chinese agriculture may be characterized by the expression, "the economy of the minute," for in truly remarkable ways it is the most efficient (if not always the most modern) in the world. Over 80 per cent of China's current population is engaged in agricultural work, and in former times the percentage was even greater. While today there are over 50,000 agricultural communes housing and employing an average of 14,700 people each, the more common organization of farming has always been based on the small family plot "smaller than the area needed to house an American farmer's tools." At the turn of the century it was estimated that if the Chinese had been employing Western styles and standards of agriculture the country could support only one half of its 1900 population. But even with nearly one billion people China is self-sufficient in food.

The most important products of Chinese agriculture are rice, grown to the south of the Yangtze, and millet and wheat, produced mostly in the North. The rice fields are located in any low-lying ground area or on terraced hillsides where sufficient quantities of water can be diverted to the walled-off sections. Perfection of dozens of irrigation techniques has led to the Chinese farmer's ability to produce amid nearly any conditions. Another important factor in Chinese agriculture is the great care taken to nurture growing plants with fertilizer. It has been said that nothing in China is wasted. Everything from human excrement to fish bones and the charred paper from exploded firecrackers is collected in various types of containers and turned in-

算盤

針灸

農業

中
國
事
物

to fertilizer, which is fed to the growing plants rather than added to soil before planting. All precautions are taken to maintain the fertility of the soil, which in the great river basins is also aided by flooding, which leaves rich alluvial deposits behind. The result is that as many as three to four rice harvests a year occur in some regions. In the southern parts of China the sunken rice paddies are separated by narrow raised embankments, on the slopes of which fruit trees and vegetables are grown.

China is now the world's largest producer of food grains. Hemp and silk production are also highly developed areas of Chinese agriculture—especially the silk farms of Guangdong Province. In northern and western China, the drier, cooler climate is conducive to large-scale livestock production.

[See IRRIGATION and RICE.]

ANCIENT IRRIGATED RICE FIELD. C. 1900

ALCHEMY

There is evidence that the Chinese were manipulating chemicals as early as the fourth century B.C. in the belief that it was possible to extend the length of human life, and even to attain material immortality. Alchemy was in practice the art of making elixirs of longevity and immortality. Through the systems of numerology, Taoist mysticism, and the traditional reverence for Nature, the alchemists believed that their work would result in success if it duplicated, or mimicked exactly the much slower processes in Nature. A real elixir could be found by analogy. The most perfect (least subject to decay) substance known was gold; therefore by association with gold, men could aspire to the same durability and longevity as the perfect metal.

The alchemists set about to produce gold from cinnabar (mercuric sulfide) in a metaphorical process that would lead to immortality of the soul. The father of Chinese alchemy was Wei Po-yang, author of *The Threefold Concordance* in A.D. 140. Even more noteworthy is the great synthesizer Ko Hung (A.D. 260-340), author of the *Pao-p'u Tzu*, or "*Old Sober-sides.*" The number of existing alchemical treatises from before the tenth century A.D. is between one hundred and two hundred. Most of these provide detailed instructions concerning the preparation of the "elixir." The sage able to produce the elixir was thought to be immediately rewarded by becoming a *hsien*, or "immortal."

Throughout its history, Chinese alchemy seems, however, to be aimed less at producing the results that would be the natural goals of a more scientifically minded tradition, than with the precise imitation of perceived patterns and processes in nature. Very often the alchemical texts in the later Taoist mystical period are instructions for internal alchemical processes rather than for processes one would pursue in a laboratory. Alchemy was linked to the understanding of the Five Elements and the passive (*yin*) and active (*yang*) principles, as well as to meditation, gymnastic, sexual, dietetic, and breathing disciplines. All of these together led to immortality, but alchemy provided the metaphoric key for the manipulation of external forces in order to re-create the perfection of nature.

[See LONGEVITY and ELIXIR OF IMMORTALITY.]

ALLIGATORS

Alligators are found occasionally on the Yangtze River and are indigenous to China. It is felt that perhaps some of the qualities attributed to the benevolent dragon by the Chinese derive from alligators. The emergence of the alligator from hibernation is seen as a good influence that heralds the coming of spring.

AMULETS AND CHARMS

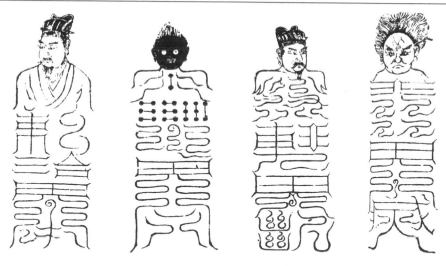

CHARMS FROM THE *Taoist Canon*, A THIRTEENTH CENTURY TEXT, DEPICTING THE MASTERS OF THE FOUR DIRECTIONS. THESE WERE USED TO NULLIFY CURSES.

The use of charms in China originates with the belief in benevolent spirits and in evil spirits. In order to check or restrain the malevolent influence of evil spirits named *kuei*, the Chinese developed an extremely elaborate system of charms to control them. The charms are all designed to command, expel, or counteract the evil done by the *kuei*. They are used for everything from protection against disease to the guarantee of a happy marriage. The charms are used in every one of China's great religions, but the first organized compendium of charms is attributed to Chang Tao-

13

中
國
事
物

ling, the first official head of the Taoist Church, who has been called "Heavenly Master" by his followers. Chang is said to have received a complete knowledge of charms and spells from the Taoist sage Lao Tzu. Chang then retired to the mountains and wrote a book on charms to expel and kill spirits, ghosts, and evil influences to restore the order of Heaven and Earth.

There are charms for every event and occasion. They are formed of materials as diverse as metallic pendants to be hung around the necks of children and paper charms that are pinned to walls or burned. There is a "charm from Hades for the soul of a person harassed by evil spirits" and a "charm for a person poisoned by doctors' prescriptions." There is a "charm of universal efficacy," as well as both Buddhist and Taoist charms curing all diseases. There are charms for the protection of one's possessions, and for the increase of one's wealth. Most often, Chinese charms take the form of colored pieces of paper inscribed with magical words invoking the assistance of a god or benevolent spirit to quell the influence of an evil one.

While numerous charms exist to undo evil, there are also those that function as a sort of insurance, so that no harm will arrive in the first place. Children are the objects of countless amulets designed to protect them from a host of evil spirits who wander the earth looking for unprotected young ones to kidnap. They wear amulets to protect them from the Dog of Heaven, who steals children. Some wear dog hair to fool the animal into thinking they are not children; some parents dress their male children in girls' clothes so that the spirits will not know they are males.

On New Year's Day, all of the paper charms are replaced by new ones. It is customary for people to hang charms for every imaginable purpose on objects throughout the house and at work during the holidays.

One of the most effective charms used is the character *chi*, meaning a dead *kuei*. Since the evil spirits, *kuei*, are vulnerable to death, when they come across this charm over a door or house, they flee in terror.

[See HUNDRED FAMILY LOCK, HUNDRED FAMILY TASSEL, and SPIRITS AND DEMONS.]

ANCESTOR WORSHIP

The worship of ancestors, according to most scholars, lies at the root of religion in China, and until recently served as the principal reason for the type of family life existing in China since ancient times. The cult of the Earth and ancestor worship predate organized religions by close to two thousand years, and formed the basis of what has been called the Chinese family religion. The Chinese believed that since there was no separation between the affairs of heaven and earth, the spirits of the dead continued to exercise an influence over the living. The critically important rituals characterizing ancestor worship are connected with funerary rites, the selection and tending of graves, and the regular offering of sacrifices—of food and incense burning, kowtowing before the grave, and beseeching one's ancestors to intervene on one's behalf. In imperial times it was not unusual for officials of high rank to retire from public life for as long as three years to mourn parents.

It was believed that if ancestors were buried on family property they would join the agricultural gods in affecting the family's harvest. Living and dead members of a family were bound together in mutual dependence. While the dead could intervene on behalf of the living in the spiritual realm, the opposite was true as well. The living, by properly conducting their rituals, could assist the spirits of the dead in their progress through various stages of the afterlife. The system insured respect for the family, and served to guarantee that people be concerned about its proper maintenance; their own future as dead ancestors was at stake if they failed. The practice of mortuary sacrifice insures one's own future while looking after one's familial responsibilities.

The number of gods invoked during funerary rites and in the course of sacrificing to ancestors is greater than during any other religious ceremony in Chinese daily life. The Buddhist and Taoist gods of heaven are prominent forces in looking after one's dead ancestors. The most important, however, is the high god, Shang Ti—or first ancestor of the Chinese imperial system. The Emperors, called "Sons of Heaven," derive their authority from their great ancestor Shang Ti—who established the right of Emperors to rule over men.

祖先崇拜　麻醉

BRIDE AND BRIDEGROOM WORSHIPPING THE TABLETS OF THEIR DECEASED ANCESTORS. GUANGZHOU. C. 1900.

ANESTHETICS

The ingredients of the various immortality elixirs are essential parts of Chinese pharmacopoeia in a history that goes back over two thousand years. The literature of alchemy is also a record of the earliest forms of Chinese medicine. Hua T'o was a famous surgeon during the Han Dynasty. He was also the father of modern anesthetics. According to the *Annals of the Later Han Dynasty*, he first applied general anesthetics by means of a drug dissolved in wine. The principal ingredient of this wine, known as "bubbling drug medicine" (*ma-fei*), is believed to have been opium. Chronicles of the time indicate that he began the practice of administering oral anesthetics when he operated on the arm of General Kuan Yu.

中國事物

APRICOTS

The scholar has reaped the reward that is due,
And homeward returns on his wearying steed,
When the blossoming apricots come into view,
He urges his charger to bear him with speed.
—Sung Tzu-ching (A.D. 998-1061)

It's obvious that, in this passage, Sung's horseman has more on his mind than the first apricot harvest. Like the cherry, the apricot, with its sweet, edible center, was symbolic of women.

The Chinese are very fond of apricots, and grow many varieties. In their diets, the edible seed is used much like almonds in the West. However if eaten in excess the fruit of the apricot was believed to harm the bones and sinews and to promote blindness and the falling of hair, including that of the eyebrows and eyelashes. The *Chinese Herbal* (*Pen Tsao*) also warns about eating too many apricot seeds because their toxicity may be strong enough to poison a dog. This runs contrary to current medical speculation in the West about the effectiveness of apricot seeds in combatting cancer.

ARCHITECTURE

PAPERCUT SHOWING UNIQUE TILT TO CHINESE ROOF STRUCTURE.

The most immediately noticeable characteristic of Chinese architecture is the widespread use of the curving roof. The origin of this graceful and beautiful architectural practice stems from at least as early as the fourth century A.D. Between the Han and Sui dynasties, Chinese roofing became immensely elaborate, with three types of dominant curves becoming fully stylistic elements for subsequent centuries; they are the full concave slope, the curving ridge, and the uplifted eave corners. The heavy tiled roofs often descend well below the top of the wall and then sweep upward.

The Chinese roof, however, is more a consequence than a basic element of the unique ideas of Chinese architecture. The roof is the result of a system in which an independent frame is strengthened by a series of corbel brackets, allowing the roof to lie against the brackets supported by the central column rather than by the entire length of the wall. Walls are not structurally significant nor are they imposing in the typical Chinese house. The sloping roof, an elevated terrace or veranda, covered hallways between buildings built around a central court; these are the central features of all Chinese building complexes.

The buildings front in a southerly direction—for practical and geomantic reasons—and usually have their face on the long side. A series of buildings is often built one behind the next along a central axis, the whole surrounded by a single wall.

The most important aspect of Chinese architecture was the notion of "modules" that could be connected, added, and compounded on existing buildings as needed. The earliest works on architecture in China stressed the human-scale needs for these dwelling units, any number of which could be added to a system of dwellings already in existence. The resulting walled-in compound with dozens of buildings along main axes, connected by covered walkways, became the most common Chinese building. The system could be applied to farmhouses as well as to palaces and temples, and an early reliance on wood and brick as the main construction materials added flexibility to both esthetic and practical considerations.

Most Chinese dwellings surround interior courts containing gardens. These formed an essential private relationship of the building and its inhabitants with Nature, and since Chinese architectural expansion traditionally took place horizontally (rather than vertically, as in Western cities), the atmosphere of harmony between man and Nature could be preserved in the most urban environments.

The most impressive examples of Chinese architecture are the great pagodas, temples, and fortified walls, many of which are still standing today. Some of the pagodas were erected as far back as the sixth century A.D. The great palaces of Kyoto and Nara in Japan also embody the principles of Chinese architecture. They were modeled on the great palaces of Chang'an which were destroyed during the An Lu-shan rebellion around 755 A.D.

Chinese buildings have also been noted for their color. In addition to brightly painted walls, columns, lintels, and beams, the Chinese paint the decoratively constructed cornices, and even the relief designs found on bricks.

[See FORBIDDEN CITY, PAGODA, and PALACES.]

ART OF WAR

BRONZE SWORD FROM THE LATE CHOU DYNASTY (770-221 B.C.)

According to tradition, Sun Tzu was a general living in the sixth century B.C. He presented a book entitled *Art of War* to his ruler, Ho-lu. What is more likely is that the author was an unknown general of the Warring States (480-22 B.C.) who wanted to confer the respectable mantle of antiquity on his work by claiming it originated in Classical times with Sun Tzu. Whoever he was, the author of the *Art of War* created a work that remains unmatched for its crisp insights and piercing analysis of man's most gruesome activity.

中
國
事
物

The book is a systematic guide for generals and their rulers, for the intelligent planning and prosecution of successful military campaigns. The book is as fresh today as ever, and eclipses many more recent military strategists who often become bogged down in the technical details of their own age. Sun Tzu penetrates this in a way that was admired by both Napoleon Bonaparte and Mao Tse-tung.

Sun Tzu believed that the most skillful warrior defeats his enemy without battle, captures his cities without besieging them, and overthrows his government without shedding blood. One of his goals was to minimize the waste and destruction of war, so that victory could be more complete. To be effective, he wrote, the commander must employ deception of all types, create false appearances to fool the enemy, and maintain a flexible, maneuverable posture in order to exploit the enemy's weakness. The final chapter of Sun Tzu's *Art of War* is a guide to the "employment of secret agents" in which every manner of deception is described and advocated. In Sun Tzu's view, the army was simply the final instrument in the successful commander's kit.

The *Art of War* is an important key to understanding Chinese military history, for soldiers and scholars have been relying on it as an ultimate authority in military affairs in China for over two thousand years. In the eighteenth century, copies were introduced to both French and Russian military hands. It has been claimed that Sun Tzu has had a clearly visible effect on Russian military strategy of this century.

ASTROLOGY

Based on the ancient twelve-year cyclical dating system of lunar years, the Chinese astrological system has been used for centuries throughout Asia as a guide for all business, official, and romantic activities. According to legend, the oriental zodiac was first established by the Buddha, when he attempted to restore order to the affairs of the world. He invited all of the animal kingdom to a summit conference, but only twelve beasts came, and the order in which they arrived, from Rat to Pig, marks the order in which the twelve years in the cycle follow one another. Each of the animals presides over an entire year, and all of the events that occur are influenced by the special characteristics of that animal.

The Chinese lunar calendar consists of twelve months, with a thirteenth added every twelve years to keep the system on an even keel. As a result, the Chinese New Year always begins on a different date in either January or February. One born during either of those months may have to look up the exact date of the New Year in question to find his or her zodiac animal. Otherwise, the chart of animal signs and all of the years for this century are as follows:

RAT	1900	1912	1924	1936	1948
		1960	1972	1984	1996
OX	1901	1913	1925	1937	1949
		1961	1973	1985	1997
TIGER	1902	1914	1926	1938	1950
		1962	1974	1986	1998
CAT	1903	1915	1927	1939	1951
		1963	1975	1987	1999
DRAGON	1904	1916	1928	1940	1952
		1964	1976	1988	2000
SNAKE	1905	1917	1929	1941	1953
		1965	1977	1989	

HORSE	1906*	1918	1930	1942	1954
		1966*	1978	1990	
GOAT	1907	1919	1931	1943	1955
		1967	1979	1991	
MONKEY	1908	1920	1932	1944	1956
		1968	1980	1992	
ROOSTER	1909	1921	1933	1945	1957
		1969	1981	1993	
DOG	1910	1922	1934	1946	1958
		1970	1982	1994	
PIG	1911	1923	1935	1947	1959
		1971	1983	1995	

*Fire-Horse years.

占星學

In traditional Chinese culture, the annually issued Imperial Almanac contained a complete guide for all of the signs, advising what times were good for certain types of behavior, what other signs would make good companions, and what days were auspicious for important political decisions. Chinese astrology functions much like the Western zodiac, with detailed horoscopes available for each sign. Each of the animal signs is listed below with an explanation of its outstanding personality characteristics.

The Year of the Rat—The aggressive rat was the first animal to heed the Buddha's call and is therefore the first sign in the Chinese zodiac. Rats are acquisitive, suspicious, and power-hungry, but are endowed with a remarkable sense of fair play and are scrupulously honest. Rats are also generous, sentimental, and quite socially adept. Rats should avoid marrying Horses, since these marriages often lead to violent death. William Shakespeare, Truman Capote, and George Washington were all born Rats.

The Year of the Ox or Buffalo—Persons born under this sign are apt to feel they should lead nations. Hitler, Geronimo, and Napoleon were all Oxen. Oxen are powerful individuals with stubborn, reliable personalities. Whether it is in the home or in government, Ox people will always want to be captain of the ship and will usually perform well when given the opportunity to display their powers. Aristotle, Walt Disney, and Richard Nixon were all born Oxen.

The Year of the Tiger—This is the most unpredictable of the signs. Equipped with a great deal of charm, Tigers often flash brightly through life without a care for the security cherished by more wary animals, and Tigers often expose themselves to great risk. Isadora Duncan, Marilyn Monroe, Charles de Gaulle, and Karl Marx were all Tigers who left their mark on the world.

The Year of the Cat or Rabbit—Extremely concerned with being well rooted, people born under this sign are not great risk takers. They avoid conflict and emotional entanglement, choosing instead security, and domestic stability. Famous people born under this sign are Albert Einstein, Andy Warhol, and Orson Welles. A Cat can be a successful business partner for nearly anyone.

The Year of the Dragon—This is the flashiest of the signs, the most likely to be bossy, loud, garish, and unfaithful. A person born under this sign is also extremely successful and popular. Dragons make excellent actors and actresses and often appear in politics with a grand gesture, as did Florence Nightingale and Napoleon III.

The Year of the Snake—People born under this sign have an inclination toward

中國事物

abstract thought and are unusually gifted in the occult sciences. Martin Luther King, Greta Garbo, Jacqueline Onassis, Mao Tse-tung, and John Kennedy were all born Snakes. The long list of famous Snakes is studded with beautiful women and great idealists. Snakes are uncommonly attractive, and the birth of a Snake daughter is considered a good omen for an oriental family.

The Year of the Horse—The Horse is among the hardest working of all animals. Horses are difficult to get along with because they consider themselves superior, cannot be defeated in an argument, and must always have their way. Horses are often successful at politics and are usually dandies, always appropriately appointed for every occasion. Khrushchev, Leonard Bernstein, and Princess Margaret are all hard-working Horses. Once every sixty years, there occurs what is known as the *Fire-Horse Year* (the most recent ones were in 1906 and 1966). Female children born in a Fire-Horse Year are considered to have brilliant futures, but bring disaster on their families. There are numerous stories circulating about the high abortion rate in Japan during late 1965 and 1966 because Japanese women did not want to bring misfortune into their families by giving birth during a Fire-Horse Year. Some better-known Fire-Horse babies were Rembrandt and Davy Crockett.

The Year of the Goat—Goats are warmhearted, disorganized, and extremely vulnerable. The Goat cannot be bound by restrictions, but will always find a natural solution. They work when they are least expected to and cannot be reached by being pushed. They are often found in the arts because of their elegance and independent creativity. Michelangelo, Mussolini, and Margot Fonteyn were all born Goats.

The Year of the Monkey—The Monkey is the most contradictory of signs. Monkey people are extremely intelligent and make close, entertaining friends. They are clever, good tacticians with a flare for deception. Lyndon Johnson, Mick Jagger, and Elizabeth Taylor were all born under this sign. A Monkey can be a barrel of laughs, but is not to be implicitly trusted.

The Year of the Rooster—People born under the sign of the Rooster are enthusiastic about details others may overlook. Roosters cannot be bossed and are best employed in a field they have cut out for themselves. Roosters are often brashly outspoken and reckless adventurers who may turn out to be dreamers. The Rooster may swagger too much for his own good, but is an excellent and popular friend. Some of the better-known Roosters are Katharine Hepburn, Ethel Merman, and Groucho Marx.

The Year of the Dog—Dogs are introverted listeners, honest, and cynical. They may not have a sense of their own values, which include dedication and a deep sense of loyalty. Although Dogs may seem to be banal at times, they are often more intelligent than the louder members of a group. Dogs are sometimes their own worst enemies because of the external anxieties through which they underestimate themselves. Their deeply critical nature predisposes Dog people to work as moralists or in law. Some of the greatest Dogs of history were Lenin, Voltaire, and Benjamin Disraeli.

The Year of the Pig—The Pig is the most reliable and honest of all signs. Pigs have great difficulty making up their minds, but once they do, they overcome every obstacle in order to carry out their decisions. Pigs are good friends and have an unquenchable thirst for new knowledge. They have a natural way in the world, but are often betrayed because of their own credulity. The great Pigs of history were either quite successful in financial affairs, or idealists who gave their lives to improve the lot of their fellow men. Among them are the first Rothschild and Rockefeller, Albert Schweitzer, and Oliver Cromwell.

占星學

光緒三十一年

夏至致日圖

表竿

圭

THE GNOMON BEING USED TO MEASURE THE SUN'S SHADOW. PUBLISHED BY IMPER-
IAL ORDER IN THE *Shu Ching T'u Shuo,* 1905.

中國事物

ASTRONOMICAL INSTRUMENTS

The Chinese were the innovators of many useful astronomical instruments. The basic and most ancient of these was the vertical pole or gnomon, which during the day casts a shadow and allows one to measure the declination of the sun, and which by night offers a reference point against which to measure the motion of the stars. The art of observing and measuring shadows cast by the sun also gave rise to the Chinese sundial and the orienting template, which allowed the angle between the shadow cast and some standard reference point to be measured.

These early astronomers also used the sighting tube to cut off extraneous light when viewing stars, and at the same time to provide a stable frame of reference against which the apparent motion of a star could be checked. The sighting tube is probably referred to as early as 120 B.C., and was certainly the subject of a later proverb about "looking at heaven through a tube."

Chinese astronomers also used armillary spheres, which make it possible to locate a particular star at some moment of observation. Chang Heng, in about A.D. 132, devised a way to make the armillary sphere rotate slowly by means of a waterwheel powered by constant water pressure, thus inventing the first mechanized orrery.

[See OBSERVATORIES and SUNDIALS AND TIMEPIECES.]

AWETO

The aweto or winter-worm grass (*Tung-ch'ung-hsia-ts'ao*; in Cantonese, *Toong ch'ooy hah ts'o*) is the strangest insect in all creation. It is actually a caterpillar that in the course of its natural development blossoms out into a plant. The vegetable fungus that takes root in the neck of the caterpillar (eventually killing it) grows upward to the height of six or eight inches, and downwards into the body of the buried aweto until the vegetable matter has supplanted all the animal tissues in the outer skin of the insect. The original form of the aweto remains intact, although to all intents and purposes it is now a plant. Once the transformation is effected, the vegetable matter then dies as well, becoming brown and brittle. The odd combination of insect and plant makes the aweto look like a wooden caterpillar that has a big horn sticking out of its neck.

Generally found in the South of China, the aweto is prized for its pharmacological value. It is boiled with pork to produce an invigorating tonic.

BAMBOO

Victorian traveler Colonel Barrington de Foublaque was especially impressed by the Chinese use of bamboo. He wrote: "What would the poor Chinaman do without bamboo? Independently of its use as a food, it provides him with the thatch that covers his house, the mat on which he sleeps, the cup from which he drinks, and the chopsticks with which he eats. He irrigates his field by means of a bamboo pipe; his harvest is gathered in with a bamboo rake; his grain is sifted through a bamboo sieve, and carried away in a bamboo basket. The mast of his junk is of bamboo; so is the pole of his cart. He is flogged with a bamboo cane, tortured with bamboo stakes; and finally strangled with a bamboo rope."

The 1,001 uses of bamboo were enumerated as early as the third century in *Chu-p'u*, the *Treatise on Bamboo*. It is without question one of the more extraordinary plants in existence, and the civilizations of a quarter of mankind would have developed on a completely different course without it.

Bamboo grows all over China, with the largest varieties appearing in Hubei,

BAMBOO. INK ON PAPER HANDSCROLL. ATTRIBUTED TO SU SHIH (A.D. 1036-1101).

天文儀器　冬蟲夏草　竹　銀行　蝙蝠

Sichuan, and Zehjiang. It flowers and bears fruit perhaps only once in one hundred years, although it is the fastest-growing plant in the world, sometimes growing as much as four feet in a single day. The Chinese used it medicinally as a tonic for the stomach, as a cure against dysentery, and as a remedy against toothache. When medical opinion proved in doubt, they would explode it in fire to drive any demons away.

The tender, new shoots of bamboo are major ingredients in most Chinese cuisine. They are delicately flavored "textured" food. One of the twenty-four classical examples of filial piety had an ailing mother whose last wish was to enjoy a bowl of soup made from bamboo shoots. None were to be found in the middle of winter. The son wept copious tears of pity in a bamboo grove and caused the hard ground to soften and new shoots of bamboo to burst forth.

BANKS

Long before the first European traders visited the Orient, the Chinese had a widespread effective system of premodern banks. The "native" banks were generally small, unprepossessing buildings, totally unlike their European counterparts. The Chinese banks accepted deposits, usually for a period of six months, and loaned money to local merchants. A key difference between Chinese banks and our Western banks was that very often the loans were unsecured in Chinese banks. Sometimes banks would accept supplies of goods such as grain, herbs, or beeswax, but it was extremely rare for real estate to be used as security. For both the borrowers and the bankers, one's age and personal reputation were the most important qualifications.

As the banks grew during the Sung Dynasty (A.D. 960-1279) they gained further revenue through the issuance of banknotes and the minting of coins. Today in China, however, banking and lending policies are conservative and anti-inflationary. All banking in China comes under the auspices of the People's Bank of China. It functions much like the Federal Reserve System as well as a conventional commercial bank. With its thirty thousand direct branches it is the largest bank in the world.

[See CURRENCY.]

BATS

Known variously as the "heavenly rat," "flying rat," and the "night swallow," the bat plays an important role in Chinese folklore and medicine. According to the *Pen Ts'ao*, or the *Chinese Herbal*, thousand-year-old bats, white as silver, are found

中
國
事
物

hanging inside the caverns of southern China. Since these creatures are believed to feed on stalactites, the bats' medicinal properties insure longevity as well as good sight. Their blood, gall, and wings are especially favored in the concoction of such elixirs. However, there is also a prevailing superstition that the hair will fall off the head of anyone who touches a bat.

The bat is not regarded with aversion in China as it is in the West. In fact, the bat is symbolic of happiness and is frequently employed for decorative purposes in China. Often it is represented in such an ornate manner that it resembles a butterfly. The popular motif of the Five Bats exemplifies the Five Blessings: old age, wealth, health, love of virtue, and a natural death. One of the most ubiquitous motifs in the nineteenth century enamels was the orange bat. The Chinese term for bat, *fu*, is a pun on the word meaning "happiness."

BEADS

Beads have been worn in China for thousands of years: It is recorded that ones of jade were popular during the reign of Huang Ti, which ended in 2597 B.C. The crowns of ancient Emperors were adorned with spherical beads, and a string of amber beads is a traditional part of court dress. Law once dictated the number of beads that could be worn by the Emperor and the officials under him, while the type of bead held in the button on an official's cap was one indicator of his rank.

The Chinese have adopted as a necklace the Buddhist rosary, an eighteen-bead strand used for invocations. The well-to-do choose beads of jade, coral, agate, or pearl for summer; in winter they switch to ivory or cedar ones. Not only used for necklaces, beads are popular in brooches, bracelets, and earrings as well.

BECHE-DE-MER

This esculent holothuria is also known as a "sea slug," "sea worm," or most pleasantly, "sea cucumber." The Chinese name it *hai-shen*, or "sea ginseng," and they prize it as a texture food for its unctuous resilience. Although it resembles a cucumber in shape, the *beche-de-mer* is actually a marine slug, any of several species of echinoderm that live in the coral reefs of the South Seas. The *beche-de-mer* is caught not by spearing or diving but by wading around in shallow water and gathering it up. The *beche-de-mer* is then quickly gutted, parboiled, dried, and often smoked. Before cooking it must be soaked for days, carefully and thoroughly cleaned, and boiled several times. After all this it may be eaten steamed with chicken or duck, or used to make a very thick soup. The taste is mild and slightly sweet.

BEES

Chinese bees are allegedly more polite than Western bees. Chinese bees are more easily handled, and their buzz is supposed to be worse than their bite. Ho Hsien Weng, a Taoist wizard, proved this when he took a mouthful of rice and blew it out as live bees which, when called back, re-entered his mouth and became rice grains again. Bees were most commonly kept by monks in their mountain temples. Their honey was used for making sweetmeats and preserves, and their wax, covered with vermilion, was used in candlemaking. Honey was used universally in China as a seasoning in cooking and is the oldest and most respected sweetener in Chinese cuisine. Chinese hives are odd-looking affairs, generally shaped like an hourglass, while others are more cylindrical in design. The tiny openings in Chinese hives are just big enough for one bee to push through at a time.

BEGGING

It is an ancient folk custom in China that twice a month, on the new and the full moon, beggars roamed the streets in ragged bands. The shopkeepers anticipated their arrival and met them at the door with small individual contributions. The consequence of neglecting this social obligation was mild enough, but extremely effective. The offended beggars would do nothing worse than hang around all day. Alternately they appealed to his mercy and cursed him for his coldness. If the shopkeeper ever hoped to see paying customers again, he gave in.

All other days of the month, the shopkeeper was protected by his payments to a beggars' organization. The printed picture of a gourd hung over the shop entrance indicated this arrangement, and no beggar would trouble a shop so marked.

Taoist philosophy made the abrupt reversal of fortunes an aspect of natural balance, and courtesy toward supplicants was an obvious corollary. You would turn down the request of a beggar, met on the road, by explaining that you carried only sufficient funds for your own journey and, regrettably, must deny yourself the pleasure of aiding your fellow traveler. Begging in China continued until the 1950s. Although begging is still common in Hong Kong and Taiwan, it is unusual to see beggars in the People's Republic.

BEGGAR "KING" DRESSED IN RAGS. C. 1900.

念珠　海參　蜜蜂　行乞

中國事物

BELLS

When Emperor Ch'in Shih-Huang-Ti in 221 B.C. established uniform weights and measures, he also established a uniform musical scale for his kingdom. His musicians first tuned musical stones, and then tuned bells to those pitches. All bells in the kingdom were to be tuned in accordance with the Emperor's bells.

According to legend, Emperor Yu the Great arranged instruments outside the palace gate so that anyone with a problem could signal the kind of attention needed. Someone who wanted to right an injustice would strike a large bell; for private business with the Emperor, the small one. The gong signified public or private misfortune; the drum indicated a message about the manners of the Empire; and the tambourine called for an appeal of a lower-court ruling.

The Chinese may have originated the art of bell founding. They considered bells and cauldrons the most valuable vessels that could be made of bronze. Containing six parts copper and one part tin, most Chinese bells are highly ornamented. The quality is so fine that they never crack; one reason may be the tiny hole the founder makes in the top.

The Chinese make two basic types of bells. One, the *chung*, has no clapper and is struck from the outside. This type of bell must be suspended. Sometimes many are placed in a frame; the *pien-chung* holds sixteen bells in its frame. It is played in Confucian temples, where it is said, "The bell speaks, the stone answers." The largest suspended bells are usually struck by long beams of wood held on a rope or a chain. The sound can be heard for miles.

The first bell clappers were wooden, and they appeared relatively early. Confucius said he wished to be "a wooden-tongued bell of heaven." Windbells, or *fengling*, have silk streamers hanging from the clappers, so that the bells ring as breezes move the streamers. These bells are often hung from pagodas.

Bells are the source of many legends and stories. The "taboo" bell of Guangzhou was cast in the mid-1600s. It had no striker, and legends warned that disaster would follow if it were struck. One day, a legend says, a skeptical official ordered the bell struck. Immediately afterward, a thousand babies died. (To counteract the evil spirit thus aroused, parents sometimes put bells on babies today.) In 1857, the British were bombarding Guangzhou and aimed shot at the bell. As it rang out, it foretold the calamity that foreigners later brought to the city.

China's most famous bell is the Great Bell of China in the Big Bell Temple west of Beijing. Fourteen feet tall and weighing more then fifty tons, it was cast in 1420 on the spot where it still rests. The ground was excavated from under it, and a temple was later constructed over it. Five volumes of classics are inscribed on the bell, which could be struck by a wooden hammer only on imperial order.

According to one of the legends about the casting of the bell, the Emperor Yung-lo called on bellmaker Kuan-yu to make a huge bell that the entire city could hear. Kuan-yu tried twice to cast the bell, but both times the metal came out honeycombed. The furious Emperor threatened to behead him if the third try did not succeed.

Kuan-yu's beautiful sixteen-year-old daughter, Ko-ai, decided to consult an astrologer to learn the cause of her father's bad fortune. On the day the bell was cast for the third time, Ko-ai suddenly hurled herself into the molten metal—the astrologer had said the casting would be unsuccessful unless the blood of a maiden were mixed with the metal. Ko-ai's shoe had fallen off in the hand of a friend who tried to stop her. Now it is said that the sound of the bell is followed by a woman's voice crying *"hsieh"* (shoe).

Three complete sets of bells have been discovered in China since 1950, the most elaborate consisting of sixty-four bells. It is part of the most extensive array of the Chou period musical instruments yet discovered in China. They are on display in the National Historical Museum in Beijing.

鐘鈴

籠鳥

BRONZE BELL OR *chung* FROM THE 5TH-4TH CENTURY B.C.

BIRDS IN CAGES

If the Chinese have ever had a love affair with any pet, it would have to be with birds. They have praised them in poems, coddled them with seed treats, and immortalized them in their art. A cat has even been seen to go up to examine a bird that was drawn standing on a spray in the most natural manner . . . .

Much in the same way that a Westerner will walk his dog for exercise, the Chinese will leisurely saunter along the streets, or stand in some square, or even squat on some green spot on the outskirts of town together with his favorite bird, who will be enjoying his freedom as much as possible in his portable bird cage. Meanwhile his distinguished owner may occupy himself with the pursuit of insects with which to feed his pet.

The lark is one of the most prized songbirds among the Chinese. Large numbers of Chihli larks are brought every year to the South of China, where they are especially preferred. Mongolian larks command a higher price in pet shops, and are referred to as *pai-ling* (one hundred spirits) because of their boisterous song. The lark's cage is round, made of neatly rounded splints of bamboo and varnished brown, with a removable bottom that is sprinkled with sand. The perch of the cage is in the shape of a large mushroom, as the Chinese evidently know that the lark does not alight on twigs or branches.

The canary is another favorite songster. It is commonly called a "white swallow," its usual light-yellow canary color being close enough to white to satisfy even the most scrupulous Chinese philologist. Very neat canary cages are made in imitation of houses and boats, as well as large squarish cages of unvarnished bamboo that are especially useful for breeding purposes.

In North China the thrush is undoubtedly the leading singing bird, although another type of thrush, *Sutheric webbiana*, is kept for fighting purposes, death or victory being its song.

The most readily available Chinese cage bird in the West is the Peking nightingale, otherwise known as the yellow-bellied liothrix. It has a gorgeous song, is lively, spirited—or as the Chinese would euphemistically say, "it is fond of life."

BIRD'S NEST SOUP

Bird's nest soup is what Chinese gastronomes call a texture food—that is, a food that is prized more for its unusual and interesting texture than for its flavor, which is basically rather bland. It is a Cantonese speciality, considered to be strengthening and stimulating and even a bit aphrodisiac, and is often served as a first course at grand banquets.

The birds' nests (*yen-wo-t'ang*, which means, literally, swallow's nest soup) are gathered three times a year from the roofs and sides of caves and caverns of Java, Sumatra, Ceylon, and the Malay peninsula, and the Philippines, and generally around the coast of the South China Sea. The nests are shaped like half of a small bowl, two or three inches in diameter, and secured to the roof or walls of the cave by the same material as the nests are made from. What this material is, the old authorities differed on; some thought it was an extract of seaweed masticated by the birds, but the very finest nests are often found hundreds of miles inland.

No less of an authority than the great Charles Darwin held the opinion that the nests were made of the natural saliva of the birds. Bird's nests have sometimes been faked out of isinglass, gelatin, or vermicelli. The best nests, when dried, are brittle, about the size of a duck's egg, weigh from a quarter to half an ounce, and are very clean and white and translucent. Real nests can be distinguished from fakes by the presence of impurities, but nests collected after the eggs are hatched are too dirty to be used as food.

The soup is prepared by soaking the nests until they soften, thus cleaning them of any down, twigs, or droppings, then boiling with flavorings.

BLIND STITCH

The blind stitch, otherwise known as the "forbidden stitch," involves a classic tale of intrigue and duplicity on the part of unscrupulous garment dealers and unsuspecting Western buyers. Shoppers were led to believe that the embroidery for the lavishly designed Mandarin robes was so painstakingly intricate that workers would go blind in the process of stitching the patterns. The myth was also perpetrated that these imperial garments were produced within the walls of the Forbidden City in Beijing. In fact, the peak age for a seamstress was nineteen, since only one eye could be used at a time for the fine detail. Needles were soft, and the slightest calluses on the fingers would impede progress. It was claimed in the tale that by the age of forty, the seamstress was often visually impaired.

[See EMBROIDERY.]

BOATS

In 1669 European traveler Domingo de Navarrete proclaimed that "there are more vessels in China than in all the rest of the known World." The fact that Chinese waters were crowded with boats of every description was also remarked upon by Marco Polo, and numerous Arab visitors in earlier centuries. A simple glance at the map of China with its thousands of miles of seacoast, navigable lakes, and riverways should put to rest anyone's surprise at the fact that in many ways the technical development, quantity, and versatility of Chinese boats were equal, if not superior, to any elsewhere in the world prior to the eighteenth century.

Almost all Chinese boats are based on the junk, a ship of any size up to two hundred feet in length that is suitable for both river and ocean voyages. The junk's bow and stern do not taper into gradual points, but are cut off abruptly, and crossed by solid walls—unlike any Western ships. Even the biggest junks used as freighters along China's rough coastal waters are more flat-bottomed than equivalent Western sailing ships of similar size. The strength of the junk construction is found in numerous solid bulkheads, which allowed a unique Chinese contribution to navigation technique. The bulkheads help form completely watertight compartments, further assisting the ship's durability. The ship-length stem and stern ribs used in junks are often "grown to shape," a practice that while known to Western shipbuilders long ago, was perfected by the Chinese. Another unique feature of the junk is the large number of masts (up to seven), which are placed according to a system unknown outside of Chinese-influenced areas: The masts are off-center—to port and starboard, rather than in a straight row along the ship's longitudinal center. They are also tilted—some forward and others aft, resulting in a fanlike shape when the junk is under full sail. Perhaps the most important characteristic of Chinese vessels, and one that was unknown in Europe until the fourteenth century, was the invention of the stern post rudder for steering the ship. It was the junk's squared-off stern shape that

PAPERCUT OF ELABORATE CHINESE RIVERBOAT.

中
國
事
物

allowed for the development of this most efficient steering system, which was eventually adopted universally. It allowed the Chinese to launch ships of greater size and maneuverability at earlier dates.

To aid the Chinese mariner on his voyages, the Chinese developed the mariner's compass, and numerous other navigational tools long before such devices appeared anywhere else in the world. Yet by the time Western ships were visiting Chinese waters regularly, the great age of Chinese maritime exploration was over. There are, however, astounding records of distances, places visited, and the size of Chinese naval expeditions, some dating back to the third century B.C., but most from the great age of Chinese exploration in the fifteenth century.

In A.D. 1170 naval maneuvers involving over seven hundred ships exceeding one hundred feet in length were observed and described by a traveler visiting the Yangtze River. But there are records of war fleets and naval battles going back to 486 B.C. Aside from the economic advantage of building a highly efficient river fleet, the Chinese were motivated to explore the oceans by tales of the legendary "Islands of the Blest," where immortals and elixirs of immortality could be found. Han Emperor Ch'in Shih-Huang-Ti dispatched a huge expedition of twenty thousand men to find the islands. The same Emperor made war with "castled ships" on the southern Yueh peoples. By the first century A.D. there is mention of one expedition containing 2,000 ships going to Tonkin, and numerous accounts of naval battles in the Philippine and Indonesian archipelagos.

The greatest name in Chinese naval exploration is that of Cheng Ho, an imperial eunuch, who in A.D. 1405 took thirty-seven thousand men and officers on an expedition to the Western seas in sixty-two ships bearing emissaries and gold. During the following years Cheng Ho mounted seven enormous expeditions in all. The Chinese fleets visited the Arabian Sea and traversed the Indian Ocean up and down the East Coast of Africa. Records of these visits astonished Portuguese explorers visiting the same regions several decades later.

[See HOUSEBOATS.]

BOOK BURNING

Ch'in Shih-Huang-Ti, China's self-styled "first Emperor," ruled for only a little over a decade, but will always be remembered for two reasons: He started the Great Wall of China, and he burned all the books, and burned some of their writers along with them. He stands accused of having had 450 Confucian scholars buried alive. His aims were two: to destroy all record of previous times and to unify China under the reformed writing system of his Prime Minister, Li Ssu. All this happened around 213 B.C., and much of the early Han Dynasty that followed was spent in trying to recover and restore the lost works.

Ch'in Shih-Huang-Ti spared a few Taoist texts (the *I Ching* among them), but Kublai Khan ordered that all Taoist works be brought to the capital and burned, not once, but twice. The first torch order went out after he supposedly saw Taoist priests bested in a debate with their Buddhist counterparts in 1258; the second after he had become Emperor of all China.

BOOK OF CHANGES

Alternately honored and despised, venerated and nearly burned, the *Book of Changes* has emerged into the twentieth century as the most beautiful and useful of the ancient books. Renowned psychologist C.G. Jung considered it a reliable guide-

焚書

易經

Prehistoric oracle bones or "dragon bones" used for divination.

book to follow on his explorations into the unconscious.

No one wrote the *I Ching*. Like most ancient books, the *I Ching* (*Book of Changes*) slowly and organically grew out of change itself—the collective genius of many generations of anonymous poets and prophets. The traditional father of the *I Ching* is Fu Hsi, legendary first Emperor of China, who ruled between 2953 and 2838 B.C. Fu Hsi is said to have systematized a divination method based on interpreting cracks formed by heating a tortoise shell. His eight trigrams, called the *pa kua*, were later expanded by King Wen and his son into the present sixty-four Hexagrams.

As Fu Hsi is also the father of cooking, hunting, and fishing, and as his successor, Shen Nung (2838 B.C.), is credited with the invention of agriculture, it should come as no surprise to find that the ancients used the *I Ching* as a kind of farmer's almanac. Sound advice on any subject from animal husbandry to funerary rites was to be found within.

Hsiao-t'un was the capital of the Shang-Yin Dynasty (c. 1465-c. 1030 B.C.), and from there over ten thousand pounds of bone and shell fragments were unearthed by farmers and archaeologists. For years local farmers had sold these bits and pieces to apothecaries, who used them in remedies for rheumatism that called for "dragon bones." They proved to be primarily records of *I Ching* oracles, inscribed by priests, and magical songs for which the music is lost. The writing style on the "dragon bones" has led scholars to date the *I Ching*'s present form from the late Shang to the early years of the Chou Dynasty.

Another indication of the *I Ching*'s age is "The Bamboo Books," a collection of bamboo tablets covered with more than a hundred thousand small seal characters, which were illegally exhumed in A.D. 279 from the tomb of King Hsiang of Wei, who died in 295 B.C. Fifteen different works were represented, some of which are now lost; among them were two books of the *I Ching* and annals from the reign of Huang Ti to 298 B.C.

One of the most important commentators on the *Book of Changes* was Confucius. He is said to have been fascinated by the work and to have worn out three times the leather straps binding his *I Ching*. He once lamented to his students that if he could add fifty years to his life he would spend them studying the book and becoming "without error."

[See Eight Trigrams and Yarrow.]

中國事物

BOOK OF DOCUMENTS

The *Book of Documents* (*Shu Ching*) is the second oldest of the Confucian Classics, preceded by the *Shih Ching* (*Book of Poetry*) and followed by the *I Ching* (*Book of Changes*). The *Book of Documents* is considered the oldest prose work in Chinese and is one of the most ancient of histories produced by any culture. The miscellany of official documents of which the *Shu Ching* is composed relate the history of the Middle Kingdom (China) from the time of the legendary emperor Huang Ti to the latter part of the great Chou Dynasty, a span of some seventeen centuries. These state papers include canons, edicts, ordinances, proclamations, mandates, speeches, prayers, and not a little poetry, as well as a few sermons on the vices of luxury and wine.

Wine especially threatened the empire. The redoubtable Wen Wang, who constructed the hexagrams of the *I Ching*, outlawed wine drinking except at official sacrifices. Perhaps it was King Wen's teetotalism that so endeared the *Shu Ching* to the late Victorian sinophiles: Dr. S. Wells Williams, who was hard to please, insisted "The morality of the *Shu Ching*, for a pagan work, is extremely good . . . ."

Confucius is usually given the honor of having edited the *Shu Ching* into one hundred books comprised of eighty-one documents, but some scholars are very dubious. Internal evidence seems to indicate that these documents were transcribed a hundred or two hundred years before Confucius' birth (551 B.C.).

BOOK OF MEDICINE

The *Book of Medicine* (*Nei Ching*) is the oldest medical text on earth. Fifty-two years after the beginning of Babylon, the legendary Emperor Huang Ti (the "Yellow Emperor," not to be confused with Ch'in Shih-Huang-Ti, who built the Great Wall) ascended the throne of China, and to him the *Nei Ching* is attributed. Huang Ti was a distinguished acupuncturist, and is considered the father of Chinese medicine. During his hundred-year reign (2698-2598 B.C.) the "Yellow Emperor" also invented the chariot, writing, the twelve tones from which music is composed, and the art of making silk cloth.

The oldest parts of the *Nei Ching* go back at least as far as three to five centuries before Christ, but most of the manuscript in our present possession dates from the beginning of the Han period, about 200 B.C. The *Nei Ching* consists of eighteen chapters divided into two parts: nine chapters of the *Su-wen (Simple Questions)* and nine chapters on acupuncture, the *Ling-shu* or *Chen-ching*. The *Simple Questions* asked by Huang Ti of his advisers are incredibly diverse, ranging from "Why do people dream?" to "Why do women have no whiskers?"

BOOK OF REWARDS AND PUNISHMENTS

In the novel *Dream of the Red Chamber*, one of the hero Pao-yu's relatives, who has retired from the world into a Taoist monastery, wanted to celebrate his (Chia Cheng's) birthday by having his son (Chia Ken) print and distribute ten thousand copies of Cheng's annotated version of the *Book of Rewards and Punishments*. In China it has been considered a very good deed to give this tract away for free for at least three centuries; it is China's form of the Gideon Bible.

Sinologist Dr. James Legge places its writing in the eleventh century A.D., toward the end of the Sung Dynasty, a dynasty that, perhaps not coincidentally, saw the first flowering of printing in the Middle Kingdom. The *Book of Rewards and Punishments* (*Kan Ying P'ien*) consists of moral maxims in which "trifling acts and villainous crimes" are wantonly commingled. For great transgressions the sinner is fined twelve years of life; minor infractions only remove a hundred days. A mere thirteen hundred good deeds will make one an immortal of Heaven; a piddling three hundred, an immortal of Earth. Any would-be immortal should "feel kindly toward all creatures . . . even the insect tribes, grass, and trees."

Occasionally the *Kan Ying P'ien* sounds an ecclesiastical note in its warnings. Wallowing in undeserved prosperity is compared to appeasing one's hunger with spoiled food, or one's thirst with poisoned wine. Finally, one must never "murmur against Heaven or find fault with men; reproach the wind or revile the rain. . . .

BOOK OF RITES

Of the Confucian Five Classics, time has been most unkind to the *Book* (or, more accurately, *Books*) *of Rites*. Long before Emperor Ch'in Shi-Huang-Ti consigned them to the flames with the rest of the Confucian classics, previous rulers had habitually deleted parts of these documents that might have proved embarrassing to their regimes. Confucius is, as usual, credited with having edited these classics, but his editorship was more than usually nominal and honorary. The texts that we have emerged from their hiding places about 135 B.C. Fifty-six sections were accidentally recovered during the demolition of Confucius' family home by Prince Kung (The

STONES INSCRIBED WITH THE WRITINGS OF CONFUCIUS, AT ONE TIME INLAID WITH GOLD.

中
國
事
物

Respectful) of *Yu*. The prince returned the tablets to the K'ung family, whose head, the scholarly Kan-kuo, proceeded to translate and transcribe them. He presented his transcription to the Emperor in 96 B.C., or at about the same time the historian Ssu ma Ch'ien actually completed the first comprehensive Chinese history.

The present *Book of Rites* is actually three books: the *I Li* in seventeen parts, the *Li Chi* in forty-nine parts, and the *Chou Li* in six. The youngest book, the *Chou Li*, was very likely written by the Duke of Chou (1130 B.C.), and it provides an exact blueprint of the dynastic bureaucracy that he played a large role in establishing. The *I Li*, or *Decorum Ritual*, consists of rules for the conduct of domestic and family life. The *Li Chi* is said to contain Confucius' views on government and is the only one of the three covered by the civil-service exams. The *Li Chi* contains regulations concerning when to add a poem to the *Book of Songs* (*Shih Ching*) and Seven Grounds for Divorce. Two of the forty-nine chapters have become books, and classics in their own right: the *Ta Hsueh* (*Great Learning*) attributed to Confucius, and the *Chung Yung* (*Doctrine of the Mean*) attributed to his grandson K'ung Chi, who according to legend was Mencius' teacher. These two books, together with the *Analects* and the *Book of Mencius*, make up the Four Books, the basic syllabus of Chinese schools since the twelfth century.

[See CONFUCIAN CLASSICS.]

BOOK OF SONGS

For knowledge, one studies the *Shu Ching*; for wisdom, the *I Ching*; but for pleasure, the weary scholar is apt to turn to the brief and vivid songs of the *Shih Ching* (*Book of Songs*). Although the oldest of the Five Classics, the *Shih Ching* is the best preserved and most complete. Scholars believed that the preservation of these songs was due to their music. Rhyme helped to fix the poems in scholars' memories, which were far less fragile or flammable than bamboo tablets or silks.

The *Shih Ching* covers fourteen centuries, and was purportedly composed over 3,100 years ago (1719-585 B.C.) It is now widely believed that the oldest section, the *Chou Sung*, was composed sometime between 1100 and 800 B.C. Confucius admits to having selected from over 3,000 poems the 311 that form the current *Shih Ching*. Six of these are known to us only by their titles, but the other 305 have been memorized by nearly every Chinese scholar since the year 136 B.C. Confucius also changed the order of the songs and "reformed" the music. Confucius is supposed to have summed up the moral of the *Shih Ching* (for all Confucian books have strict morals) in this single, immortal phrase: "Think no twisty thoughts."

[See MUSIC and POETRY.]

BOWING

A much less formal gesture than its European equivalent, the bow in China is a ubiquitous form of greeting. Among acquaintances it is generally performed without the use of the hands. The head bends only slightly and the body even less. The same motions made with the hands clasped over the chest indicate a more formal occasion, such as paying respects or offering thanks.

[See KOWTOW.]

BRIDGES

The Chinese were great innovators in the field of bridge building. They pioneered the design and use of the segmental arch and the suspension bridge long before Europeans. There is evidence of segmental arch bridges in the work of master bridge builder Li Chun (A.D. 610), while this same type of bridge does not appear in Europe until around A.D. 1340. Another Chinese innovation is the high nearly circular moon gate or moon bridge.

The most famous Chinese bridges, however, are suspension-type bridges constructed of either bamboo or iron. In Kuaxien there is a six-span suspension bridge crossing the Min River, each span measuring some two hundred feet. While this remarkable and famous bridge is constructed of bamboo, there are iron chain-link bridges in existence that date back to the seventeenth century and evidence of iron chain bridges built as long ago as A.D. 580. The use of the iron chain links was not adopted in European bridge building until well after the beginning of the eighteenth century, and it is possible the techniques involved were learned from the Chinese. A German architectural book printed in the year 1725 depicts a Chinese suspension bridge as an example of how to hang a level (nonsagging) flat roadway from the links and arrive at a true suspension bridge rather than the simpler catenaries, where the deck follows the curve of the suspension cables.

BRONZE

The art of molding and chiseling bronze goes back to the beginning of Chinese history. Among the best specimens are the bronzes from the Shang and the Chou Dynasties. According to the *Shu Ching*, the famous Nine Tripods were cast during the Hsia Dynasty, and sent as tribute from the Nine Provinces to the Son of Heaven. The

BRONZE VESSEL MADE BY YING LING-TE DURING THE SHANG DYNASTY (1766-1122 B.C.).

中國事物

tripods bore a map of each province, along with other demographic data. Since bronze is practically imperishable, the earliest pieces are becoming more, rather than less, numerous.

The first bronzes were the simplest in form and design. Those that were made during the Three Dynasties (Hsia, Shang, Chou) are considered to be the best, while all other models are regarded as being inferior in execution. Ch'in and Han bronzes were fairly uninspired, although there was a new burst of creativity in bronzemaking during the T'ang and the Sung. After the form, decoration, and inscription have been considered, the Chinese connoisseur will evaluate the patina of the bronze. The color and the brilliance of the piece depend partly on the alloy used—gold or silver with lead or tin—and partly on the conditions in which the bronze lay buried. The nature of the soil and the water with which the bronze might have come into contact can be crucial factors in deciding whether it is a masterpiece or whether one should dig on.
[See NINE TRIPODS and VESSELS.]

BRUSHES

In China the artist and the calligrapher share the same instrument: a round, responsive brush tipped with a fine point. This brush, often confusingly called a "hair pen" or a "hair pencil" by early translators, was brought to its present state and named *pi* by General Meng T'ien, who supervised part of the building of the Great Wall. The stem of the general's brush was made of mulberry wood and the tuft of deer's hair covered with goat's hair. This sounds more reliable than another account, which tells of a brush made by the legendary Huang Ti from black rhinoceros horn and ivory, and the "downy beard of a certain grass."

Ch'eng Miao, a contemporary of General Meng T'ien developed a kind of stipple brush made of soft wood frayed at one end into a stubbly point. The brush didn't work very well with lacquer and was abandoned long before the introduction of ink, with which it wouldn't have worked in any case. Brushes of some sort go back to the Neolithic period in China. Pottery shards four thousand to five thousand years old excavated in Honan in 1898 show unmistakable signs of having been painted with a brush. A brush dating from the period of the Warring States was found in a grave in Changsha in 1954.

Ch'ing scholar Liang T'ung-shu listed thirty-six varieties of brushes, using tufts of mouse whiskers, gorilla, tiger, and mongoose hair, pheasant feathers, and other natural animal fibers. The best brushes are made of rabbit fur, but chicken down and the hair of very young children have been used, as have the bristles of pigs and the hair of deer, goats, and foxes. Brushes are happiest when kept capped, which keeps them from drying out. A row of such caps is called *han-lin* (brush forest), and so are scholars who have passed advanced civil-service exams.

BUDDHISM

The first great foreign religion to mingle with indigenous Chinese religions and become a dominant force was Buddhism. The religion had been evolving for several hundred years when Indian monk Bodhidharma popularized it in China in A.D. 527. Buddhism, in its Mahayana form, captured the emotional needs of the Chinese, and within two hundred years became a major influence in Chinese life. The images of Buddha, along with relics of the boy of Sakyamuni, and the *Sutras* (Buddhist sacred texts) spread through China rapidly.

Buddhism also brought a host of new gods, which became intermingled with local deities and gods in the Taoist pantheon. The most important of these were Amitabha and Avalokitesvera, who became gods capable of assisting man in the process of metempsychosis— one of the main tenets of Buddhism. In the Buddhist conception, the wheel of life proceeded with souls transmuting from one incarnation to the next until sufficiently purified to literally "get off the reincarnation merry-go-round" and attain the permanently blissful state of Nirvana in which the individual is merged with totality.

With its complex web of deities and a different image of Heaven and the life process, Buddhism filled a timely gap between the official state religion, Confucianism, which had become a rigid and abstract system of preserving respect for antiquity and custom, and the highly volatile and superstitious popular religion that Taoism had become.

Buddhism and Taoism meshed quickly, borrowing each others' ideas and styles, even rituals. The Taoists absorbed new Buddhist gods and altered their temples so that by the late seventh century they were building temples in a style similar to those of Buddhists. The Buddhists, meanwhile, adopted Taoist gods, merging them with their own and contributing styles of meditation that could evolve only against a background of Taoist teachings on nature. Thus evolved the Ch'an school of Buddhism, which in Japan became Zen Buddhism. The result for China was a remarkable syncretism, where the Chinese people have blended the ethics of Confucianism, Taoism, and Buddhism, and make use of what each religion and its philosophical premise has to offer.

The most characteristic elements of Chinese Buddhism are the schools of contemplation, of which there developed hundreds of forms, each replete with monasteries. Until recent times, China was dotted with Buddhist monasteries housing not only living monks, but also temples in which unbroken successions of the founders of the twenty-six great Buddhist schools were immortalized. Each temple contained hundreds of images and texts to go with them, explaining in great detail the identity, birth date, lineage, and accomplishment of the monk in question. The greatest Buddhist monks, however, were those who had demonstrated a proclivity toward performing magic. In this, too, they resemble the Taoist "immortals" or *hsien*.

BUTTERFLY

A common embroidery, painting, and porcelain decoration, the butterfly symbolized many things to the Chinese mind. It is an emblem of joy, of summer, and of conjugal felicity.

Taoist philosopher Chuang Tzu was a chief propagator of lepidopteran tales. One is of a young student who, in a romantic pursuit of a beautiful butterfly, chanced upon a magistrate's daughter in a secluded garden. He was struck by her beauty, and he determined that he would make her his wife. In this story we see that the butterfly was something of a Chinese Cupid, and for this reason, perhaps above others, this insect has been a favorite romantic symbol of poets and painters.

CALENDARS

One method of labeling cycles of time involved the "twelve stems" and "ten branches." The ten branches probably began as names for the traditional ten-day Chinese week, though that connection has been lost, and they are often interpreted as the products of *yin* and *yang* on one hand, and the five elements on the other. The twelve branches are associated with the months, and the twelve symbolic animals of the Chinese

毛筆 佛教 蝴蝶 日曆

中國事物

zodiac. When combined in two-character combinations consisting of one stem and one branch, the two sets of characters yield a sixty-term cycle. We are most familiar with this as a way of naming years—we often hear, for example, about the "Year of the Horse." But originally this sixty-term cycle was used to number days. This cycle of sixty days fell into two thirty-day cycles, and could also be divided into six ten-day "weeks." The use of the sixty-term cycle to name days is as old as the second millennium B.C.; its use to name years does not appear until the first century B.C.

These intermeshing cycles made for a complex calendar that required continuous checking and frequent intervention in the form of extra days, extra ten-day weeks, and sometimes even an extra sixty-day cycle. As an agrarian people, the Chinese were very concerned with the accuracy of their calendar. As an instrument for maintaining vital harmony with the heavenly cycles, the calendar had a religious as well as practical function: With every change of dynasty, the calendar was reformed. The skills needed to calculate the calendar and keep it in accord with the seasons and the solar and lunar cycles were, at times, regarded as state secrets.

One problem confronting calendarmakers is that the solar cycles and the lunar cycles do not fit neatly into one another: The solar year does not consist of an even number of lunar months, and so a calendar based on one cycle will always come to disagree with the other. In other words, a lunar calendar cannot predict the seasons, and a purely solar calendar cannot predict full and dark moons. Calculating eclipses also requires an understanding of both cycles.

The Chinese calendarmakers and astronomers were fascinated with what have been called "resonance periods," the length of time it takes one cycle to move from agreement with another, through disagreement, and back to agreement. It was commonly thought that complete agreement had existed only once in the past, at the beginning of the cosmos, and would exist only once in the future, at its end.

[See CYCLE OF SIXTY.]

CALLIGRAPHY

To the Chinese, writing and painting are not two quite separate arts, but each is a logical extension of the other. Where the two meet is calligraphy. Calligraphy and painting harmoniously occupy the same scroll, and painters appropriated seals from the world of commerce for use in their own realm as calligraphic miniatures. Poets took as much pride in the execution of their work as in the content. For over a thousand years, from the T'ang Dynasty to the Ch'ing, a scholar's handwriting weighed heavily in his score on the civil-service examinations. Until quite recently even in the smallest Chinese village a *Hsi-tzu-t'a* (Pagoda of Compassion for the Characters) could be found, for the purpose of reverently burning scraps of paper with writing on them, in hopes of communicating with the spirit world. A Chinese artist will commonly not say "I'm painting a painting" but "I'm writing a painting."

Chinese may differ from other languages in being written for the eye and not, until relatively recently (around A.D. 500) at all for the ear. The earliest examples of writing come from pottery shards dating back to 4000 B.C. From the time of the Shang Dynasty on, we have a fairly complete visual record of the evolution of Chinese script. Characters whose beginnings are found on the oracular bones and tortoise shells of An-yang probably formed the earliest script (*ta chuan* or *chuan shu*, great seal), which was reformed in 800 B.C. by an imperial historian named Shih Chou. Of his *chou-wen* script we have a few examples on bronze. Li Ssu, Prime Minister under book-burning first historical Emperor Ch'in Shih-Huang-Ti (219-206

書法

EIGHTEENTH CENTURY "RUNNING SCRIPT" CALLIGRAPHY OF THE CHARACTER *fu*, MEANING GOOD LUCK.

B.C.), devised the next great revision, which was called *hsiao-chuan* (small seal script).

The invention of the writing brush (around 200 B.C.) and the gradual switch from lacquer to ink led eventually to the more fluid Han script called *li-shu*. *Li-shu* was the character used when Ts'ai Yung and the Academy of Calligraphy carved the Confucian Classics on stone tablets destroyed during the Tung Ho rebellion of A.D. 190. Ts'ai Yung once wrote: "Calligraphy is a releasing...nothing could be more perfect."

Ts'ai Yung was also a master of *fei-po* (flying white), a kind of *ts'ao-shu* (shorthand script) "the parentage of which," averred the *Hsuan-ho Shu-P'u*, an eleventh-century encyclopedia of calligraphy, "is the subject of much controversy." *Ts'ao-shu* has been literally translated "grass script" (or sometimes even "plant script"), but what it really refers to is "draft hand." A kind of shorthand that originally may have been used for first drafts and notes from dictation, *ts'ao-shu* quickly became a favorite of Zen painters and calligraphers, and drunken poets. *Ts'ao-shu* retained its function as shorthand, and was modernized by Chang Chih of the later Han Dynasty, who joined the characters together into one continuous line.

Compromise between a more conventional script and the often all-too-telegraphic *ts'ao-shu* resulted in the introduction of two more scripts: the *k'ai-shu* (or *chen-shu*) of Wang T'zu-chung of the first century A.D., and *hsing-shu* by Liu Te-sheng of the second. In the third century A.D. Wang Hsi-chih, the father of Chinese calligraphy, composed his classic *Lan-t'ing-hsu (Orchid Pavilion Commentary)*. A copy of this on stone was accidentally discovered by a monk, who found it at the bottom of a well where it had apparently lain since the invasion of the Tartars some three hundred years before.

[See INK.]

CAMELLIA

On the stairway fragrance assails the bosom;
In the garden flowers light the eye.
Once the spring heart is like this,
Love comes without bounds."
—Hsiao Yen (A.D. 464-549)

Because the camellia is indigenous to the subtropical regions of southern China, the ancient Chinese who inhabited the North did not become aware of it until their civilization spread to the South. Feng Shih-k'o noted four centuries ago that there were over one hundred different kinds of camellias being cultivated in the Yunnan, with some trees growing to over twenty feet. The most-prized camellia is the *Pao Chu* (precious pearl), otherwise known as the *Camellia japonica*. It was this flower that was introduced to England from China in the seventeenth century. Another favorite is the *Ch'a Hua* (tea flower), which the Chinese love to brew.

CANAL LOCKS

Canal locks in China grew out of a double need: to control and vary the flow of water, and to move boats between waterways with different water levels. The Chinese had three ways of doing this: the double slipway, the flash lock, and the pound lock. The first two are so old that no record survives of their origin, but they probably arose from devices used to control water in times of flooding, or to direct water into irrigation channels.

The *double slipway* is related to the spillway. At the bottom of a channel wide enough to take a boat easily is built a ramp that rises to a peak, then drops away, like the roof of a house. There is a capstan on either side of the channel: Boats are dragged, by ropes attached to the capstans, up one side of the spillway, and then allowed to skid down the other.

The *flash lock* is related to the sluice gate used to direct water from one channel to another. Boats going downstream wait by the lock until a head of water has built up, and there are enough boats to justify releasing it. When the gates are opened, the boats move rapidly downstream. This device is especially useful for helping boats over shallow stretches of river, and seems to have been in use by the last part of the first century B.C. Boats bound upstream are hauled by ropes attached to capstans—but when the flash locks are opened, upstream-bound boats have to wait until the rush of water subsides.

The *pound lock* is the sort of lock we are most accustomed to. A boat is brought into an enclosure, a gate is closed, and water is allowed to fill or drain to move the boat with little risk from one level to another.

The earliest mention of pound locks in China dates to the late tenth century. They were built to help prevent the damage larger boats often suffered in going over double slipways. After the fourteenth century, bigger boats and ships generally took the sea routes, and canal traffic gradually was dominated by smaller vessels. The pound locks were no longer needed, and flash locks and double slipways again became the usual forms of lock.

There are many legends about heroic rulers who introduced irrigation to Chinese agriculture, but locks were perhaps too recent to attract any legends. A pointed comment in the *Shen Tzu* says: "As for those who protect and manage the dikes and channels of the nine rivers and four lakes, they are the same in all ages; they did not learn their business from Yu the Great, they learnt it from the waters."

CARP

Picture yourself on a boat on the Yellow River during the third month watching the *yu* swim upstream, fighting the current, having to jump the cataract of Wu Men in order to reach the spawning ground. The carp is the fish that the Chinese consider most likely to succeed. It is not only a favorite decorative motif, but also is especially esteemed as a symbol of vigor, endurance, and power. Children were taught that carp leaping over the waterfall would become transformed into dragons—*ch'ih lung* (tender dragons). Scholars who passed the imperial examinations were referred to as "fish-become-dragons." The carp is the longest-lived of fishes, some living to be several hundreds of years old.

CARPETS

The Chinese have been trafficking in rugs for over a thousand years, since the silk route opened up the Celestial Empire to trade with the Arabs. As recently as 1925, it was estimated that as many as a half-million camels were engaged in carrying wool destined to be woven into carpets in China. Tibetan, Mongol, Gansu, and Xinjiang wool from fat-tailed sheep was preferred, and caravans traveled relatively unmolested since bandits found it hardly worth their while to plunder this smelly merchandise in such bulk. The treasures became apparent only after Chinese craftsmen wove their magic spells, dyeing, incising, and embossing the carpets with inspired exacti-

中
國
事
物

tude. Upon their primitive looms—a large one costing perhaps the equivalent of ten dollars—the Chinese have managed to produce masterpieces of color and style that cannot be rivaled with expensive Western machinery.

Unfortunately, the deep, luxurious pile of a Chinese carpet does not always cover a strong and finely knotted foundation, so the carpets were not often very long-lasting. Serious collectors prefer to display their great carpets on the wall. Modern Chinese carpets that are seen in store windows today are by and large forget-table, sometimes even regrettable, coming in enormous sizes and in cartoon colors. Traditional craftsmen would restrict themselves to the use of the five sacred colors— usually a combination of black, blue, red, white, and yellow. The intermediate shades of green, purple, or orange are rarely in evidence.

One unique carpet form in China is the pillar carpet. It is a very long, narrow carpet that is wrapped around a pillar. The patterns are designed to meet in a circular fashion. Most often the elements in the design of Chinese carpets are identical to those found in other arts, such as porcelain, painting, or ivory. Animals are often represented, especially the dragon, the phoenix, the elephant, and the horse. Flowers are more naturalistically depicted than on Persian carpets. Buddhist and Taoist emblems abound, and the Hundred Antiques are *de rigueur*.

CARVING

The carving and cutting of semiprecious stones were done with a great deal of deliberation and flourish. Agate, cornelian, lapis lazuli, marble malachite, and crystal were usually cut into figurines, while Shanxi amethyst and turquoise made

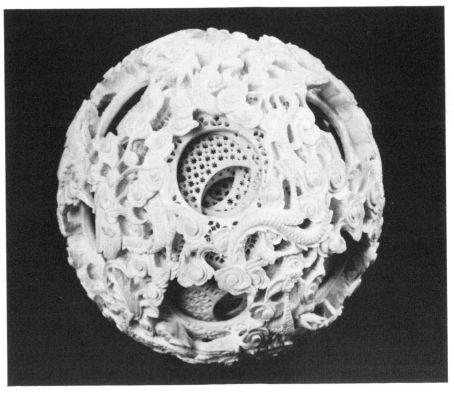

INTRICATELY CARVED IVORY MARRIAGE BALL.

the best beads. Carvers would ponder their design for several months before even attempting a single stroke. A rough-shaped stone might suggest a dragon—but the top of the piece would indicate that the best approach would be for the dragon to be coming around the mountain. A favorite motif for scholars was a vase of red and variegated white agate that was carved into a cluster of three fishes frozen in the act of springing into the air to become dragons. This was to inspire the literati to greater heights of achievement in their quest for degrees on the Dragon List.

Coral was widely used during the Ch'ing Dynasty for combs, snuff bottles, mouthpieces of pipes, tubes for feather holders, and for buttons on hats of officers. During the eighteenth century the Chinese preferred to carve coral that was pale in color, although by the nineteenth century the deep-pink variety was favored. Fourteenth-century writer Chou Ju Kua describes how it was fished for on the coast of Maghreb with grappling irons: "Although they are not always sure to get the whole tree, they will get a branch." The Chinese use the term *sheng* to apply to coral of a clear, bright, and lively color that was alive and growing when hauled in from the sea. *K'u* coral, being already dead, had a dull appearance.

The English word for bamboo stems from the Malay *bambu*, which adequately describes the sound of bursting bamboos when a grove catches on fire. It is perhaps the favorite wood of the Chinese carver because it requires the least amount of work. The hollow wood with its incredible natural gloss can easily be transformed into both useful and decorative items. Chou Ch'eng of the Sung Dynasty could carve palaces, landscapes, figures, animals, birds, and flowers on a small piece of bamboo with such delicate lines that his work was considered miraculous.

Sandalwood has always been in great demand in China, both for carving and as incense. The earliest figures of Buddha were made of sandalwood. Chou Ju Kua writes that it was brought to China from Persia in the tenth century. There was a heavy tax placed on its use, but that didn't stop the Chinese. "Its smell catches the breath and its taste is bitter and pungent...in burning it surpasses all other incenses." And what you couldn't appreciate with your nose, you could admire visually.

[See IVORY, JADE, and SOAPSTONE.]

C A S S I A

In former times, the three Kings were true and pure;
It was with them that the fragrant plants abided:
Mountain peppers mixed with cassia,
Also, garlands of melilotus and valeriana.
—Ch'u Yuan (342-278 B.C.)

The bark of the *kuei*, or cassia, also known as Chinese cinnamon, is one of the most delicious items in the Chinese pharmacopoeia. Its fragrant flowers are used to flavor other medicines, to disguise foul odors, and as a cosmetic preparation for the hair and skin. It grows extensively in the warmer subtropical regions of southern China. A related tree, *Yueh Kuei*, is sometimes depicted as the Tree on the Moon.

C A T S

Domestic cats probably arrived in China from Egypt early in the Han Dynasty (206 B.C.-220 A.D.). They were soon firmly entrenched in Chinese society. It is a fact that cats once held high official rank.

中國事物

During the Ming Dynasty, in the late fourteenth century, a Chinese Emperor conferred titles on his favorite cats. One of his cats was known as the "Bandit-Suppression-Commander-in-Chief" in recognition of his meritorious service in destroying rats in the palace. Within the palace, in fact, a special Cat Bureau was established, with several court eunuchs in constant attendance, assisted by special

富貴耄耋

DECORATIVE MOTIF WITH CAT. FROM THE *Kissho zung Kaidai.*

chefs who prepared royal feasts for the kitties. Cats in the imperial family wore golden earrings and tags that allowed them special privileges. Anyone who captured or insulted these cats was subject to immediate decapitation.

According to popular Chinese belief, the soul of a cat is the composite of the souls of nine Buddhist nuns who during their previous lives failed to observe the doctrines of their religion. Consequently, Chinese cats have always enjoyed greater consideration than Chinese dogs, and were rarely mistreated.

CEDRELA

Otherwise known as the Stinky Cedar, the cedrela is a red, fine-grained mahogany-like wood. The leaves are fed to silkworms. During times of famine the Chinese would eat the cedrela themselves, although it was never their first choice. Taken internally, cedrela works to alleviate menstrual disorders. It is also applied as a rinse to promote hair growth. Cedrela is a main source of scent in China. Boughs of cedrela were hung in latrines to freshen the air.

CELESTIAL PRINCIPLE

T'ai chi SYMBOL DEPICTING UNIVERSAL DUALITY, SURROUNDED BY THE EIGHT TRIGRAMS. CH'ING DYNASTY JADE.

The idea of the Celestial Principle, *t'ien li*, existed in Chinese philosophy since the Chou Dynasty (1030-256 B.C.). It is a concept underlying most subsequent Chinese philosophy. Sometimes considered to be the soul of the Universe, the Celestial Principle is that which preceded Creation in the Chinese cosmology.

The Celestial Principle is a force prior to the existence of any other, and is the mythical source of the organic process. It is combined with the "immaterial vapor" *ch'i* to form the substance *chih*, from which the Ultimate, the Primal Monad *t'ai chi* evolved. *T'ai chi* contains the eternal opposites *yin* and *yang*, from which all the Natural forces spring.

[See GREAT ULTIMATE PRINCIPLE and YIN AND YANG.]

中國事物

CELIBACY

Marriage was universal in China. One was betrothed without any choice, and propagation of the family was one's principal responsibility. Although for the young bride marriage might resemble slavery, women who chose to remain celibate would frequently implement this decision by leaping into a well. Suicide was almost the only social alternative.

A widespread movement, begun in the early nineteenth century among women employed in the silk industry, was called "Girls Who Do Not Go to the Family." They pressured authorities into providing homes and lived there, remaining virgins and refusing to enter into marriage. The movement was dissolved only by the social disruptions of the late 1930s.

For the most part, religious celibacy was taken much less seriously. The Chinese adopted the monastic aspects of Buddhism, but provided some colorful variations on the practice. Chinese literature contains numerous examples of lusty young men blundering into nunneries never to be heard from again, and monastic life frequently provided a convenient way to evade taxes. During the reign of Emperor Shih-tsu (A.D. 424-51), his entourage stopped the night at a Buddhist temple. Unfortunately the monks, after imbibing too much wine, unveiled a number of unmonastic items, including secret apartments designed for conducting illicit love affairs with ladies of rank. The Emperor rewarded his hosts by razing the temple.

[See TAOIST SEX.]

CHECKERS

Chinese checkers may be one of those historical oddities in which a practice or commodity, extinct in its home country, is reintroduced there through a foreign source. Everyone insists on crediting the Chinese with it, although it first appears in recorded history in Sweden about 1880, as a variation to the obsolete game of *halma*. From Europe it may have returned to China via Japan. Anywhere on earth Chinese checkers is played on a board shaped as a six-pointed star. Each player tries to be the first to move the fifteen pegs or marbles in the "home point" to the point on the opposite side of the star.

CHERRY

> Bewitching the blossoms of the spring grove,
> Poignant the meaning of spring birds;
> Spring breeze brings love thoughts—
> Gently parts my skirt of gauze.
> —Anonymous, fifth century

In our country—and indeed, all over the world—the poetical comparison of cherries to lips is common. To the ancient Chinese poets its beauty was considered equal to the ruby and the sapphire, and the fruit, like the apricot, is emblematic of the fairer sex.

The *ying t'a* is grown extensively along the Yangtze Valley, and is known both for its delicious fruit and delicate spring blossoms. Chinese cherries are smaller than Western varieties. The leaves, roots, branches, and flowers of the cherry tree are utilized in various potions and medications prescribed in traditional Chinese medicine.

CHESS

Edward Falkener in his 1892 classic *Games Ancient and Oriental and How to Play Them* asserts that *ch'u-hsiang-ch'i* (game of the science of capture) was devised 279 years after Confucius by the King of Jiangnan, to amuse his soldiers during a long winter siege in the Shaanxi province.

> ...And thus we find in this game not only elephants, cavalry, infantry, and war chariots, but a fortress in which the King and his counselors are entrenched, and from which they direct operations; a fortress belonging to the enemy, which they have to storm, and a wide river between the two armies, which can be crossed only with difficulty. The elephants, being supposed unable to cross, are left behind to protect the field against any of the enemy who might get across and we see them moving slowly and heavily up and down with measured tread.

While a *ch'u-hsiang-ch'i* set contains the same number of pieces as European chess, the pieces are quite different. Instead of a queen, there is a pair of mandarins, or counselors; our bishops have evolved from a pair of mighty war elephants. The Chinese use only five pawns, or foot soldiers, to the European eight, but the Chinese arsenal boasts artillery in the form of a pair of cannon, as would benefit the inventors of gunpowder.

A *ch'u-hsiang-ch'i* board, like an ordinary chessboard, is ruled off into sixty-four squares, but there the similarity ceases. The great Yellow River of China divides the board into two kingdoms eight squares wide by four squares long. All of the pieces may cross this river—except the elephants, mandarins, and kings. Each king and his counselors are confined together in a fortress consisting of the four squares

Two villagers of the Hebei district as they begin a game of chess. C. 1876.

中國事物

which, in a European set, are occupied by a king and his queen and their two pawns.

Chinese chessmen travel along the lines instead of in the squares, so their starting lineup contains nine to our eight; the king in the center, flanked by a pair of mandarins, then elephants, knights, and lastly rooks. The cannon occupy the second intersection up from the knights, and the five pawns are staggered to cover the row of artillery ahead.

Both *go* (known in China as *wei ch'i*) and *ch'u-hsiang-ch'i* were formerly played on paper boards, which in addition to being portable, often had wide margins for making notes. Contemporary Chinese play on boards similar to ours, of wood or stone. *Ch'u-hsiang-ch'i* is played incessantly everywhere in New China, having received an unfair advantage when mah-jongg was banned as "gambling."

CHILD REARING

In some parts of China, when a child learned to crawl he was inserted in a pair of bifurcated pants weighted with sand or dirt. It was reported that the child stolidly accepted this treatment and seemed none the worse for it. Tolerance, though, marked all aspects of the relationship between parent and child. Children were accepted among adult affairs and figure prominently in all the festivals. Legend says the later the children stay up on New Year, the longer their parents will live. Much the same tolerance was reflected in the sharing and absence of sibling rivalry among Chinese children.

The young child also had important dealings with the gods. Male infants were frequently dressed in female clothes to deceive any god bent on disrupting the home. Since a female would become a part of the family she married into, the troublesome deity would pass her up. A male child might even wear a dog collar on the assumption that the gods were truly absent-minded.

The practice of infanticide was sanctioned by one of the Confucian tales of filial piety in which a man finds he cannot support his wife, child, and aged mother. He digs a hole to bury the child so the mother's milk can be used to nourish its grandmother and finds, instead, a pot of gold.

The expense of raising a female child, only to have her marry into another family sometimes prompted parents to kill her at birth, but Western sources almost certainly exaggerated the incidence of infanticide. The Chinese believed that to bury a child under three would visit death on an older member of the family, so a child under three who dies was disposed of wherever convenience dictated. Some towns built baby towers to receive them. Missionaries benefited by interpreting this as infanticide.

In China today the local governments are responsible for providing health clinics, as well as child-care and maternal health-care facilities. Day-care and infant-care centers are available to all working parents. The fees are very nominal.

[See EDUCATION, FAMILY, and FILIAL PIETY.]

CHOPSTICKS

The strangest chopsticks in history turn up before the Sung Dynasty (A.D. 960-1279) in the records of royal gifts; they were part of a traveling set with a spoon, and all three pieces were carved from rhinoceros horn. At other times special chopsticks were made from precious materials like amber and jade. Everyday chopsticks are bamboo or hardwood, and fancy sets are sometimes made of ivory or bone tipped with silver. Centuries ago it was widely believed that the presence of poison in a dish would blacken the silver, but this test is not very reliable, as the sulphur contained in eggs will do the same.

The use of chopsticks has been, until recently, confined to the Orient, but it must also be remembered that even forks were fairly uncommon in the Occident until the sixteenth century. While the nomadic Mongol carried on his belt a little case containing chopsticks and knife, his European counterpart had to make do with a knife, fingers, and perhaps a crude spoon. A more elaborate traveling kit used by both Mongols and northern Chinese contained chopsticks, knife, two-tined fork, spoon, metal cup, and tongue scraper. Lacquerware spoons and chopsticks date back to the former Han Dynasty (206 B.C.-A.D. 9).

An ordinary Chinese place setting consists of chopsticks, a flat-bottomed porcelain spoon, and a rice bowl, which can also be used for soup or tea. The Chinese term for chopsticks is *k'uai tzu*, which is a homophone, with the character meaning "hasten" or "hurry," but chopsticks can be frustrating until the knack for their use is acquired. The extra-long chopsticks used for cooking and serving can be downright intimidating to a beginner. The most efficient way to eat rice with chopsticks is to hold the bowl close to the lips, and use the sticks like a broom to sweep the grains into one's mouth. It is not considered mannerly to wind noodles around chopsticks as if they were spaghetti on a fork.

CICADA

Cicadas are neither crickets, locusts, nor grasshoppers. The cicada, or "scissor grinder," as it's known to the Chinese, sings throughout the summer to attract the female (a silent partner). Since the Chinese love noise as a rule, and complete silence signifies only gloom to them, the cicada is particularly appreciated for the din it emits. Chinese insomniacs often rely on the concertos of the cicada to lull them to sleep in the hot months. As autumn approaches, however, the melancholy last rites of these insect Carusos inspire such a deep sense of nostalgia that the Buddhist precepts regarding the impermanency of life are invariably brought to mind. In fact, the cicada symbolizes immortality and reincarnation to the Chinese. The cicada spends the first four years of its seventeen-year life cycle underground as a larva, then comes out in the form of a mobile pupa, splitting down the back and emerging a perfect insect. It is for this reason that in ancient times a piece of jade, carved in the shape of a cicada, was placed in the mouth of a corpse before burial.

The cicada's music is produced by the vibration of two flaps or lamellae situated in the thorax of the male insect. Chinese children make a sport of its capture, applying a sticky substance to the end of a bamboo pole, and poking it among the higher branches of trees where the *sz-sz-sz-sz* of the cicada betrays its presence. Once caught, the insect has a straw tied around its abdomen, so as to irritate the sounding apparatus and make it sound off even more.

The Chinese use the skin of the cicada as a medicine for convulsions, as well as for fever in children. Needless to say, the bitter mixture of cicada skin and hooked creeper (*Nauclea sinensis*), forced down the throat of the unwilling child, produces an altogether different kind of musical refrain.

CITRONS

Chinese citrons are ornamental fruits that are chosen especially for their interesting shapes and their pleasing fragrance. *Citrus medica* is a hardy species of oblong fruit that can grow even in the brutally cold North of China. It has a green-and-yellow

養兒育女

筷子

蟬

枸杞

中
國
事
物

peel that is thick and wrinkled, and can be kept for a long time as a table plant in a bowl, on a tray, or in a basket. Another well-known citron is the so-called Buddha's Hand (*Citrus sarcodactylus*), which has a thick rind that displays ten or twelve elongated lobs resembling fingers. The Chinese quince, which is a familiar shrub in the West, is mostly grown for its showy flowers. Its large peachlike fruits are beautifully tinged with red and green.

CITRUS

The Celestial Kingdom is probably the original home of the sweet orange, the mandarin orange, the tangerine, and the kumquat. There are altogether over eighty varieties of oranges growing on the southeastern coasts of China, and on neighboring islands. Very little of the orange peel would actually be thrown away. Servants, children, and ragpickers would gather the peels up, dry them, and sell them in bulk to druggists who used them for medical purposes. Canton oranges (*ch'eng*), from which the Seville orange is derived, were prescribed for lobster poisoning, pinworm, and breast cancer. Orange seeds were thought to be effective against urinary problems. The *loquat* is a fruit that is probably indigenous to central-eastern China. It is principally grown in the Tangxi District in Zhejiang, where orchards stretch for miles into the distance. The juiciest variety of this citrus fruit is known as the *p'i-p'a*. Lemons are commonly ornamental; however, they are used as a seasoning in the cooking of southern China. Citrus fruits would be given as presents for their scent, and as good-luck omens to be hung outside the home.

CIVIL-SERVICE EXAMINATION

"All walks of life are lowly, only the scholar stands high." So reads an old Chinese proverb. In imperial China wealth and prestige were dependent on power, and in their rigidly stratified society the only path upward was through the civil-service examination system, which the Chinese called, figuratively, the Ladder to the Clouds (*pu-pu ch'ing-yun*). The imperial examination system graded and licensed students with patents of scholarship. Such academic degrees brought privilege, and at the top of the ladder, appointments in the clouds.

Essentially, the ladder to the clouds had four rungs. First an examination held in one's district capital, followed by triennial exams in the provincial capitals. Then on to the imperial capital for triennial exams. Those who desired a higher distinction could take a palace examination on bended knee in the presence of the Emperor.

A civil-service candidate would begin a course of study as a teen-ager, learning the philosophical, historical, and poetical classics of Confucianism. At about twenty-three he would come to the district capital, pay a stiff fee, and win his degree after writing for a day and a night in a small cell. This degree, called *hsiu-ts'ai* (flowers of talent), gave the minimum elite status. He might then travel to his provincial capital carrying along his candles, writing instruments, and food. He would enter a large area filled with perhaps thousands of examination cells, each measuring no more than six feet deep and three feet wide. He would then be thoroughly searched, since cribbing was rampant and ingenious scholars had been known to transcribe the classics on their underwear. This exam lasted three days, conferring the title of *chu-jen* (promoted scholar). The decisive step was the metropolitan exam held in the imperial capital under the Board of Rites. As many as thirty-five hundred *chu-jen* would pursue the *chin-shih* degree, which conferred the right to hold office. Of these, 10 percent would pass, becoming poets, historians, or chancellors in the provinces.

ROWS OF EXAMINATION CELLS. C. 1900.

In theory the system is quite meritocratic. In practice the local gentry (high officeholders or nobility) were those most likely to send their sons up the ladder to the clouds or to buy degrees for them. Still it provided remarkable social stability, and all aspirants for office, weaned on the Confucian ideology of filial piety and imperial loyalty, aimed their ambition not at revolution but at service to their ancestors.

China brought the era of the imperial examination system to a close in 1905. After a series of humiliating defeats, beginning with the first Opium War, China began to feel socially and technologically backward. In 1872, an official, Li Hung-chang, argued that scholars "have confined themselves to the study of stanzas and sentences and are ignorant of the greatest changes of the last several thousand years."
[See EDUCATION.]

CLOTHING

Clothing serves two essential purposes in China: to protect the wearer from the weather and to indicate his position in society. Two garments are the basis of all Chinese dress; all others are variations on the theme. One is a pair of loose-fitting trousers, adopted from the example of mounted barbarians in the fourth century B.C. The other is a blouse or jacket, which sometimes grows into a long robe. The common people dress in cotton dyed brown, black, or indigo. The wealthier ones choose

中
國
事
物

richly colored silks, which have been produced in China for perhaps four thousand years. The silks are often patterned like damask or lavishly embroidered.

The Chinese invented the layered look. In the winter, leggings, open in back and fastened at waist and ankle, are worn over the trousers, with the excess material from the trousers sticking out behind. Layers of jackets, quilted or fur-lined or bolstered with silk or cotton wadding, are donned on cold mornings, then shed as the day grows warmer. The weather is described according to the number of garments needed to combat it—a two-coat or a six-coat cold day. As many as twelve might be worn if it's frigid enough. In the summer a single robe of silk, cotton, or grasscloth suffices, along with the trousers. When it rains, coats of finely woven straw of palm leaves keep off the wet.

In China a girdle was something that functioned more like a pocketbook than a corset. An essential part of every costume, it encircled the waist like a belt and was a convenient way to carry odds and ends that one needed during the course of the day.

PORTRAIT OF A WOMAN IN FORMAL ATTIRE. C. 1920.

公
雞

Hung from the girdle or attached to it might be a fan sheath; a snuff box; a watch-case; a set of chopsticks; and a purse to hold money, keys, and perhaps a knife. The finest girdles were decorated with buckles of jade, gold, or other precious material.

The *cheongsam* from southern China has come to symbolize the Chinese woman to Westerners. A long sheath-style dress, its side seams are slit to a point above the knee and it has the small upright collar characteristic of Chinese garments.

Chinese robes have long, full sleeves that are very useful. They serve as muffs in the winter (the Chinese don't wear gloves), and they are handy for carrying small objects. In China a man doesn't pocket an object, he "sleeves" it.

Many bright colors may vie for attention in a single Chinese outfit; they are not thought to clash. Men tend to wear darker shades—a deep purple jacket over a bright blue robe would be a typical combination. Pink, green, and pale blue are feminine colors. White is the color of mourning. Gold symbolizes wealth and good fortune, while red is joyous; one doesn't wear red for twenty-seven months after one's parents die. Yellow was the Emperor's color, worn only by the imperial family.

Confucius said that careful regulation of dress, among other things, will enable a sovereign to rule righteously. Taking this seriously, the Emperors regulated every item of official and ceremonial costume, down to the proper buttons for caps. The color of the silken robes, the motifs embroidered on them, the shape of the hat, and the style of the girdle all indicate an official's rank and standing in court. At one time the regulations even specified the date on which the officials must switch from summer to winter attire.

The lavish embroidery on the ceremonial robes has symbolic significance. The most ancient insignia on state attire depicted the Twelve Ornaments, signs of power and authority. Only the Emperor was allowed to wear all twelve. One imperial robe was described as having waves (the sea) embroidered at the hem, with a mountain (the earth) rising from them, and clouds (the heavens) above. Dragons representing the Son of Heaven—the Emperor—sat among the clouds, ruling the whole.

Ming Huang, a T'ang Emperor, decided that court vestments in his day had become too luxurious and expensive. He ordered a bonfire made, which consumed vast numbers of silk garments and jeweled ornaments. Later in his life, however, he repented and resumed his lavish mode of living.

As people are prone to imitate those they perceive as their betters, colors and styles once reserved for high officials gradually filtered down to the everyday folk. But the Chinese have great respect for tradition, and fashions overall change very slowly. A person can wear a garment handed down by a parent or a grandparent with little fear that his contemporaries will consider him out of style.

COCK

The red comb on its head needs no adorning.
It struts, its body covered in snow white feathers.
All of its life it dares make few utterances,
But when it crows, ten thousand doors burst open.
—T'ang Yin (A.D. 1470-1523)

Pictures of a red cock are commonly found pasted on house walls in China, since the *kung-chi* is supposed to protect homes from fire. And since ghosts usually turn in around sunrise, it is believed that the cock chases them away. Therefore, the image of

53

中國事物

a white cock is used at weddings, funerals, and even at childbirth to discourage demons from making themselves known. The Chinese attribute five virtues to this felicitous fowl. He has a crown on his head, which is a sign of his literary genius; he has spurs on his feet, which make him a mean contender in close combat; he is courageous; he is benevolent, because he always clucks to the hens when he scratches up a grain; and he's faithful, because he never loses track of time. Cocks have been fighting in China since time immemorial, or at least since coined currency went into circulation.

PAPERCUT OF COCK.

COMPASS

The power of the lodestone to attract iron was known in China as early as 500 B.C. The first use of the directional properties of the lodestone seems to have been in the art of geomancy, or *feng-shui*. The first pointers were shaped like spoons, and rotated on the polished surface at the center of the geomancer's compass. The form of the spoon established a link with the Dipper, which also points north.

The spoon was gradually replaced by a figure, often a fish or tortoise, suspended on a pivot. This figure was in turn replaced by a magnetized needle. A final mutation was the use of a needle, or a fish, suspended on the surface of a bowl of water.

The shift from lodestone to magnetized needle took place during the fifth century A.D., but the shift from land use to maritime use of the compass did not take place until at least the middle of the ninth century. The reason for this may well be related to the fact that soft iron does not retain magnetism very long, while steel does —and that the maritime use of the compass for long voyages had to wait on the development of steel needles.

[See GEOMANCY.]

CONCUBINES

The system of concubinage can only be understood in a social structure that prized the continuity of the family above all else. Marriage was arranged, the compatibility of the new couple was assumed, and their principal mission was to produce a male heir.

Suppose, then, that the husband and another woman fell in love. Rather than disrupting the family, the woman might choose to be absorbed into it as his concubine. The husband could give her fine rooms to live in and every luxury he could afford, she might prove instrumental in the propagation of the family, but she would not alter its formal structure.

Admittedly the system lacked a reciprocal outlet for the wife, but she was compensated by virtue of her stature in the household. She was legally mother of all the children born to any of her husband's concubines. She selected wives for her sons, even if she were childless. Her enormous social power was unaffected.

Concubines, too, held a reputable social position. They wielded their share of influence over China's history, having figured in the collapse of a number of dynasties. One of the most infamous of these was Wu Hou, the Empress, who rose to power in the eighth century by usurping every office of the state after having ruled from "behind the curtain." She was a cruel, vain, and licentious woman, and was said to be a devout Buddhist. It is recorded that she died of ennui at the age of eighty-two. Her life story is remarkably reminiscent of the last Dowager Empress of China, Tzu Hsi, who also reached the Dragon Throne by way of the imperial bedchamber.

CONFUCIAN CLASSICS

As soon as Chinese children graduated from fairytales and stopped believing in Liu the Barbarian or in Big-Eyes Yang, they were presented with the Classics. These ancient texts were quite different from the spoken language, being archaic and extremely concise in expression. Students were required to memorize the main Confucian Classics, to be thoroughly familiar with ancient and modern poets, and to be able to compose original verses in the style of specific periods. Although the mechanical process of memorization was arduous, the Classics provided the budding scholars with a rich store of images and formulas of thought that could be decisively applied in real-life situations.

Su Tung-p'o (A.D. 1036-1101), one of China's greatest poets, exemplified this fresh approach to the Classics by teaching his sons first to write compositions of many words and few ideas, and then finally to write compositions of many ideas and few words. One of his sons asked him the point of the exercise. Su Ting-p'o replied: "Consider the marketplace. There are many goods displayed that are available to

羅盤　妾侍　儒教經典

55

中
國
事
物

me. All I need is one thing: money. Now, in terms of literary composition—if I first have ideas, then all the classical and historical books will be at my disposal. The main thing in composition is to have ideas."

The required reading list for the Chinese civil-service examinations included the following classics: The Five Classics (traditionally supposed to have been written or compiled by Confucius)—the *Book of History*, the *Book of Rites*, the *Book of Changes*, the *Spring and Autumn Annals*, and the *Book of Songs*; the Four Commentaries (containing the opinions of Confucius)—the *Analects*, the *Great Learning*, the *Doctrine of the Mean*, and *Book of Mencius*; the *Official Dynastic Histories*; and the *Ancient Book on Arithmetic*.

CONFUCIANISM

The Master said: "What the superior man seeks is in himself. What the inferior man seeks is in others."

The Master said: "The superior man, in the world, does not set his mind either for anything or against anything; what is right he will follow."

The Master said: "When we see men of worth, we should think of equaling them; when we see men of contrary character, we should turn inward and examine ourselves."

—Analects

At the time that Greek civilization was at its height in the Mediterranean, one of the greatest philosophers of all time appeared in China. Confucius (551-479 B.C.) was to influence the pattern of Chinese civilization for the next twenty-five hundred years until the coming of the twentieth century. The Chinese referred to Confucianism as *Ju Chiao* (The Teaching of the Learned) in keeping with the Master's belief that man was the only fit topic for the reflection of a sage. To Confucius' moral and social teachings were added ceremonies for the worship of ancestors, as well as various state rituals. Although Confucius was essentially a humanist, he nevertheless recognized the supremacy of heaven. His theories of the cosmos, however, were closely linked with ethics, since man was regarded as being in harmony with the universe.

[See CONFUCIAN CLASSICS and PHILOSOPHERS.]

CORMORANT

A distant cousin to the pelican, the cormorant may be found in different parts of the world, but nowhere has its unique fish-catching abilities been better explored than in the Orient. Cormorant fishing has been mentioned in Chinese annals as far back as the Sui dynastic history (A.D. 581-618).

The main fishing haunts of this odd-looking black bird are stretches along the North River above Guangzhou. The Chinese fisherman sets out with a pair of cormorants perched on either end of his punt. The birds are attached to their master, less by sentiment than by hempen cords that are fastened around their throats so as to discourage them from swallowing any of their catch.

At a given signal, the cormorants will glide gracefully into the water, darting swiftly after fish or eel, nipping them with their strong, hooked beaks, and swallowing until their pouches contain their full limit. The fish are then disgorged once the birds are back on board.

CORMORANT FISHING NEAR THE SHORE. C. 1907.

儒教　鷺鷀　化粧品　官場生活

COSMETICS

A "painted woman" was once considered a scandal in Western countries, and a subtle hand with cosmetics is still favored. But Chinese women considered putting on heavy makeup to be as natural as getting dressed in the morning.

The women applied a coat of white powder to make their complexions more fair, then added deep pink rouge to lips and cheeks. Beautiful eyebrows were arched to resemble a willow leaf, usually tweezed away, and redrawn with pencil or charcoal.

Gala events called for more elaborate makeup than usual. On only two occasions did a Chinese woman forego cosmetics: when she was in mourning and on her wedding day.

COURT LIFE

When the Emperor selected his concubine for the evening, a eunuch was sent to the woman's apartment. She was wrapped in a red cloak and escorted to the Chamber of Divine Repose. The eunuch removed the red robe and left her naked at the foot of the Emperor's bed. It might be assumed that this practice was emblematic of extreme sensual indulgence. However, it was instituted in the Ming Dynasty when a concubine brought a length of yellow cord, tucked under her embroidered gown, and tried to

中
國
事
物

strangle the Celestial Emperor in his sleep. So the pleasures of life in the imperial court were closely related to politics.

As if to symbolize this, governmental business during the Ming was conducted from sometime after midnight until shortly before dawn. The sight of so many spectral figures slipping through the dark streets of the Forbidden City must have set a curious tone to the assemblies.

Through the long history of the Chinese court there were periods of unparalleled enlightenment. One Emperor of the Han Dynasty invited everyone in the empire to apply for a position at court. Tung-fang Shuo responded and became such a great favorite he was spared the death penalty when he returned to the palace drunk one evening and relieved himself in the upper hall. He was stripped of rank as punishment and once again became a commoner, but he remained at court and regained favor.

There were also periods of extreme rigidity and nefarious intrigue. At the end of the Ming Dynasty, for example, a hundred thousand eunuchs ran the court. To see anyone of rank required payment of a "squeeze" to his subordinate. To obtain an audience with the "Son of Heaven" would be an extremely costly progression. And always there were the magnificent spectacles, great fights staged between bears and tigers, and women of legendary beauty.

[See DYNASTIES, EMPERORS, and GOVERNMENT.]

COURTESANS

At times in early China it was improper for a lady to play a musical instrument, or to appear too learned, or, in fact, to appear at all. Courtesans filled the gap. They were expert at singing and recitation and had a very high standard of performance. The world of the nightclub singer or movie star is the closest parallel in Western life.

The courtesan differed from the prostitute in that the courtesan courted with more than cash. The novel *Chiu-wei-kuei (Nine-Tailed Tortoise)*, which describes life in the 1930s, indicates a man might have to spend several months and three thousand or four thousand dollars before bedding what was supposed to be a woman of easy virtue.

There is a story of a famous courtesan who refused a young man's advances. He persisted, raising his offer to one hundred thousand pieces of cash for the privilege of spending the night with her. Still she declined. The following day he told the courtesan that all night as he slept, he dreamed they were united in love. Presumably he intended to resume courting her with this confession. Instead the courtesan promptly demanded the one hundred thousand pieces he had promised her.

COURTS

Underlings of the mandarin will shame the litigants and the mandarin will not hesitate to extract confessions under torture from even the innocent part.

—Li Kuei

Although the average Chinese had many legal rights under the imperial system, and in theory could petition all the way to the Emperor for a redress of grievances, the court system operated in a way very different from ours in the West.

The lowest courts were the district courts, presided over by a magistrate who handled all governmental and judicial matters in the district. From there one could appeal to departmental, circuit, or provincial courts.

The trials that took place were not trials as we know them, for the object of law was not so much to punish the guilty as to create social harmony. A local magistrate who had a heavy caseload was seen by his superiors as being ineffective at creating harmony among the populace. For this reason hearings were short. Neither party was allowed the advice of counsel, and the accused was considered guilty until proven innocent. Torture was freely used to extract confessions. Such a system naturally encouraged people to resolve their differences before they wound up in court, where both the innocent and the guilty were perceived as troublesome, obstinate, and unable to get along.

The main concern of law in China today is to maintain Communist Party standards of social and political morality, which is in direct contrast to the legal system of the West, which focuses more on the questions of procedure and violations of specific laws. According to the constitution of the People's Republic, cases that originate in the lower courts can go as high as the Supreme People's Court for final adjudication, however the exercise of appeal currently exists mostly in theory. Lawyers per se are rare in China.

[See LAW.]

娼
妓

法
庭

COURTROOM SCENE. C. 1900.

中國事物

CRANES

This bird is a common emblem of longevity in China, and is often depicted beneath a pine tree, also a symbol of age.

No bird except the phoenix gets splashier coverage in Chinese mythology than the Manchurian crane. It is the patriarch of the avian kingdom, and the favored mode of air transport for immortal beings. For this reason, the figure of a crane, wings outstretched, often adorns the face of coffins, to convey the departed's soul to heaven.

CRICKETS

"When the ancients painted swans and tigers, they turned out looking like ducks and dogs," wrote Mei Yao-ch'en in the Sung Dynasty. "But now I see these painted insects successful both in feeling and in form. The walkers truly seem to walk, the fliers truly seem to soar, the fighters seem to raise their limbs, the chirpers seem to swell their chests, the jumpers really move their legs, the starers really fix their eyes!"

Despite their avowed fondness for insect themes in art and literature, it is nevertheless true that Chinese entomologists did their best research in the sporting arenas

DECORATED GOURD CRICKET CAGE WITH A CARVED JADE COVER. LATE EIGHTEENTH, EARLY NINETEENTH CENTURY.

where cricket fights were held. Never has scholarship owed so much to the passion for gambling.

Cricket fighting is a grand old pastime dating back to the T'ang Dynasty (A.D. 618-906). Scores of volumes, both contemporary and classical, have been written on the subject of Chinese crickets. The crickets are classified according to various types, and graded according to their fighting strength. Such apocryphal topics as the best diet for the insect gladiators and the best urns to keep them in are discussed in minute detail.

The popularity of the sport reached its height in the last decades of the Sung Dynasty when the Emperor and his officials were so preoccupied with insect fights that they completely neglected affairs of state. In some of the provinces, magistrates accepted farm taxes in the form of crickets during the autumn quarter, the peak of the cricket-fighting season.

Cricket fights were usually conducted in a bamboo arena the size of an ordinary abacus—that is to say, in a rectangular box about two inches tall, eight inches long, and four inches wide. The top of the arena was covered by a screen made of netting over a fine, polished split bamboo frame. At each end of the arena was a sliding door through which the gladiators entered. In the middle of the box was another sliding door, separating the two insects. The door was removed and the crickets were prodded into mortal combat. The fight could last for thirty minutes or for thirty seconds. Usually the crickets were matched according to size, and their weights were taken before the bout.

Cricket fighters were housed in cages of porcelain, jade, ivory, bamboo, or gourd, and fed anything from fresh shrimp to hard-boiled eggs. During hot days the urns were kept in the cool, dark corners of the house. In winter the urns were covered with cotton. Despite these precautions, few crickets would survive the winter. Depending on their fight record, they might be buried in an ordinary box, or enshrined in a coffin of gold.

[See GRASSHOPPERS.]

CRIMINAL PUNISHMENT

The criminal in China was liable to face punishments quite different from those meted out in our society, yet in general Chinese authorities made an effort to fit the punishment to the crime. Punishment was determined by the degree and the severity of the crime, in much the same way that we distinguish among first-, second-, and third-degree murder.

A first-degree murder or a robbery combined with a murder was punished by beheading the offender. Decapitation was far and away the most serious punishment, since the Chinese believed that one's spirit would enter the afterworld in a state of disfigurement and shame—a literal loss of face. An accessory to murder would face strangulation, while an attempted murderer would be whipped and banished to another province, often to hard labor.

Rape, a second major crime, was also punishable by decapitation. Significantly, it was felt that a woman must resist for a rape to occur, and there are recorded cases of offenders being let off because the woman feigned sleep during a rape, and therefore did not resist.

Arson was usually punishable by whippings or banishment, but if fire were to touch imperial property or buildings, then death by strangulation was the required penalty.

鶴
蟋
蟀
刑
罰

中國事物

PAPERS ATTACHED TO CANGUE EXPLAIN THE CRIME AND SENTENCE. C. 1900.

Certain other crimes were treated quite differently than they were in the West. A perjurer or misleading witness was slapped on the cheek with a leather slipper or a piece of bamboo. Although divorce was legal, it was often a punishment to the woman. Women were required to be totally faithful, but men were not. Wives could be punished or divorced for barrenness, sensuality, lack of filial piety toward in-laws, loquacity, thievishness, jealousy, distrust, or incurable disease.

During the Cultural Revolution many political criminals were "rehabilitated" at communal work farms. Often mediators were assigned to mete out intense criticism and monitor self-criticism. The community was engaged to practice ostracism of an offender in order to aid in rehabilitation. Today such practices still exist, but imprisonment is quite common as well as death and terms of hard labor. The death sentence is often carried out at the time of sentencing.

[See COURTS, FIVE PUNISHMENTS, LAW, and TORTURE.]

CURRENCY

貨幣

The first medium of exchange used in China was probably the cowrie. These shells were strung together to form units of an accepted value during the reign of the Shang Kings (c.1550-c.1030 B.C.). Little is known of the systems of exchange or the methods of valuing these cowrie strings.

During the Bronze Age an unusual medium of exchange emerged. Agricultural tools such as knives or shovels were commonly exchanged as barter, and in time small imitation tools were made in bronze, deliberately for monetary purposes. Over time these coins became smaller and more stylized, and by the sixth century B.C. some of the states were minting coins in the shape of circular discs.

Disc-shaped coins, usually with a square or circular hole for stringing together, were used throughout the imperial period. Although generally they were copper coins of a single denomination, gold ingots were used in major transactions. As the use of coins became widespread during the Han Dynasty (206 B.C.-A.D. 220), barter became less important and was used only in periods of economic uncertainty.

The first attempt at printing paper money took place under Emperor Han Wu Ti (around 100 B.C.), although it would be a thousand years before the use of it became widespread. During this time a remarkable counterfeit-prevention method was invented. Bills were manufactured from the skins of a certain species of white deer found only in the Emperor's hunting preserves.

There was a more widespread emergence of banknotes in the ninth and tenth centuries. This owed much to the contemporary development of printing, the shortage of copper, and the needs of commercial establishments for a medium of exchange that could be handled more easily than unwieldy strings of copper cash. Bills of exchange and letters of credit issued by businesses soon evolved into modern bank-

COINED CURRENCY FACTORY SCENES. FROM THE *T'ien Kung K'ai Wu.*

中
國
事
物

notes, and by the eleventh century the government took over the issue of paper currency. However, the dangers of issuing too much paper money were widely ignored, and during the Sung Dynasty (A.D. 960-1279) periods of inflation were frequent. During the Mongol Dynasty years later, Marco Polo made reference to Asian peoples who were "idolaters and subjects of the Great Khan, and used Paper money...."

In 1948, after a terrible period of fiscal collapse due to corruption and mismanagement, China centralized the monetary system. By 1952, the People's Bank of China became the central note-issuing bank. The common currency in New China is called *renminbi* (people's currency). The principal denomination is the *yuan*. The *yuan*, in turn, is divided into ten *chiao*, while the *chiao* divides further into ten *fen*. Only the *fen* are issued in coin form.

CYCLE OF SIXTY

The Heavenly Ruler T'ien Huang had twelve brothers, ten of whom were kings, while the Earthly Ruler Ti Huang also had 10 brothers. Toward the close of his life the former said to the latter: "Let us combine the brothers of our two families, and thus establish a chronological order for naming months, days and hours."
—Edward T.C. Werner, *Dictionary of Chinese Mythology*

The ensuing system called the Cycle of Sixty was designed by the legendary Ta Nao (2698-2598 B.C.), a minister to Huang Ti. The brothers of the Heavenly and Earthly Rulers became the Ten Celestial Stems and Twelve Terrestrial Branches used in the computation of time by the Chinese since the Han Dynasty (206 B.C.-A.D. 220).

Chinese chronology divides time into three great periods extending over 24,192,000 years. These are divided into cycles of sixty years, sixty being the lowest common multiple of ten and twelve. Each of the sixty years is named after a combination of the ten stems and twelve branches, correlated with the progression of the Five Elements: water, wood, fire, earth, and metal; and with the progression of twelve animal names of Chinese astrology. The entire cycle is repeated after sixty years, and the cycles are numbered. The year 1984 will be the first year of the seventy-eighth Cycle of Sixty. The system is used to denote twelve hours of the Chinese day, and the twelve points of the compass.

Because the cycle runs its course in sixty years and has to be repeated, Chinese historical dates are often given by a double designation, using the cyclical-year number as well as the name and number of years of the reigning Emperor.

CYCLES

The role of cycles and the observation of cyclical change had a profound effect on the development of Chinese philosophy and science. The Taoists were captivated by the cyclical changes in nature, the celestial cycles, and the ever-recurring process of decay and renewal. The *I Ching* and the philosophies of change are all metaphorically attached to the rhythmic ebb and flow of things. Even Neo-Confucian philosopher Chu Hsi (A.D. 1130-1200) commented on the importance of cycles: "There is no other event in the universe except *yin* and *yang* succeeding each other in an unceasing cycle."

CYMBALS

Like drums, gongs, and bells, cymbals were part of an army's technical and psychological armature. Generals could use their sounds to direct troop movements. During night attacks, soldiers rubbed together many pairs of cymbals to frighten and confuse the enemy.

Although China is reputed to be the oldest cymbal-making country, the *Yueh*, a classic on Chinese musical instruments, written by Ch'en Yang in A.D. 1101, indicates that they may have entered China from Tibet.

The boss, or circular center section, of Chinese cymbals can be up to one inch thick. The diameter of the boss is three times its thickness; the diameter of the cymbal as a whole is about seven times the diameter of the boss.

Because of their high proportion of brass, Chinese cymbals have a rather brittle sound. Actors as well as musicians use small cymbals to draw attention to an important speech; the players strike cymbals several times before speaking.

MUSICIANS PLAYING CYMBALS, DRUMS, AND GONGS AT WEDDING FEAST. FUZHOU. C. 1910.

DECIMAL SYSTEM

One of the key elements of the decimal system is place notation, in which a number is written according to how many ones, tens, hundreds, and so on, it is made up of.

六十甲子　甲子　鈸　十進制

中國事物

There are examples of place notation in China that go back as far as the thirteenth century B.C.

Early Chinese place notation used names for each place—as though we wrote 321 by saying "three hundreds, two tens, and one." This affected the systems of weights and measures, which may have begun to use decimal divisions as early as the sixth century B.C.

By the third century A.D. the system of decimal place names began to be extended to fractions, so that decimal fractions could be written. There is also evidence that multiplying by tens and hundreds was understood as moving the number a "step up," in much the same way that we speak of "moving the decimal point."

The other key element of the decimal system is the use of zero, which makes calculation much easier. The earliest Chinese practice was simply to omit the name of the unneeded place: This was useful in tabulation, but not in arithmetic, which had to await the borrowing of the zero symbol, perhaps from Arabia.

The old decimal naming system is still used today in literary writings, and for reading numbers out loud, but in science and mathematics only arabic numerals are used.

DECORATIVE DESIGNS

Unbroken, undecorated space is as anathema to the Chinese craftsman as it is to a modern billboard advertiser. Fortunately, in their art, pottery, gardens, and so forth, the Chinese artist aims for aesthetic harmony.

CHINESE INTERLOCKING DECORATIVE PATTERN.

The Chinese are attracted to extremes in color and sound, and the striking design and vibrant color of their porcelain are appreciated worldwide. Designs are used everywhere to decorate storefronts, temples, bridges, memorial arches, stationery, carpets, clothing, and other items.

The simplest type of design is the meander or key pattern, which derived from archaic pictographs depicting clouds and thunder. It has been used in pottery and other arts as a border design for thousands of years. Other common patterns include herringbone, fish roe, octagons and squares, trelliswork, honeycomb, ring designs, and flowered and starred designs. Many of these arabesque and diaper patterns are similar to different lines of European heraldry and probably reflect common historical nature worship.

The swastika, similar to the key pattern, is a design found in most cultures, and in China it is seen on the stomach of idols, the eaves of houses, on carpets, and on other objects. In India the swastika was the monogram of Vishnu and Siva and was probably imported to China by the Buddhists. The swastika has its crampons directed toward the right, and its opposite, the sauvastika, is directed toward the left. Both signs are found on the footprints of the Buddha.

DEER

The deer is believed to live to a very great age, and the god of longevity, Shou Lao, is frequently pictured mounted on a buck. The deer is also believed to be the only animal capable of finding the fungus of immortality, *Ling Chih*.

The horns of the deer hold the same important position in Chinese pharmacology that they formerly held in European medicine. The soft internals are pulverized and made into pills, while other parts are boiled into jelly. They are believed useful as a stimulating aphrodisiac and as an astringent or a tonic.

Yak were also formerly common in China, and herds of deer were said to follow this animal, guided by the movements of its tail. Buddhist and Taoist monks use the yak's tail, or chowry, as a fly whisk, keeping the dust of the world at bay.

DICE

Dice were used in both divination and gambling. Chinese dice are numbered from one to six and arranged the same way as ours, but the four and the one are colored red. The Chinese substitute a bowl for our cup from which to throw the dice. Different games are played with different numbers and sizes.

Dice are used in a board game that seems to be a nineteenth-century precursor of Monopoly. Players throw dice in order to determine whether to move upward or downward on a large paper diagram listing all the different titles and dignitaries (of which there were many) of the Chinese Government.

DICTIONARIES

The Chinese, strictly speaking, have no alphabet. This makes their dictionaries a little peculiar. The earliest dictionary, the *Erh Ya*, is traditionally ascribed to the Duke of Chou (twelfth century B.C.), but was probably compiled during the second century B.C. The *Erh Ya* that has come down to us is a book of synonyms in ten chapters.

Another ancient dictionary is the *Shih Chou P'ien*, compiled around 800 B.C. The courtier, Shih Chou, supposedly codified a variety of writing systems into a standard vocabulary of some nine thousand or ten thousand characters, but his work is entirely lost. Other analogical dictionaries grouped together words that sounded alike but carried different meanings (homophones), which gave them the frivolous look of being huge collections of puns.

Eventually, dictionaries organized according to the words' meanings gave way to dictionaries organized according to how the words were written. The first of these was the *Shuo-wen*, attributed to Hsu Shen of the second century A.D. He arranged 10,600 characters according to 540 radicals, giving a brief history of each. Someone later added a guide to pronunciation, probably during the T'ang Dynasty. By the

中國事物

Ming Dynasty the number of radicals had been reduced to the present 214. The radicals function as roots to the word's meaning and are themselves ordered according to the number of strokes required to write them. These kinds of dictionaries, therefore, require you to know how to "spell" a word or recognize the radicals in order to look it up.

Linguistic breakthroughs during the fifth century A.D. made it more practical to organize dictionaries according to sound. For both of these Buddhism was responsible. The Buddhist dictionary *Yuh Pien* (A.D. 543) introduced the system *fan ch'ieh*, which made it possible "phonetically" to represent the pronunciation of a character.

Modern Chinese dictionaries generally combine a phonetic dictionary with an index of radicals, making it possible to look up the meaning of a word from its pronunciation, and its pronunciation from its written form.

[See CALLIGRAPHY and LANGUAGE.]

DIVINATION

> . . . to unravel what is confused and search out what is mysterious; to discover what is deep and reach to what is distant thus determining what will be fortunate or unlucky, there is nothing greater than the milfoil (yarrow) and tortoise.
>
> —Confucius

The Chinese, like all other ancient and classical civilizations, developed highly complex systems of divination. In the belief that spirits and gods know the future, divination was used to find out these secrets and communicate them to men.

The earliest and most popular form of divination was by heating a tortoise shell and observing the way it cracked when a hot point was touched to it. Tortoise shells with as many as seventy-two different divining points have been found. During the Chou Dynasty (c. 1030-256 B.C.), the ultimate work on divination was composed, introducing a new system involving hexagrams and their interpretations. The system used six alternating odd and even numbers to indicate the divine will and its response to any serious question. This evolved into the text known as *I Ching (Book of Changes)*. The book is considered the greatest manual of divination ever written.

Despite the apparent comprehensiveness of the *I Ching*, a host of other divination techniques abounded in China until recent times. Some are:

Physiognomy: Certain Taoist priests—notably the followers of a blind Tao-shi, who lived between A.D. 780 and 805—foretell characteristics and temperament by examining the lines and structures of the faces of those who come to them.

Celestial divination involves techniques similar to Astrology, as it is known in the West, but consists of calculating the relations of much more complex systems: the nine divisions of the celestial sphere, the five planets, the six constellations, the five sacred mountains, and the four great rivers of China.

Casting lots: By either placing one hundred numbered and polished bamboo slips in a tube and shaking them until one falls out, or by shaking a box with ten coins, one of which is marked, and noting the order in which the marked coin falls out, a person can kneel before an appropriate god and learn the correct action to take in the future. The numbers and the coin position are keys to the "drawn" verse in a book that goes with the lots. This system of casting lots is similar to the *I Ching*, but has tremendous variations based on local custom throughout China.

Divining blocks: Mostly made of bamboo or wood, divining blocks are tossed before a deity in sequence; by observing which sides are up (much like dice), a series of combinations leads to a cross-referenced commentary indicating whether the action contemplated is in divine favor or not.

Omens are also drawn from the cries of birds, by the consultation of chopsticks in a bowl of water, the dissection of written characters, and by examination of finger joints, as well as by countless other techniques.

[See ASTROLOGY, BOOK OF CHANGES, FORTUNE-TELLING, and PALMISTRY.]

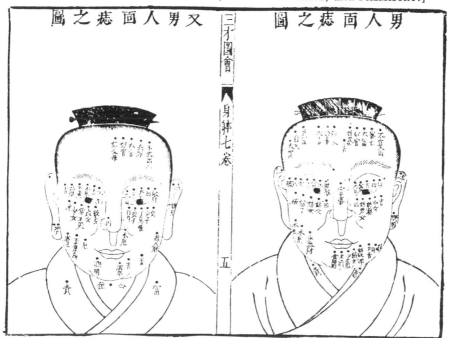

SIXTEENTH CENTURY DRAWING DEPICTING THE SCIENCE OF PHYSIOGNOMY. FROM THE *San Ts'ai T'u Hui.*

DIVORCE

According to the Confucian codes, there were seven justifications a man might have to divorce his wife: barrenness, adultery, jealousy, theft, disobedience toward her husband's parents, an incurable disease, or a shrewish tongue. If the wife's parents had died, however, she couldn't be divorced because there would be no family to take her back. The husband couldn't divorce her while he was in mourning for a parent, and if she had mourned the customary three years for his parents, he couldn't divorce her at all. The code also provided that, had the husband been poor when he married and grown wealthy in the course of their life together, he could not send his wife back to her family. Thus, although divorce was left to the discretion of the husband and was not a matter of official concern, it was probably infrequent. There would be little reason to antagonize the wife's family when one could select a concubine without risking social opprobrium.

For the wife, the situation was much different. If through abuse, she had suffered broken bones, the law might intervene, but she had no other grounds for divorce. Only when her husband's misbehavior was flagrant enough to disgrace her family

中國事物

could a bride expect them to avenge her.

Marriage laws were rewritten in 1950 and divorce was finally made available to women. The general trend, however, is now toward family mediation so that, after a brief thaw that undid the ills of the arranged-marriage system, divorce is again difficult to obtain.

[See CRIMINAL PUNISHMENT and MARRIAGE.]

DOCTORS

The Chinese doctor of old was a curious combination of quack and naturalist. He had no medical exams to pass, and no qualifications were necessary. He may have even failed in business before taking up the healing profession. All that he required was a book of prescriptions, preferably obtained from a retiring practitioner. "Beware of taking drugs from a doctor whose family has not been in medicine for three generations," was the only consumer-protection wisdom of the day.

Traditional medical concepts were based on a philosophical understanding of the human body, which was regarded as a microcosm of the universe. Good health was actually a state of harmony among the different "virtues." Doctors of the Sung period recognized five important organs (heart, liver, spleen, lungs, and kidneys) that were related to the five elements. Methods of treatment included massage, punctures made with a silver needle at specified points, and drugs and beverages of various kinds. A popular recipe for curing malaria recommended the use of a fly found on a dog. "Take one dog fly. Remove the legs and wings. Roll it in wax so as to form a pellet, which is to be taken with cold rice wine on the day of the attack."

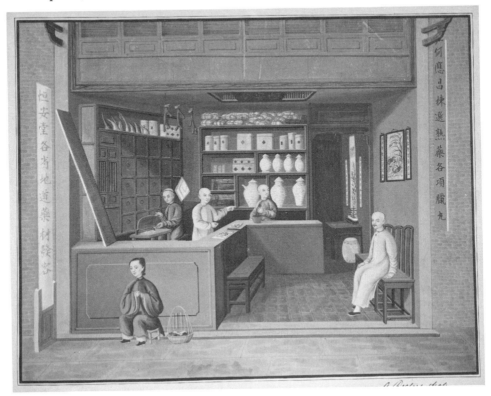

DOCTOR'S SHOP. C. 1830.

From 1949 to 1965 the number of doctors in China trained in Western medicine rose from twelve thousand to two hundred thousand. However, the integration of Chinese and Western medicine is the ideal in China, and doctors are often trained in both disciplines. In rural China where doctors are not available, "worker doctors" or "barefoot doctors" spread the word about preventive medicine, birth control, and hygiene. They are able to treat and diagnose simple illness, while as much as 85 per cent of their medicines are herbal.

[See Acupuncture and Herbology.]

医
生

狗

DOGS

A monk asked Chao-chou Tsung-shen, a Chinese Zen master: "Does a dog have Buddha nature or not?" Chao-chou got down on his hands and knees, wagged his tail a bit, then replied (to the best of his abilities): "Would you repeat that question?"

Regardless of whether they have Buddha natures, sport Taoist tails, or are canines of the Confucian school, the classic Chinese dog has been around for over four thousand years. In A.D. 565 a Chinese Emperor gave the name of Chi Hu (Red Tiger) to a Persian dog that used to ride sidesaddle with him. In A.D. 620 a dog and a bitch only eight inches high were presented to Emperor Kao Tsu. These precursors to the modern Pekingese were so intelligent that they were trained to lead a horse by its reins, and to carry lit torches for their masters at night. The cult of the lapdog in China reached its peak in the middle of the eighteenth century. Beijing had thousands of these "sleeve dogs," and the imperial court had a large staff employed as a pooper-scooper brigade.

Dowager Empress Tzu Hsi made a special effort to develop standards for the breed. She decreed: "Let the Pekingese wear the swelling cape of dignity around its neck. Let its forelegs be bent so it won't feel inclined to wander away from the imperial precincts. Let it be taught to refrain from gadding about. Let its color be that of a lion to be carried in the sleeve of a yellow robe...." Its recommended diet was "sharks' fins, curlews' liver, and the breast of quail."

When Beijing was being sacked by the British in 1860, Tzu Hsi gave strict orders that all the palace dogs be killed. A few were captured, however, and one of them was presented to Queen Victoria. Later, a few more specimens were obtained and a normal breeding program was begun in the West.

The Chinese fighting dog is one of the strangest-looking dogs in the world. In fact, it doesn't even *look* like a dog, bearing a strong resemblance instead to a diminutive hippopotamus. Its muzzle is blunt, its coat is piglike and unpleasant for other dogs to mouth, and its teeth are curved like scimitars, making it next to impossible to disengage its jaws after a hold has been established. The breed has been kept in China for centuries, but it has not been recognized by any of the major canine organizations in the West.

Contrary to popular opinion, the "chow" did not receive its name because it was one of the principal items in the diet of the Chinese. The most probable explanation is that it simply means "Chinese dog," since the Chinese who lived around Guangzhou were once known as Chows. In fact, the chow was nothing more than your average mongrel, and it did not become the breed it is today without the conscientious intervention of the English, who took the dog to heart.

At the Fourth Annual Exhibition of the Chow Chow Club at the Royal Aquarium in London in 1898, the program noted: "Every dog has his day and the chow-chow is having his now. Nevertheless, we venture to predict a long life for the

中
國
事
物

club because it is certain that when the chow-chow is bred from good stock and domesticated, it is a very jolly dog and quite unlike the species you meet in the Far East."

DOMINOES

At least three centuries ago, the Chinese invented dominoes. They may have been derived from Chinese dice, which also have the one and the four spots in red, and Chinese playing cards must have certainly derived from them, as the cards not only have the same number of spots as the dominoes, but also bear the same names. A Chinese domino set will have thirty-two "bones," eleven of which are matched pairs called the "civil series." (The remaining ten are "military.") Ancient sets were made of ebony, ivory, or bone.

Dominoes, like dice, were once used in divination, and are popular in both China and Korea for both games and gaming. The clacking of the bones is said to sound like castanets in crowded casinos. *Shih Tsai, P'ai Chiu,* and *T'ien Chiu* are played with dominoes and dice, and *T'ien Chiu* can also be played with cards.

DONKEY

The donkey gets a bad name in most cultures, and the Chinese is no exception. The donkey is a universal symbol of stupidity. In light of its usefulness as a work animal and its occasional presence on the Chinese dinner table, we might expect the lowly donkey to fare better in mythology than it does.

The donkey appears neither in the Cycle of Sixty nor in the twenty-eight Chinese constellations, and the saying, "Year of the Donkey, Month of the Horse" means never.

Since no reference to the donkey occurs in China before A.D. 168, it may be assumed that this animal was imported to the country. It is possible, however, that it is an offshoot from the onager or wild ass from Mongolia.

DOOR GODS

The legend of the door gods goes back to Emperor T'ai Tsung (A.D. 627-40) of the T'ang Dynasty. The Emperor was haunted by spirits passing back and forth through an arch formed by a bent peach tree. Two of the Emperor's ministers offered to stand guard fully armed at night to protect him from the demons. When after several nights the nightmares ceased, the Emperor thanked his faithful servants, and had pictures of them painted on either side of the door leading into the palace. Ever since, on New Year's Day everyone in China posts pictures of the two armed *Men Shen* on the left and the right sides of their doorways.

The door gods became associated with the host of household deities honored in China until recent times. They are closely linked with the protective functions exercised by the gods of the six directions and the god of the kitchen.

[See SHADOW WALL.]

DRAGON

The Chinese dragon, unlike its Western counterpart, is a benevolent monster, and has been worshiped since primitive times as *Lung Wang* (the Dragon King), in charge of rain. The dragon is chief of the four supernatural creatures, the others being the unicorn, the phoenix, and the tortoise. It has been speculated that the physical appearance of the dragon is based on some prehistoric animal, but also that it resembles

骨
牌
驢
門
神
龍

Donkeys used as work animals. From the *T'ien Kung K'ai Wu.*

中國事物

alligators (found in some Chinese rivers), as well as smaller serpents and lizards.

The dragon lives part of the year in heaven and part in the mud underground. Most dragons inhabit the watery depths of the sea and rivers, and popular tradition has four dragon Kings ruling over the four seas surrounding the habitable earth. The dragon was originally the symbol of fertile rain, and the regenerative power of heaven, but beginning with the earliest literature, dragons were appropriated by the

蒼龍散子
一二四

rulers of China as emblems of imperial power. Many of the early emperors were said to have dragon fathers and terrestrial mothers. The emperors became known as "dragon faced" men who sat on the "dragon throne" and ascended into heaven on the back of a "dragon." The imperial dragon was depicted as having five claws on his foot rather than four, like dragons of the more pedestrian variety.

Because of such an overwhelming association with power, dragons came to symbolize success, wealth, and importance. The *I Ching* uses the dragon to signify wisdom. Physically, however, dragons are an amalgam of nine different beasts. It is believed that there are in fact nine different types of dragon, each inhabiting a different type of environment and in charge of different powers. The only harmful variety of dragon is the *chiao* which is scaly and resides in the marshes high in the mountains. For its strength, the dragon is always shown pursuing a pearl, which is called the Pearl of Potentiality. If lost, the pearl leaves the dragon helpless and incapable of action. The portrayal of the dragon trying to swallow the sun has often been used by magistrates to signify the impossibility of their dealing unjustly.

While the cult of the dragon in China is widespread due to imperial appropriation of the mythical animal, it remained popular as a water deity also. Sailors and boat owners traditionally beseeched the dragon for safety on water and for wealth. The dragon was held responsible for storms and droughts, as well as being in charge of the confluence of two rivers. Peasants prayed to the dragon and made earthen dragon images to bring rain in times of drought. Floods were also the dragon's domain, and were controlled by the proper sacrifices.

The teeth and bones of the dragon are considered among the rarest of medical substances. They are gathered from the bones of mammoths and other prehistoric beasts occasionally found in China, and they are ground into a fine powder and sold for a very high sum.

DRAWING

The distinction between drawing and painting does not strictly apply to traditional Chinese pictorial art. The two methods are considered to be identical and are both referred to by the same term, *hua*. In Western terms, Chinese "drawings" might best be described as pictures in which the linear brush stroke is predominant, while the calligraphic brush stroke is used in "paintings." Buddhist and Taoist artists favored the precise linear technique in their drawings of iconographic subjects because it was believed that any deviations were sacrilegious and robbed the drawings of magic and potency.

Soft brushes were made from goat hair, stiff ones from rabbit hair or wolf hair. The brushes came in different sizes and different widths, and sometimes several would be fastened together in a row to produce a flat wash effect on a large area. Ink had to be freshly ground by rubbing an ink stick on an inkstone. The brush would be allowed to soak up just enough ink to cover an exact surface of paper—whatever was required to render flower petals, leaves, or rocks in a garden. Now would the Chinese artist be ready to strike with his brush? Not quite. In order to be proficient in drawing, he would first have to serve an intensive apprenticeship in calligraphy. This would begin at the age of six or seven, when a child would spend two hours a day on his calligraphy lesson. He would graduate to doing stone-rubbing reproductions of T'ang and Sung calligraphies, both those schools being noted for their structural qualities. At the age of ten or twelve, the budding artist would move on to the Wei Dynasty to perfect the stele rubbings that are distinguished for their austere stylistic

中國事物

elegance and semi-archaic flavor. At fifteen or sixteen, the apprentice would begin copying the earliest forms of Chinese writings, usually rubbings from stone drums and ancient bronzes. Meanwhile he would also be practicing the use of a heavy steel brush, a pointed steel rod the size of a large brush, without any support in order to develop strength and steadiness in his arm and wrist. The Chinese believed that copying and lifting weights were the best forms of training in the graphic arts.

Both calligraphy and drawing share the same qualities—that of a restless yet rhythmic movement, with the ever-present yet undetectable life force behind it. The clouds on paper are always filled with the breath of wind, the ripples on a pond strive for stillness, garments on figures flutter symbiotically, and limbs turn this way and that. Now having mastered all this, the student may begin to draw acorns falling, birds in flight, and the arrival of the seasons.

DRUMS

Carried in the forefront of the fighting, the drum shared with the flag a place of honor in battle. "The drum was used to beat the assembly, and in the advance, the bell as a signal to halt," records the *Art of War* from the fifth century B.C. Six-foot drums, pulled in ox-drawn wagons, were sometimes at the head of a battle formation. The drummers, frequently madmen recruited from prison, struck the drums with clubs or whips. Drums had an important role in religious ritual, too. The *Book of Songs* describes a hymn performed to drum accompaniment. Written records mention drums as far back as the Yin (Shang) period (c. 1350-1030 B.C.). Legend gives them a much longer history as far back as 3500 B.C., when they were supposedly introduced from Central Asia: Ancient writings refer to drums as barbarous instruments from Turkestan and Tibet.

The body of most Chinese drums is wood, and it is often built up in sections like a barrel. A membrane, called the head, is stretched over each end. Made of thick cowskin or pigskin (although even the skin of fish has been used), the heads are nailed

PERFORMANCE OF RITUAL MUSIC WITH DRUMS. C. 1900.

to the body of the drum. Most Western drums, in contrast, use metal bands to attach the head, which allows the head to be tightened and thus tuned. Because the tension of the heads cannot be adjusted, Chinese drums cannot be tuned. The heads are often painted or varnished to keep the skins taut under varying atmospheric conditions.

An earthenware drum may have been the first Chinese drum. A baked clay pot was filled with bran and the top covered with skin. A smaller version, without grain inside, still exists today as the *po-fu*. Another drum, the *ping-ku*, resembles a tambourine. The body is just three inches high; the head diameter is nine to fifteen inches. The rim is lacquered red and the skins are decorated. The body of the *t'ao-ku* drum is pierced by a stick, which forms its handles. When the player twirls the drum on the stick, beads suspended on the body swing up and strike the heads. The *t'ao-ku* evolved into the small clapper drums used today by beggars and street hawkers.

Although the bronze gong drum was used as early as the fourth century B.C., tradition says that General Ma Yuan invented it to help him conquer northern Indochina in 43 B.C. Ma Yuan placed the gong drum under a waterfall. The din of water falling on the bronze head persuaded the enemy that reinforcements were on the way. They promptly fled. Gong drums were considered sacred. Sometimes a little hole was drilled in the side of the drum to allow spirits, believed to inhabit the drum, a way to escape. Owning a gong drum became a status symbol, too. The bigger the drum, the more favorably it reflected on its owner.

Chinese drums are an important part of Chinese music and theater and are occasionally included in twentieth-century Western orchestral music. Aaron Copland scored a Chinese drum in his "Concerto for Piano and Orchestra" in 1929, and Roger Sessions called for a small Chinese drum in his Third Symphony, written in 1957.

DUCK

Across the mist flowers and grass appear far and hazy,
How I regret we came here not by the same path.
Just where we stop our oars and chance to meet,
Mandarin ducks fly off into the swift current.
—Chu Ch'ing-yu (A.D. 826)

With its mauve feathers, flecked with gold, the gaudily plumaged mandarin duck has for centuries been a favorite subject for Chinese artists. Observing the bird's monogamous habits, the Buddhists held it in high esteem for its fidelity and connubial affection. Chinese chefs have even higher regard for the Pekin white duck's gastronomic virtues, although the method of preparing the world-famous Peking duck dates back only to the turn of the century. The Chinese wore duck-shaped amulets for protection against drownings, and for extra luck would don duck-shaped life jackets—actually buckles that were made of jade, depicting two ducks entwined by lotuses. Duck's Day was celebrated on the fourth day of the New Year when traditionally all the public bathhouses would reopen for business.

DWARFING PLANTS

The intimacy between plants and people was an integral part of Chinese life. Households that could not afford the space for a garden went one step farther in aligning themselves with nature—the table culture of dwarf plants. This art—called *P'en tsai*, and later the Japanese *bonsai* when it was introduced to Japan—focused on the land-

77

中
國
事
物

ELEGANTLY SHAPED BAMBOO IN CHINESE GARDEN. C. 1905.

scaping of floral scenes in miniature. Although it is believed that *P'en tsai* was developed during the T'ang Dynasty, its origins are not precisely known. Dwarf plants were frequently depicted in Sung paintings, and as motifs on porcelains of the sixteenth century.

Curiously enough, the seemingly grotesque and awkward twisting of miniature trees against a rock setting was an accurate depiction of actual Chinese landscapes. Conifers and maples were preferred trees for miniaturization, as well as evergreens and Japanese apricots. The process of dwarfing would take years of diligent pruning and constricting. The principal means of reducing a plant's growth was through the confinement of its roots. The main root is removed so the plant must survive on the surface, auxiliary-root system.

DYNASTIES

The Western Capital is in turmoil,
Wolves and tigers create chaos.
Once again I leave the Central Realm
Cast myself to the Ching barbarians.
Family and relatives face me in grief,
Friends pursue and cling to me.

朝
代

As I leave the gate, all is desolation:
White bones cover the plain.
—Wang Ts'an (A.D. 177-217)

Over the past two thousand years in China there have been hundreds of Emperors, thousands of millions of individuals, and countless rebellions, but only one system of rule: the dynasty. Just as the Shang fell to the Chou, the Chou to the Ch'in, the Ch'in to the Han—and on and on—the classic cycle of change would continue until the last dynasty, the Ch'ing, was replaced by the republic in 1911. The cycle was classic, and totally unique among all the civilized countries of the world that somehow managed to reach the twentieth century intact. A dynasty would lose its Mandate of Heaven at the hands of a popular rebellion. A new dynasty with a new Emperor would be installed. There would be a vigorous period of new ideas and an active reform of the old. This would be modeled, nonetheless, closely and carefully on some earlier dynasty. Finally, the new rulers would become jaded, transmuting enlightenment into lust and hedonism. The eunuchs in the Imperial Court would man their posts, exerting their squeeze through corruption and intrigues. The countryside would once again become the stage for rebellion. Starvation and injustice would take its toll. The cosmos would shudder, certain freak meteorological manifestations would alert the people to the fact that the Mandate of Heaven was about to be transferred to a new dynastic contender.

Chinese dynasties were divided into two types: the *cheng* and the *p'ien*, the principal and the partial dynasties. The former ruled the entire country, while the latter would exert influence only on portions of the Middle Kingdom. There were over twenty-four principal dynasties in the period from the Chou to the Ch'ing, and an undetermined number of minor ones.

Kao Tzo, founding emperor of the Han Dynasty in 202 b.c., and Emperor Ching the fifth sovereign (d. 140 b.c.). Both from the *Sun Ts'ai T'u hui*, 1609.

79

中國事物

THE DYNASTIES OF CHINA

HSIA			c. 2000-1600 B.C.
SHANG			c. 1550-c. 1030 B.C.
	Western Chou	c. 1030-711	
	Eastern Chou	770-256	
CHOU	"Spring and Autumn" period	722-481	c. 1030-256
	Warring States period	480-222	
CH'IN			221-207
	Former (Western) Han	206 B.C.-A.D. 9	
HAN	Hsin	9-23	206 B.C.-A.D. 220
	Later (Eastern) Han	25-220	
THREE	Shu (Han)	221-263	
KINGDOMS	Wei	220-265	221-265
	Wu	222-280	
	Chin	265-316	
SOUTHERN	Eastern Chin	317-420	
(Six	Liu Sung	420-479	
Dynasties)	Southern Ch'i	479-502	
	Liang	502-557	
and	Ch'en	557-587	265-581
	Northern Wei (T'o-pa)	386-535	
NORTHERN	Eastern Wei (T'o-pa)	534-543	
DYNASTIES	Western Wei (T'o-pa)	535-554	
	Northern Ch'i	550-577	
	Northern Chou (Hsien-pi)	557-581	
SUI			581-618
T'ANG			618-906
	Later Liang	907-922	
FIVE	Later T'ang (Turkic)	923-936	
DYNASTIES	Later Chin (Turkic)	936-948	907-960
	Later Han (Turkic)	946-950	
	Later Chou	951-960	
Liao (Khitan Tartars)		907-1125	
Hsi-hsia (Tangut Tibetan)		990-1227	
SUNG	Northern Sung	960-1126	960-1279
	Southern Sung	1127-1279	
Chin (Jurchen Tartars)		1115-1234	
YUAN (Mongols)			1260-1368
MING			1368-1644
CH'ING (Manchus)			1644-1911

Hsia Dynasty (c. 2000-1600 B.C.)—The Hsia Dynasty belongs to the prehistory of China, and although Chinese tradition speaks often of the Hsia it really doesn't tell much about them. Supposedly they descended from the Yao and the Shun peoples, who were, in Confucian mythology, virtuous rulers from a prehistoric golden age. The archaeological evidence is that the Hsia existed in Southwest Shanxi Province. They were skilled in working with bronze and they also developed a primitive agriculture. A written language predated the Hsia but we do not have evidence of their use of it. Many questions about them remain unanswered.

Shang Dynasty (c. 1550-c. 1030 B.C.)—The history of Chinese civilization really begins with the Shangs. How they came to precedence over the previous cultures is unknown, but by 1600 B.C. they were established in northwestern Henan and towns near Anyang. The several cities of the Shangs were probably quite large, consisting of rectangular houses surrounded by walls of tamped earth.

Their accomplishments were impressive. They discovered or invented sericulture (silk production), horse breeding, wheeled chariots, a logographic script of over a thousand words, and advanced agriculture to feed their population of five million.

The Shang worshiped deceased rulers and ministers and in these practices we can see the beginnings of Chinese ancestor worship. They also consulted oracles, sometimes by reading tortoise shells and bones. Many of these "oracle bones" have been found. They would burn a depression into the bones so that cracks formed in them. From the shape of these cracks the future was foretold. Later, the question and the answer would be written on the bone.

The Shang Dynasty apparently collapsed under the weight of its own decadence. The last Shang King, Chou Hsin, has been called a Chinese Nero, and by one historian, "a debauching monster." During the popular rebellion that ended in the establishment of the Chou Dynasty, Chou Hsin put on his finest robes and set fire to his palace, perishing in the flames.

Chou Dynasty (c. 1030-256 B.C.)—In 1028 B.C. Wen Wang led an army into Henan and captured the Shang capital, bringing to life the odd period known as the Chou Dynasty. The Chou had ruled a small western realm, in Shanxi, and probably came from Tibetan and Turkish stock, later intermarrying with the Shang. Because they were a small minority, faced with ruling a huge, unmanageable territory, the Chous divided China into nearly a thousand fiefdoms. The lords of these little kingdoms were chartered, much like feudal lords in medieval Europe, and represented a family or clan. They owed their allegiance to the central Chou capital of Shaanxi but within their little walled provinces, their power was nearly total.

Perhaps the most interesting accomplishment of the Chou was in the field of religion, where they abolished human sacrifice and systematized the worship of ancestors. Moreover, because the head of the family took over the performance of religious services, thousands of Shang priests literally became unemployed. In finding a new place for themselves in society these priests evolved into something like the scholars of the later eras. They became specialists in traditional morals and religious celebrations, resolving legal disputes and organizing local festivals and sacrifices at the appropriate times of year. In short, China gained a social class with the unique functions of defending tradition and creating social harmony. This was also a time of great social and intellectual ferment. The ideas of Confucius and Lao Tsu were widely circulated.

As the centuries rolled by, the rulers became less effective and the empire grew weaker and weaker. The feudal system began to dissolve as the larger states con-

朝
代

中
國
事
物

quered their neighbors. By the third century B.C. only fourteen states remained of the original thousand. The stage was set for the reunification of the empire under Shih-Huang-Ti, the Tiger of Ch'in.

Ch'in Dynasty (221 B.C.-207 B.C.)—Ch'in was an unlikely province to produce the conqueror of China. It was a barbaric western region, somewhat isolated from the civilization and etiquette of Confucian China. Like the other provinces, they were often at war with each other and the hated Hsiung-nu, the steppe people of the North. As late as 361 B.C. Ch'in was not represented at the formal conference of feudal rulers.

But their isolation did help them become great soldiers. They were famous for their horsemen and mounted archers, and developed battering rams and siege equipment for attacking walled cities. By 318 B.C. they had defeated the provinces of Han, Chou, Wei, Yen, and Ch'i. In 312 B.C. they defeated Ch'u. In 293 B.C. they beat Han and Wei again. Though the reports are probably exaggerated we can be sure that these battles were murderously destructive. It is estimated that over one hundred thousand Chou soldiers were executed after surrendering to Ch'in in 260 B.C.

It was on the fields of war that King Cheng gained the title, the Tiger of Ch'in. But it was his ferocity in government that has made him one of the most interesting, and least-liked figures in Chinese history. His chief adviser, Li Ssu, was a leading proponent of legalism, which in direct conflict with Confucianism, held that men should act in their own self-interest. Accordingly, private land ownership grew, destroying the feudal system, while leaving military power in the Emperor's hands. He introduced a harsh legal code, as well as severe taxation systems (to pay for public works like the Great Wall), slavery, and corvée labor (mandatory public service). But he earned the harshest enmity of historians when he ordered the burning of all classical Chinese writings, a great setback for advanced philosophical thought in the East.

Though detested by the Confucian historians that followed, it must be said that Ch'in was a vigorous and even spectacular leader. He undertook great public works, which secured the Empire and improved the economy. He developed the governmental pattern for future dynasties, dividing the empire into thirty-six provinces, each commanded by a triumvirate consisting of a civil officer, a military officer, and an imperial attaché who reported only to the Emperor. On the River Wei he built a new capital and around it he constructed imitations of each of the provincial capitals he had conquered, and peopled them with slaves, dancing girls, musicians, and the wealth of conquered lands. This must have been an incredible spectacle; nearly twenty-eight miles of the riverbank were covered with castles and royal gardens. Sadly, these were burned to the ground by the conquerors who followed.

When he died, Ch'in Shih-Huang-Ti was buried and it is said his concubines and any workmen who had been in the tomb were sealed in with him. Like many strong leaders in history, Ch'in's empire did not outlast him. His sons proved to be weak leaders and by 209 B.C. the empire was again divided and under attack by Liu Pang, who would establish one of the most popular dynasties in Chinese history, the Han.

Han Dynasty (206 B.C.-A.D. 220)—Liu Pang, along with a general named Hsiang-Yu, conquered the Ch'in capital at Shenyang in 209 B.C. Liu was a simple, peaceful man who avoided seeking revenge against Ch'in officials and soldiers. However, when Hsiang-Yu and his troops arrived, they had different ideas. The city was sacked, the tomb of Ch'in was broken open, and an area the size of New York City was burned to the ground. This aroused such resentment that Liu Pang was forced to fight Hsiang-Yu's army for the throne. After his victory Liu Pang assumed the throne and declared a general amnesty for all. The people so loved this compassionate man that all Chinese soon came to call themselves the Sons of Han.

Though they had conquered the Ch'in, the Han dynasty maintained the same political organization, this time dividing the empire into thirteen provinces. Under the guidance of his chamberlain, Lu Chia, Liu Pang was persuaded to practice Confucian ideals of patriarchal government. It is during this time that Confucianism became the ruling philosophy in China and Confucius was called the "uncrowned ruler of China."

The Han rulers made great strides in unifying the intellectual, political, and economic life of China. Emperor Wu established the first university for training Confucian scholars, underscoring the need for a civil-service system based on merit rather than position of birth. This marked the beginning of the civil-service examination. Han Wu-Ti (140-87 B.C.) also set up the government monopolies in the salt and iron industries and standardized the currency. Despite an interruption when Wang Mang seized power in 9 A.D., the Han Dynasty lasted nearly 430 years. Furthermore, the functional bureaucratic system they introduced was to survive rebellions, governmental breakdowns, and reform movements, and last well into the twentieth century.

Three Kingdoms, Southern, and Northern Dynasties (A.D. 221-581)—Following the downfall of the Han Dynasty in A.D. 220, China went through nearly four hundred years of upheaval and indecision. For most of this time the country was divided into two or more competing kingdoms, each controlling a particular region. Immediately following the Han was the period known as the Three Kingdoms (*San Kuo*). The three hostile states were the Wu in the South and the Southeast, including the Yangtze Valley; the Wei in the North and the Northwest, with its capital on the Yellow River; and the Shu in what is now in the province of Sichuan, in control of the Southwest. It is interesting to note that these areas conformed to the basic economic divisions of the country.

The bloody conflicts among these kingdoms provided the colorful material for that classic Chinese epic, *Annals of the Three Kingdoms*. In A.D. 265 the Wei emerged victorious, and for the second time in its history China was unified under a dynasty that came to be known as the Chin. The Chin did not last very long, however, and in its place a motley band of "seventeen" dynasties rabble-roused in the North. Only three of these were Chinese; all the others were of Turkic, Hunnish, and Mongol stock from Central and Northeast Asia. Not surprisingly these "barbarians" gradually adopted the more civilized Chinese way of life, acquired Chinese names, married, and settled down.

Sui Dynasty (A.D. 581-618)—Wen-Ti defeated the remnants of the northern Chou Dynasty in 589 and unified China for the first time in nearly four hundred years. He drove out many of the foreigners, including Turks, Tibetans, Indians, Mongols, and Huns, who had been nipping at Chinese territory.

After four hundred years of division, governing China was no easy task. Northern and southern Chinese, though they shared the same written language, had developed regional dialects (Mandarin, Wu, Min, and Cantonese), and communications were difficult. However, Wen-Ti was a vigorous leader who undertook great public works, including the Grand Canal. This exacted a great toll on the Chinese people in the form of taxes and forced labor, and combined to make the Sui Dynasty an unpopular one. When Li Yuan took over in 617 the regime was so weakened that

朝
代

中國事物

the T'angs were able to establish power and begin a three-hundred-year reign. Ironically, the great accomplishments of the Sui, in unifying China and constructing a superior canal system, also led to its downfall.

T'ang Dynasty (A.D. 618-906)—The T'ang era was truly China's golden age: a period of stability and great political reforms, combined with high accomplishments in arts and poetry. When the T'ang came to power they immediately set out to equalize land holdings among the Chinese. This involved instituting an in-kind tax system, whereby the peasants could pay taxes with grain and produce, significantly cutting the power of the moneyed classes. Under T'ai-Tsung this policy of social welfare was furthered with a relaxed penal code and a governmental system that emphasized the power of civil servants rather than provincial military officers or aristocrats. In addition T'ai-Tsung founded the first literary academy, and the study of classic Chinese literature became the official prerequisite for the civil-service examinations.

China was expanding her territory and trade at this time. Arab traders from India and the Malay Peninsula established contacts in Guangzhou, and by the close of the eighth century as many as four thousand foreigners lived there. In 751 the Arabs erected a minaret that still stands.

This must have been a very exciting period. Under T'ai-Tsung (780-805) the Chinese capital at Xian was a bustling intellectual center for a country of perhaps fifty-five million people. In the capital city there were representatives of many faiths: Christians, Buddhists, Taoists, Mohammedans, Zoroastrians, Magians, and Manicheans. Of course, Confucianism was still the official faith, but the Chinese, always very practical toward religion, felt that as long as Confucian traditions were observed in public one could practice any faith in private.

This heterogeneity lasted for nearly a hundred years. But under Wu-Tsung (841-47), a furious campaign of persecution against Buddhism began that culminated in the destruction of nearly forty-six hundred monasteries. This drove the Buddhists underground, where they created many secret societies that resisted the regime in subtle and occasionally direct ways. The An Lu-shan rebellion of 850 began the downfall of the dynasty. The dynasty's cohesion was further weakened after the breakdown of land reform in 780. As the large landowners grew more powerful, they began to assert themselves militarily, and by the beginning of the tenth century the empire disintegrated.

Five Dynasties (A.D. 907-60)—After the fall of the T'ang Dynasty, a profusion of small, belligerent states fell upon the glittering remains of the greatest civilization in the world. From the North came the single most important force of the time, a Mongol tribe called the Khitan Tartars. They lost no time in razing the T'ang capital, but they built their own capital on roughly the same site. This became Nanjing, the Southern Capital, and was the beginning of modern Beijing as the capital city of China. The new dynasty, the Liao, managed to survive the alternately rising and falling fortunes of the other states, and even endured the establishment of the Sung Dynasty, from whom they received handsome tribute for a time. Eventually, however, the Liao became completely absorbed in Chinese culture, proving once again that the Chinese are less a race than a continuous civilization.

Sung Dynasty (A.D. 960-1279)—The Sung Dynasty can be divided into two periods. The first epoch ended in 1127 when the Tartars conquered the northern half of the country and established the Chin Dynasty. The Southern Sung Dynasty then lasted until 1279, when Kublai Khan established the Yuan Dynasty.

Perhaps the greatest Sung Emperor was Chao Kuang-Yin, who, like the Roman

朝
代

Emperor Claudius, was crowned by his guards, who finding him drunk, threw the yellow robe over his shoulders and proclaimed him emperor. Under Yin and the later Emperors, China reached what has been called its "Periclean age." In the universities of this period in China long histories were written and speculative philosophies were investigated. Wang An-Shih advocated concepts that could almost be called socialist. The contemplation of nature's beauty, reflecting the influence of Taoist and Zen thought, became the major theme in Sung art.

Yet throughout her long history China remained vulnerable to outside attack, particularly from the North, and this period was no exception. The Emperor, Hui-Tsung (1101-26), adopted a fatal policy of playing his enemies against one another. The Chin Tartars were encouraged to attack the Khitan Tartars, to whom the Sung had been paying tribute in order to avoid being attacked. As soon as the Khitans were defeated, the Chin predictably turned South and soon all China above the Yangtze was in their hands.

Chin Dynasty (A.D. 1115-1234)—The Chin (Kim Tartars or tunguts) were the ancestors of the Manchu Dynasty, and they controlled northern China for nearly a century. Their first conquest was over the neighboring Khitan Tartars, who called themselves the Iron Dynasty. For this reason the Chin took the name "Gold Dynasty," and their fierce warriors rode into the battle with the cry "Iron Rusts, Gold Endures" upon their lips. The reign of the Chin however, was very unstable and in 1207 they were faced with an unstoppable invader, Genghis Khan (1162-1227).

He began his conquest of China in 1207 and after four years had conquered the provinces of Zhili, Shanxi, and Shaanxi. In 1212 he destroyed ninety cities so completely that, according to legend, "a horseman could ride over sites without stumbling." It is estimated that a million people perished during the campaigns of this relentless conqueror.

Genghis' son Ogadei continued the tradition after his father's death. The beleaguered Chin moved their capital around regularly under Khan's attacks but to no avail. Emperor Junin-li was defeated by Ogadei in 1240. Junin-li held out in his palace fortress until all his soldiers died and only women guarded the walls. Then he set fire to the city and burned himself alive in the palace. Mangu Khan, son of Tuli Khan, Ogadei's brother, then led the fight against the weakened Southern Sung Dynasty and was followed by Kublai Khan, who defeated them in 1279. This began the Mongol or Yuan Dynasty.

Yuan Dynasty (A.D. 1260-1368)—

> In Xanadu did Kublai Khan
> A stately pleasure dome decree
> Where Alph the sacred river ran
> Through caverns measureless to man
> Down to a sunless sea.
>
> —Coleridge

The great Kublai Khan, praised by Marco Polo, ruled from the China Sea to the Strait of Malacca. He conquered territory as far south as Burma, and was only defeated by the Japanese, who routed his attacking forces in 1281.

Although all the Khan had gained their reputation through military exploits, Kublai took a great interest in art and literature and in public works and economics. He deepened and widened the Grand Canal and furthered the use of paper money

中
國
事
物

(with inflationary results) during his reign.

His last years were clouded by a war against his cousin Kaidu, who was aided by the turncoat General Nayam, who had been Kublai Khan's military adviser. When Nayam was finally captured he was beaten to death Mongol style, wrapped in a sack so the blood would not splatter.

Following Kublai Khan was his grandson Timur, who died without an heir in 1307. The next thirteen years were prosperous ones for China, under Emperors Wu-Tsung and Jen-Tsung, both of whom worked at eliminating the differences between Mongols and Chinese. They were followed by five weak rulers, the last of whom was assassinated by the ex-Buddhist priest, Chu Yuan Chung, in 1368, establishing the Ming Dynasty.

Despite their record of relentless violence and warfare, the Mongol rule was distinctive in many respects. Tibetan Buddhism rose to prominence when Kublai proclaimed the first Dalai Lama. And in the Yuan court, theater became the most popular art form, leading to a profuse output of plays and novels that have become Chinese classics.

Ming Dynasty (A.D. 1368-1644)—The Ming Dynasty is characterized by a great restoration of native Chinese culture, partly as a reaction against the previous century of Mongol domination. Particularly under Hung-Wu (1368-98), there was tremendous innovation in Chinese dress, art, and architecture. The Chinese rebuilt their bridges, temples, shrines, tombs, and rock gardens, and reconstructed the walls of five hundred cities. They built, at this time, the Forbidden City in their capital, Beijing. With this emphasis on the past, however, came a great turning inward and a near xenophobia in foreign relations.

Immediately after the overthrow of the Mongols the Chinese had been quite expansive, annexing Manchuria as they drove the Mongols north. Like the Portuguese ten thousand miles away, the Chinese were also embarking on a great period of maritime exploration. In 1405 a eunuch admiral, Cheng Ho, led sixty-three ships to the Indian Ocean and returned with the captured King of Ceylon, who was made to pay homage to the Emperor. The explorations ended by 1430 and the oceans then belonged to the Arabs, the Portuguese, and the Japanese pirates. All during the 1500s the Portuguese and the Russians tried, for the most part unsuccessfully, to establish relations with the Ming court. Once again China was coming under siege, this time from traders and the more modern civilizations in Japan and the West.

In addition, China had internal problems. The great public works of the fifteenth and sixteenth centuries required a burdensome level of taxation to support a vast civil-service bureaucracy. When taxes became too great the peasants lost what land they had, selling out to the great estates, and producing a rebellious poor class that made the Ming vulnerable to internal rebellion. When Manchuria seceded in 1618 under the Kim Tartar leader Nurhaci, the stage was set for the last great dynasty, the Ch'ing, or Manchu.

Ch'ing Dynasty (A.D. 1644-1911)—The Manchus had been defeated by Ogadei Khan (son of Genghis) in 1240, but three hundred years later they were on the move again. Their leader, Nurhaci, conquered the Liaodong Peninsula in 1582, and by 1618 Manchuria was under his control. Taking advantage of an internal rebellion, the Manchus marched into the Ming capital of Beijing in 1644 and established the Ch'ing Dynasty. Shun Chih, who was only six at the time, became the Emperor of a nation that by now numbered nearly seventy million people. At this time, the empire was divided into the eighteen provinces we know today.

The history of the Ch'ing era is one of continual fighting against outsiders and great internal stresses caused by China's rapidly growing population. Under K'ang Hsi (1661-1722) Jesuit missions were established in China. The priests served the regime as mapmakers, court astrologers, and weaponmakers—all rather strange occupations for missionaries. The relations with the Christians remained peaceful for a time and the Catholic Church was hoping to establish a beachhead in China against the Byzantine Church. However, by 1725 the missionaries were thrown out, apparently because more and more European traders and pirates were arriving and claiming to be missionaries also.

During the eighteenth century internal revolts were infrequent and this helped lead to great population increases. By 1800 China had well over two hundred million people. But the outside world continued to push into China. Moslem uprisings in Turkestan became endemic after 1736, and by the time of the Tao-Kuang Emperor (1821-50) the dynasty was near collapse. The British had taken Hong Kong, and the Mohammedan revolts in Turkestan and Yunnan had cost hundreds of thousands of lives. The Taiping rebellion of 1850, and the numerous subterranean groups sprouting everywhere foretold the disintegration of a whole society that was to occur. During the reign of Wen-Tsung (1851-61) Japan's development began to supersede China's and the Japanese began the attacks on Chinese territory that would continue until 1945. During the Sino-Japanese War of 1894, Korea and Formosa were lost.

The picture that emerges is of a society that was not equipped militarily or philosophically to survive the nineteenth century. The glorious Confucian culture with its emphasis on hierarchy, order, and harmony was no match for the ambitions or armaments of its more modern neighbors. In its final years the regime became a ludicrous parody of imperial greatness, ruled by a terrified and superstitious woman, Empress Tzu Hsi. She had imprisoned the Emperor in 1898, and upon her death in 1908, appointed two-year-old Pu Yi to the throne. This only further strengthened the regime's internal opponents and made abdication inevitable. On February 12, 1911, Regent Yuan Shih K'ai renounced the throne and declared a republic. China had entered the modern age.

EDUCATION

The first book handed to the Chinese child when he began his schooling was the *Three Character Classic*. It is written in rhyme, in lines of three words each, and it begins with the phrase, "Men at their birth are by nature radically good." Numerical series followed: the three powers, the five virtues, the six kinds of grain. And all of this stern fare was to be memorized!

Confucius considered intellectual accomplishment of little value unless it was accompanied by emotional discipline, which produced a well-adjusted member of society. This uniform and formidable approach to education knit the country together so firmly that its long succession of conquerors scarcely affected its essence.

Competitive examinations for governmental positions represented the apex of this system. They date back to earliest history, although they were modernized around a.d. 1000. The exams lasted anywhere from one full day up to nine days. The candidates were assembled before dawn, according to a description of one exam. As soon as it was light enough, two themes for prose essays and one for a poem were carried around on long poles to be copied down. A portion of the grade was determined by how quickly the essays were completed.

In China today about 90 per cent of the young children attend primary school.

中國事物

The curriculum is very much like that of the schools of the West with the addition of politics, calligraphy, and a foreign language, usually English. During the atrociously misnamed Cultural Revolution of 1966, advanced education fell into severe decline, but by 1975 colleges began to reopen and are now staffed at one half their pre-1966 capacities and growing. Entrance examination is again the criterion for entry, but some preference is given to students with peasant-worker backgrounds. Higher education is free in China; this includes books, food, housing, medical care, and pocket money.

[See CIVIL-SERVICE EXAMINATION.]

MODERN WOOD CUT BY SHANGHAI FACTORY WORKER, TENG TAI-HO, ENTITLED "OUR WORKER-TEACHER IS FINE."

E G G S

The Chinese have never been puzzled by the riddle of "which came first . . . ?" For them it is always the egg, potent symbol of fertility and rebirth, good luck and happiness, whose smooth, round, cornerless shape denotes tranquillity. The egg is perfectly balanced between *yang* (the white) and *yin* (the yolk). The Chinese smoke, steam, salt, marinate, and dye the eggs of chickens, ducks, geese, quail, squab, and plover, boil them in tea, and bury them in limy clay. They were apparently the first to hatch eggs artificially in incubators made from wicker baskets lined with cotton or felt and suspended over the fireplace.

When an infant is about a month old the Chinese celebrate this event by shaving his head and sending hard-boiled eggs dyed red to their relatives and friends, who are then expected to respond with gifts for the child. Other special occasions are celebrated by cooking "egg sheets"—thin crepelike pancakes of pure egg.

Tea eggs are eaten at New Year's, or anytime as a between-meal snack. They are prepared by boiling eggs for an hour, then letting them cool and cracking the shells to form a crackled pattern, and boiling for two more hours with salt, tea, and star anise, until they have become soft again. Tea eggs will last for a day or two without refrigeration if they are kept in water, and are just as delicious cold as hot. Eating tea eggs at New Year's is a piece of sympathetic magic to roll good luck into the home for the year, just as the eggs can roll.

Eggs pickled in brine, which remain liquid, are so salty that they are used primarily to season other foods such as congee. Salty eggs will keep for quite a long time, as long as the brine doesn't start to ferment, and they are generally ready to eat after about three weeks of total immersion.

Thousand-year-old eggs are usually served cold, as an hors d'oeuvre. These are duck eggs that are coated with a kind of limy clay that chemically cooks them—in six to ten weeks, though, not a millennium. The lime soaks through the eggshell, turning the yolk a deep, dark green and the white a transparent bluish brown, and giving the whole egg a rich, creamy texture like an avocado's. Thousand-year-old eggs taste more fishy than eggy, but with a flavor of such mellowness and depth that most people are content with just a few bites. Others are content with none at all.

EIGHT AUSPICIOUS SIGNS

Although it is obvious from Buddhist iconography that the Buddha had exceptionally long earlobes, not too many people are aware that the Enlightened One wore on the sole of his foot the Eight Auspicious Signs that symbolize the sacred teachings. The signs include the Wheel of the Law, the Conch Shell, the Umbrella, the Canopy, the Lotus, the Jar, the Fishes, and the Mystic Knot. This last is a symbol of longevity, because it is endless like a true lover's knot.

EIGHT CYCLICAL CHARACTERS

A great deal of space in Chinese almanacs is devoted to fortune-telling. Although Western nations have evolved numerous methods for predicting the future, from tarot cards to tea leaves, the Chinese cannot be matched when it comes to matters of great portents. The Eight Cyclical Characters are four pairs of characters in the Chinese horoscope that represent the year, month, day, and hour of one's birth. By considering their mutual affinities, the good or bad aspects of any undertaking can be determined.

EIGHT DIRECTIONS

The Eight Directions are derived from the position of the Eight Diagrams or Trigrams in the cosmic scheme of things. During a séance, the Chinese medium will close her eyes, and join her open hands with the fingertips touching and the thumbs separate. In this manner she forms the Eight Directions, each of which contains all the spirits to

中
國
事
物

be found in the universe. The medium will deliver the message to her client, then blow lightly into the tunnel of the Eight Directions to establish contact with the spirit. She may then relay the news that Great-grandfather is complaining that the kitchen god is unhappy, that the door god appears to be unhinged, or even that the ancestral tablets are disgruntled.

EIGHT IMMORTALS

The "*Pa Hsien*" or Eight Immortals are Taoist representations of historical figures who have attained immortality. They are seen individually, or in a group, sometimes crossing the sea in fragile boats or on rustic bridges on their way to the Taoist paradise.

Chung Li-ch'uan was able to revive the souls of the dead with a magic fan. Chang Kuo-Lao traveled on a magical white horse, which he folded up and put away at night. Lu Tung-Pin was granted a magic sword as a reward for overcoming ten temptations. (He couldn't resist the sword, which was his eleventh temptation.) He is the patron saint of barbers. Ts'ao Kuo-chiu always carried a pair of castanets on his person because he wanted to be prepared for any emergency. He is venerated by those in the theatrical profession. Li T'ieh-Kuai was on intimate terms with the spirit of Lao Tzu, whom he used to visit in the celestial regions. One day Li returned to find his body missing, so he had to settle for the physical form of a dying beggar. The body came complete with a crutch, so Li had to limp through the rest of his existence. Han Hsiang-tzu was borne by his teacher to the Magic Peach Tree so he could taste the immortal peaches. He fell from the branches, and would have been killed had he not bitten one on the way down. Lan Ts'ai-ho is of uncertain sex, but may have been a woman who wandered about in tattered garments begging her way. She carries a basket, and is the patroness of all gardeners. Ho Hsien-ku was a lady who lived near Guangzhou, and was revered for the long distances she went to procure dainty bamboo shoots for her ailing mother. Ho's only food was mother-of-pearl, which gave her the desired immortality.

DRAWING OF THE EIGHT IMMORTALS. FROM THE *Kissho zung Kaidai.*

EIGHT INSTRUMENTS

The Chinese use a unique system to classify instruments. While Western instruments are grouped by the way they are played, Chinese instruments are divided into eight classes by the material they are made of. Emperor Shun (2225-2206 B.C.) is credited with making the eight divisions, which are believed to correspond to the eight trigrams (*pa kua*) of Fu Hsi. An entire system of correspondence was then set up. Just as the Chinese saw a relationship between instrument and material, so they perceived a connection between instruments and the external world:

Material	Instrument	Cardinal Point	Season	Phenomenon
gourd	mouth organ (*sheng*)	northeast	winter to spring	thunder
bamboo	pipes (*p'ai hsiao*)	east	spring	mountain
wood	wooden fish (*mu yu*)	southeast	spring to summer	wind
silk	zither (*ch'in*)	south	summer	fire
clay	globular flute (*hsuan*)	southwest	summer to autumn	earth
metal	bell (*chung*)	west	autumn	dampness
stone	sonorous stone (*ch'ing*)	northwest	autumn to winter	heaven
skin	drum (*ku*)	north	winter	water

As the classification reveals, the notes of Chinese music are closely bound up with the materials that produce them. A substance and its sound are like body and soul. Individual notes, in isolation and slowly fading away, are much more important in Chinese music than in Western music. Perhaps the intimacy of sound and matter explains why three of the eight categories are idiophones—instruments without membranes (drums are thus excluded) that produce notes by vibrating after they are struck. To the Chinese, these are melody-making instruments. To Westerners, they are just part of the rhythm section, buried in the percussion corner of an orchestra.

EIGHT RULES

The observance of the Eight Rules was assumed to alleviate any moral or spiritual dilemmas. The Eight Rules are filial piety, politeness, decorum, integrity, fidelity, sense of shame, fraternal duty, and loyalty. Incorrigible Chinese, however, are vilified with the expression "Forgetter of the Eight," a term of abuse that was frequently painted on walls or posters outside the evildoer's residence.

EIGHT STEEDS

For the Chinese the horse is a symbol of speed and perseverance. Clever lads were referred to as "one-thousand-*li* colts." Stupid ones were called "turtle's eggs," imply-

八仙　八儀　八大規律　八駿

91

中
國
事
物

ing illegitimacy, since turtles were believed to conceive by thought alone, without any action.

The most famous team of Chinese horses were the Eight Steeds of Emperor Mu, who used to cruise all over his realm in his chariot in 746 B.C. The Eight Steeds are a popular art motif, and are carved from various materials, including ivory. One of the eight is depicted as rolling on his back, overjoyed at finally being retired from government service.

EIGHT TRIGRAMS

When the reliability of omens derived from beam sagging and floor creaking came to be questioned, the Chinese discovered the efficacy of reading the cracks on a heated tortoise shell. The Eight Trigrams are said to be representations of just such cracks. The actual discovery of the Eight Trigrams was attributed to Fu Hsi in the twenty-ninth century B.C. These are eight groups of lines; each group consisting of combinations of three broken or unbroken lines, arranged in three ranks. They formed the basis of the Sixty-four Hexagrams in the *I Ching*, or the *Book of Changes*, an ancient Chinese system of wisdom, philosophy, and divination.

[See BOOK OF CHANGES.]

THE EIGHT TRIGRAMS AS ARRANGED BY THE LEGENDARY EMPEROR FU HSI.

EIGHTEEN PROVINCES

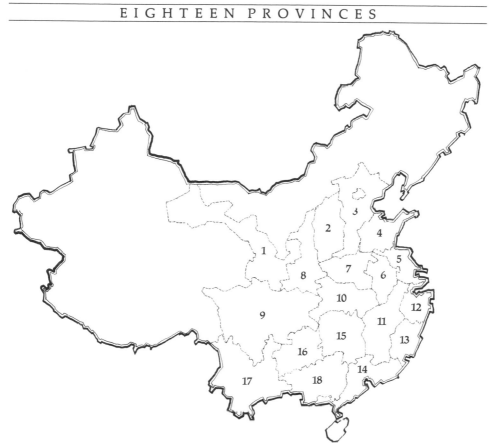

八卦 十八省 靈丹

THE EIGHTEEN PROVINCES OF CHINA ARE 1. GANSU, 2. SHANXI, 3. HEBEI, 4. SHANDONG, 5. JIANGSU, 6. ANHUI, 7. HENAN, 8. SHAANXI, 9. SICHUAN, 10. HUBEI, 11. JIANGXI, 12. ZHEJAING, 13. FUJIAN, 14. GUANGDONG, 15. HUNAN, 16. GUIZHOU, 17. YUNNAN, AND 18. GUANGXI ZUANGZU.

While China is conventionally divided into eighteen provinces, throughout her history the number of governmental units has varied greatly. Under Ch'in Shih-Huang-Ti, the first Emperor (221-207 B.C.), the country was divided into thirty-six, and later forty-one provinces. During the Ming Dynasty (A.D. 1368-1644), the number of provinces was as low as thirteen before the Ch'ing Dynasty established the eighteen provinces in the seventeenth century.

The Chinese land mass slopes from east to west, and the great rivers flow down this slope. In the valleys of the Yangtze and other rivers are where Chinese civilization began, and the nearby provinces—Shaanxi, Shanxi, Henan, and Sichuan—have been recognized as geographical units throughout Chinese history.

ELIXIR OF IMMORTALITY

Because the Chinese believed that heaven and earth were continuous, and the worlds of men and spirits intermingled according to a prescribed system, it seemed feasible for men to attain material immortality. As early as the third century B.C. the search for immortality dominated the concerns of Taoist alchemists, who thought that the "Order of Nature" in which impure matter could be made into gold, or incorruptible

中
國
事
物

essence, could be transposed to the "Order of Men," so that mortals could become *hsien* (immortals).

It was believed that the alchemist who made the elixir would be immortalized immediately and ascend into heaven. Philosopher Huai Nan Tzu discovered the elixir in 122 B.C.; he was whisked off to join the blessed immortals so fast that he spilled the cup containing the elixir. His barnyard animals sipped up a few drops and found themselves joining their master in the heavens.

Various substances were thought to contain longevity-producing ingredients. Ginseng root and *Ling-chih* mushroom were believed to confer immortality if ingested according to the proper ritual. The most seriously pursued substances were metallic—cinnabar (mercuric sulphide) to be exact. The processes of cinnabar were clearly mystical, and it was believed that an alchemist who could produce the pure substance gold from cinnabar would quickly join the immortals.

The Elixir of Immortality was concocted of something called "sublime cinnabar" according to the great alchemical synthesizer Ko Hung (A.D. 260-340). Ko Hung knew how to prepare nine varieties of "divine cinnabar," any of which could produce gold, lead to immortality, or resuscitate the dead of less than three days. Ko Hung's "flower of cinnabar" contained the following: realgar (arsenic disulphide), alum (aluminum and potassium sulphate), rock salt (sodium chloride), "lake" salt (ammonium chloride), urea, oyster shells (calcium carbonate), "red stone fat," soapstone (magnesium silicate), and lead carbonate. The mixture was sealed with a paste containing seven minerals and it was heated for thirty-six days. If it were ingested for seven days the alchemist would become immortal. If instead it were added to mercury or lead, it would result in the production of gold.

Because gold was the most perfect, incorruptible, and durable long-living metal known, it too could confer longevity and immortality. Various attempts to ingest gold were recommended and attempted by those seeking immortality. The most popular method was to eat off of gold plates and drink from gold goblets—thereby ingesting small quantities of metal. Softened gold was also made into pills that could be taken orally. Another technique was to age wine with gold stored in it for long periods—thereby producing something called "gold juice."

[See ALCHEMY, FUNGUS OF IMMORTALITY, GINSENG, and LONGEVITY.]

EMBROIDERY

The Chinese have probably decorated with embroidery for almost as long as they've worn clothes. The art is said to be at least four thousand years old. As soon as the Chinese learned how to make silk, they figured out how to use it for this colorful and often exquisitely wrought needlecraft. During the eighteen-century, embroidery reached its peak as an art form.

Just about every article of clothing a person might wear is embroidered—shoes, pajamas, purses, caps, jackets, and robes (especially ceremonial ones)—along with items not meant to be worn, like altar cloths, banners, and wall hangings. Rainbows of colors are used to create geometric patterns, calligraphic characters, animals, and plants. Dragons parade across gentlemen's backs, flowers twine around ladies' hems, phoenixes rise on elegant coats. Most designs are symbolic, conveying a good wish to the wearer or showing his rank in the court or the military.

Chinese embroidery requires diligence and patience. A silk jacket might take several people two years to complete, and an elaborate robe or a theatrical costume more than twice that. As many as twenty thousand stitches have been counted on a spectacle case only two inches wide and six inches long. For projects where both sides might be seen, a frame is set up to hold the fabric being decorated. Two workers on opposite sides push the needle back and forth to each other, creating mirror image designs; there is no right and no wrong side to the final piece. The best work is done with such precision of detail and subtlety of coloring that even on close inspection it is hard to distinguish from a painting done in oils or watercolors. Each feather in a bird's wing, each hair in a tiger's fur can be picked out.

[See BLIND STITCH and TWELVE ORNAMENTS.]

刺
繡

皇
帝

SILK AND METAL THREAD EMBROIDERY FROM THE CH'ING DYNASTY (1644-1912).

EMPERORS

The Emperor was regarded in Chinese society as the "Son of Heaven," and great power and responsibility came with this title. According to the "mandate of heaven" the Emperor was responsible for the prosperity of the earth's inhabitants and could expect in return loyalty and obedience from them. This required the Emperor to deport himself in a way that was worthy of his unique position.

During the Han Dynasty (206 B.C.-A.D. 220) great steps were taken to differentiate the Emperor from the rest of society, and many future Emperors were raised under conditions created to enhance the dignity and authority of the imperial house. The Emperor dwelt in the innermost part of the palace, sealed completely from any lowly influence of the outside world. His world was run by eunuchs who administered the palace and often held high government positions, by courtiers waiting in

中
國
事
物

attendance, by women who attended to all his needs, and by staff scholars who looked after religious duties. His food was specially prepared (and tasted to prevent poisoning), and he was dressed in the finest robes, each with its own political or religious significance. His daily activities often included endless ceremonies of court and shrine, as well as consultations with government officials. When he died, a majestic mausoleum would be prepared for his burial with all appropriate solemnity.

Traditionally, the government structure had two parts: the provincial offices throughout the empire and the central administration in the capital. The main responsabilities of government rested with two very senior officials who approximated a modern Prime Minister, and through a network of junior officials, received decrees signed by the Emperor, and through a network of junior officials, received reports to bring to the Emperor's attention. Below these officials were the major offices of state, which we might think of as cabinet posts. Their responsabilities included astrology, religious ceremonies, record-keeping, security, legal administration, foreign relations, tax collection, care of the imperial palace and staff, and direction of public works.

In practice the government and the imperial-succession process were a bit more chaotic. Many of China's imperial houses were founded as a result of foreign invasion or internal chaos, and often the mandate was conveyed from one member of the imperial house to another through intrigue and bloodshed.

Over the history of the empire, there were both great and unworthy owners of the throne. In general it may be said that the great Emperors occurred early in any dynasty and that the greatest Emperors led the most progressive, aggressive, and expansionist eras. The more inward-looking, defensive dynasties, particularly the Ming and the Manchu, tended to produce Emperors who at best developed the highly refined sensibilities in art and literature, and at worst gave themselves over completely to hedonism and decadence.

[See DYNASTIES and GOVERNMENT.]

ENAMELWARE

Enamelware or cloisonné requires the use of metal ribbons or wires, which are soldered or glued to the metal body to form the desired patterns. The individual cells or *cloisons* then must be repeatedly filled with enamels, fired, sanded, and polished.

The art of enameling was introduced to the Chinese by Arab traders, who brought it with them from Byzantium. The Chinese name for enamel is *Fa-lang*, which is derived from Folin, the old name for the capital of the Roman Empire of the East. The *Ko ku yao lun*, a well-known book on antiquities published in 1459, described the new art form in the following manner: "The body of the piece is made of copper, decorated with designs in colors made of materials fused together. We have seen urns for burning incense, vases for flowers, round boxes with covers, wine cups, and the like, but they are only fit for use in the ladies' inner apartments, being too gaudy for the libraries of scholars of simple tastes. It is also called the ware of the devils' country."

Actually there is controversial evidence that a crude form of cloisonné might have been made during the T'ang Dynasty, although it wasn't until the Ming that the Chinese felt confident enough to make great advances in this field. The Golden Age of enameling was the eighteenth century under imperial patronage. In the nineteenth century, the quality of cloisonné began to deteriorate again when great demands arose for pieces to be imported to the West. Holes in the enamel were filled in with wax, and later on, when the wax melted, these unsightly pits would become visible. Most of the collectibles today, such as ashtrays, cigarette boxes, napkin rings and salt-and-pepper sets, belong in this class. Yet a well-executed piece of enamelwork is one of the most exquisite examples of Chinese innovation and craft.

ETERNITY AND LONGEVITY SYMBOLS

The term *t'ai chi* refers to the origin of all created things and is represented by a circle equally divided by a curved line. The circle, or ring, is a symbol of eternity and its divided parts represent the primary constituents of life, the male and the female principles (*yin* and *yang*, respectively).

A ring has no beginning and no end and to the Chinese is emblematic of dignity and authority. In ancient times the Emperor would use a pair of rings—one perfect, the other defective—to indicate his pleasure or displeasure with royal officers.

Like the ancient Greeks, the Chinese admire the love song of the cicada. In the life cycle of this insect, which passes the first four years of life in an underground larval stage before emerging in pupal form, the Chinese find a metaphor for immortality and resurrection. For this reason a cicada, carved in jade, used to be placed in the mouth of a corpse before burial.

The Chinese have numerous symbols for longevity, including peach charms, which are worn by children to bind them to life. The gentle, smiling star-god of longevity is pictured surrounded by mushrooms that give immortality, and holding the fruit of *P'an t'ao*, the peach tree that blossoms every three thousand years. The *shou* is a familiar symbol of longevity. This character is seen in all the arts and crafts of China as a decorative motif. There are over one hundred ways of writing it, and occasionally an entire garment will be embroidered with the different forms. It was considered a rare token when the Emperor granted his ministers copies of this character written in his own hand.

FOUR EXAMPLES OF THE *shou* OR LONGEVITY SYMBOL.

ETIQUETTE

A British consul, describing a banquet held by a Chinese warlord in a distant province, observed how delicately the fierce monarch dined, touching his food only with his right hand. "After the meal was over," the Englishman noted with dismay, "he blew his nose with the left-hand fingers, and royally wiped them on the attendant's trousers."

The Chinese term for etiquette is *li*. The original meaning of *li* was "to sacrifice." The word was extended to encompass the rituals surrounding the sacrifice and then to cover any ceremonial behavior. Much of the code reflects practical courtesy: A person carrying a load has right of way on the street regardless of rank, and in

中
國
事
物

passing any object two hands must be used. Some of the provisions are only an expansion of what a Westerner would consider conventional politeness: The correct way to demand repayment from someone in your debt would be to request a loan from him for your own use.

Some aspects of Chinese etiquette may have contributed to life's complications. It was improper to speak to someone without removing your spectacles, to the obvious disadvantage of nearsighted businessmen. It was also considered impolite to greet anyone while mounted on a horse, a sedan chair, or a wheelbarrow—common forms of transportation. The prospect of dismounting and remounting with every greeting would have kept everyone on foot, but for the expedient use of fans. If, in passing, you raised a fan in front of your face and prevented eye contact, there was no rudeness in continuing on your way—at least not among equals. If, however, you saw your employer headed toward you and you wished to avoid the inconvenience of causing him to dismount, or the impoliteness of ignoring him, you were left with little choice but to duck into the nearest alley.

EXORCISM

Along with divination and the use of protective charms, exorcism forms a crucial pillar in the practices of the Taoist popular religion. When the everyday protection accorded by prayers and charms breaks down and illness or unexpected death result, it is quite common for people to seek out a Taoist priest and arrange for exorcism of the demons or malevolent spirits causing misfortune.

The procedure for exorcising demons is performed by one or more priests who chant an efficacious formula specifically designed for the ills they wish to dispel. A charm with mystical diagrams and words is prepared and given to the person seeking the exorcism—often it is burned in the course of the ritual. The power of the charms depends on which gods or entities are being summoned to help rid the person or the premises of evil. One Taoist demon-expelling charm goes as follows: "Chang, the Heavenly Master, is here, and commands the thirty-six spirits of the Dipper, the spirits dwelling in the Sun and Moon, the seven gods of the Great Bear, all the heavenly host, and the spirit of the sea monster that rescued Kuei-hsing from the watery depths. Banish, therefore, all fear." Insanity and suicide were the most critical events popularly believed to require exorcism.

FALCONRY

Select fine arrows and call for falcons,
All have heard of our uncommon skill;
Rout the fox and close in upon the pheasants,
Flush out the ancient hills and mounds!
—Lu Lun (c. A.D. 770)

The Chinese characterized eagles, falcons, and all other birds of prey with the term *ying*, a written symbol that depicts the act of one bird swooping down upon another. Ancient Chinese texts record the sport of falconry as far back as 200 B.C. It was a favorite amusement of the Emperor and his court throughout history. The Mongols were especially devoted to falconry. According to Marco Polo, Kublai Khan employed no less than seventy thousand men for his hawking excursions. Falcons, kites, and other predatory birds were taught to pursue their quarry, and there were eagles of such size and strength that they were able to take on wolves.

驅邪　訓鷹捕獵

鎮宅神英

鎮宅除邪是神英

逐日捉拿狐狸精鬼怪開音不見面妖邪奔走出了邊此英買在他家去諸邪一見心裡驚

Falcon with his prey. From *Researches Into Chinese Superstition* by Henri Doré.

中
國
事
物

FAMILY

The Chinese believed that their lives continued in the lives of their children, so a failure to produce offspring meant the death of all one's ancestors as well as the end of the family line. Parents were expected to spend their lives building up enough wealth so their children could prosper, and the filial child, in turn, worshiped his parents. If the parents failed their responsibilities, however, this did not lessen the children's filial duties or the obligation to his children.

In the traditional family, everyone worked for the family as a whole. If someone kept part of his wages, he would be condemned by the other members of the family. A merchant who had to do his business outside the household could spend what was necessary for his living expenses, but he would be expected to account to the head of the family regarding the amounts spent.

According to the precepts of Confucius, government should be based on the same principles of virtue and moral example that worked within the family. The concern should be for harmonious human relationships, whether in business, social relationships, or matters of state. Then, it is believed, all affairs will resolve themselves harmoniously.

[See ANCESTOR WORSHIP and FILIAL PIETY.]

FANS

Hardly anyone in China goes about without a fan. So much a part of everyday life are fans that the wealthy gave them to the poor as an act of charity. Criminals have carried them to their executions. Fans are a popular symbol of China in the West, and the making of fans for export has employed thousands of people in recent years.

Traditionally, fans are carried suspended from the waist or stuck in a sock top, a sleeve, or the neck of a jacket. They are used mostly in the warmer months, but they have more functions than just cooling—they flit away flies, they dust off chairs about to be sat upon, they emphasize points in conversation, and they convey messages to friends.

In imperial China, men carried folding fans, a type introduced to China from Japan in the eleventh century. Men's fans commonly have twenty or twenty-four ribs

FAN OF GILT-EDGED PAPER MOUNTED ON IVORY. MADE FOR THE EUROPEAN MARKET. EARLY NINETEENTH CENTURY.

of horn, bone, sandalwood, bamboo—or, more expensively, ivory, tortoise shell, or mother-of-pearl. They are covered with paper or silk and are often decorated with painting and/or calligraphy.

A woman's fan is round and fixed, not folding. This kind has been used in China for many hundreds of years, far longer than the folding type. The round fans are made of silk, paper, straw, feathers, or a southern China palm tree's appropriately fanlike leaves. Feminine fans have at least thirty ribs.

Different fans were considered appropriate for different seasons, and those concerned about such things took care not to be seen with the wrong sort. A deserted wife in China was once called "an autumn fan," since, like the fan, she was cast aside at the end of the pleasant season.

FEASTS

There were a great many feasts on the Chinese lunar calendar for which the celebration itself was sufficient justification. The Double Yang Feast, on the ninth day of the ninth month, was celebrated by drinking wine and taking a walk in the hills. The Lantern, Moon, and Wedding feasts were particularly important because they were among the few occasions when women could venture outside with propriety.

The Lantern Feast falls on the first full moon and marks the conclusion of the New Year celebration. The last leftovers are consumed. The holiday was observed as far back as A.D. 700, and the lanterns have sometimes been decorated with delicate figures that turned in the draft from the flames. The basic idea was to have lanterns everywhere. A legend tells of a Ming Emperor who set out so many lanterns that even Buddha came from heaven to see.

The Moon Feast was celebrated on the night of the full moon in the eighth month, the equivalent of our harvest moon. An impressive feast was prepared, including round sweet mooncakes stacked thirteen to the plate for the number of lunar months. It was the moon's birthday and, in the interest of fertility, a woman might address a question to the moon concerning her future. The old man, or the moon maid (who shared lunar tenancy with a rabbit and a three-legged toad), would pass along the answer in the fragments of a conversation accidentally overheard. The most important event during the Moon Feast is the writing of poetry.

The Wedding Feast required consumption of meals prepared by both families. Late into the evening, the bride and groom's room was filled with young relatives and friends who teased them with the intention of keeping them awake. When the last guests finally left, the pair were served another bottle of wine and two vegetable dishes. The exhausted couple were expected to drink the wine and eat still one more plate before retiring.

FESTIVALS

Festivals celebrated heroes, honored ancestors, and popped up for any good reason. There was a Festival of Kites, at the end of which the kites were cut adrift to carry off impending disasters. A Festival of Flowers was held on the twelfth day of the second moon, when women and children would cut out colorful paper favors and hang them from flowers and flowering shrubs to insure a fruitful season.

The Dragon Boat Festival occurred on the fifth day of the fifth month in memory of Ch'u Yuan, a very popular statesman who drowned himself in a river after having been falsely accused. He was a much-loved courtier, and the people sent boats out in search of the body. The catastrophe has been commemorated as an

中國事物

annual holiday since around 295 B.C. The Dragon Boats raced amid fireworks and the accompaniment of men beating gongs and drums. *Tsung* (rice and meat wrapped in leaves) is thrown in the river then to placate the gods.

The Festival of Departed Spirits occurred in autumn and honored the souls of those who died an unnatural death or had no family to offer the ancestor rites for them. It was thought that these departed spirits would continue to wander the earth until guided from it. Processions with lanterns followed the banks of rivers to convey the souls of those who drowned.

The Festival of the Tombs is a similar rite, which occurred in spring. The ancestors' graves were cleaned, the plots weeded, and the ancestors were offered a meal. In the Ming Dynasty, pieces of gold and silver, paper, and mock money; and earlier, paper houses, bowls of food, and replicas of farm animals were burned on the theory that they were transformed into the real thing as they passed through the smoke into the invisible world.

ENAMELED PLAQUE DEPICTING THE DRAGON BOAT FESTIVAL. CH'ING DYNASTY.

FILIAL PIETY

Mao-ying left his family when he was eighteen. When he was forty-nine he returned, having overcome gravity and the need for nutrition and having found the *tao*. His father beat him for his lack of filial piety.

Filial piety originated in ancestor worship. It was thought that a departed spirit that was not properly honored would bedevil its living kindred. It's sometimes assumed that Confucius created the concept of filial piety, but in fact Confucius complained that filial piety had come to mean nothing more than the support of one's parents. In his teachings he sought to revive the precepts of earlier days when parents were also treated with great reverence.

Good health was a demonstration of filial piety, because the body was a gift from one's parents. A selfish attachment to one's wife and children over one's parents manifested unfilial behavior. The classic *Tales of Filial Piety* recount heroic acts such as those of the child who lay naked in his parents' bed at night so the mosquitoes could gorge themselves before his parents retired.

孝心　指甲

CHINESE SON AND HIS BRIDE PAYING RESPECT TO HIS PARENTS. C. 1900.

Author Pearl Buck presented an interesting example of filial piety: If a son jumps into a rushing river to save an unknown stranger and drowns in the process, his American parents would feel at least some pride at his heroism along with their grief. If he were the son of a Chinese couple they would feel tremendous shame that he would throw his life away meaninglessly and bring them grief—thus lacking basic filial piety.

Although filial piety is in eclipse in China, it was the basis for a remarkably stable political structure. It may be the only traditional concept in modern social structures that has effectively accommodated the needs of the elderly.

[See ANCESTOR WORSHIP.]

FINGERNAILS

One way to identify a person of gentility in China was by his or her fingernails. Many people, both men and women, cultivated at least one nail of inordinate length, particularly on the left hand. It was a sign that they, somewhat like a worker who wears white collars rather than blue, needn't concern themselves with manual labor, where such an ornament surely would get in the way.

To protect their precious nails, those who had them would sometimes wear special fingernail cases. Simple ones were made of bamboo. For people who wanted to show off a bit more, there were fancier versions of silver or gilt, set with gemstones.

中
國
事
物

FINGERPAINTING

The brush was invented as early as 4500 B.C. Paper was invented around A.D. 100. But it wasn't until the T'ang Dynasty, some six hundred years later, that Chinese painters discovered the finger. In the history of Chinese painting there have always been enterprising artists who tried to substitute the brush with some other instrument, but never with any lasting results. Even lotus stems were in vogue for a while. Fingerpainting, on the other hand, came into its own in A.D. 750, and evoked the highest admiration of the Chinese public. They even regarded it as being superior to brush painting. Hands had to be clean, nails kept long and flexible, and although some painters would cheat—especially in the application of watercolors to the lighter areas of a painting—an authentic fingerpainted work could not easily be brushed off as being mechanically derived.

The greatest fingerpainter was said to be Wu Wei, although none of his work survives. He was so accomplished that he could paint cats "that would keep any house entirely free from rats." He was also inordinately fond of drink. One night he was summoned by Emperor Hsien Tsung to the palace to demonstrate his skill. Unfortunately, Wu Wei was too drunk to stand and had to be carried into the Imperial Presence. "Draw a spring among the pinetrees," was the command. Wu Wei fell on his knees and knocked over an ink pot. In a moment, however, using just one finger, he produced a charming picture on the floor. The Emperor pronounced it divinely inspired, and Wu Wei won the day. Fingerpainting had arrived.

FISH

Legend has it that the natures of fish and birds are interchangeable, and stories of fish transformed into birds are common. The fish is most significant as an emblem of freedom, and, as evidenced by the many fantastic goldfish varieties, was much appreciated for its aesthetic qualities. In water the fish moves easily in all directions and is often seen as a symbol of harmony, connubial bliss, and emancipation. A pair of fish is regarded as emblematic of the joys of sexual union, and is a common wedding gift. The character *yu* which represents fish, sounds like the word for "abundance." All formal banquets in China are concluded by the arrival of a large fish.
[See CARP.]

"THE PLEASURE OF THE FISHES." YUAN DYNASTY SCROLL DATED 1291.

FISHING

Next to rice, fish constitutes the principal food product available to most Chinese, and fishing has always been an essential part of the Chinese economy. Over a thousand varieties of fish are caught throughout the lakes, rivers, and coastal waters of China. The fish is an emblem of wealth and abundance, and is cultivated for pleasure as well as for food. Over sixty varieties of carp are raised as goldfish to be kept as pets in aquariums, gardens, and tanks that are commonly found throughout China.

It is believed that the Chinese were taught how to fish by the legendary Fu Hsi (2953-2838 B.C.), who was the first to make different kinds of nets and to teach the people how to use them. Progress was rapid, with numerous innovations developing over the centuries. Along with complex irrigation and agricultural techniques resulting from the early management of rivers and lakes came the notion of fish farming. China's reservoirs are full of hatcheries dating back hundreds of years, but the most impressive technique is that of raising fish alongside young rice in the submerged rice paddy. By the time the rice is harvested the fish are large enough to catch and eat. For the large river- and oceangoing fishing boats used by huge fishing fleets an innovation in the storage of fish helped keep the fish fresh until they were sold at market. Since Chinese junks are regularly equipped with watertight compartments that could easily be flooded, some junks began to fill their holds with water in order to keep the fish alive until they reached their port.

By the time of the Han Dynasty, the management of fisheries and the control of water products were brought under government control in China. While the waterways police concentrated largely on the allocation of irrigation water and its taxation, they also inspected water purity, controlled pollution in fishing waters, and regulated the seasons of fishing—all over two thousand years ago.

In addition to fishing, the Chinese contributed greatly to the knowledge of pearling and pearl diving. Some of the world's richest pearl fisheries were located around Hainan Island in Guangdong Province. Pearl diving was a thriving business in the region as far back as 111 B.C. The people of Huzhou have been credited with the discovery of pearl cultivation by implanting mother-of-pearl into the oyster. They attribute the invention to a thirteenth-century inhabitant. The production of cultivated natural pearls has become the main source of pearls in the world today, and has alleviated the lot of the pearl diver.

[See PEARL DIVING.]

FIVE ATMOSPHERIC CONDITIONS

Chinese weathermen didn't have to rely on satellite reports to plot the weather. The Five Atmospheric Conditions (rain, fine weather, heat, cold, and wind) could be deduced from the interactions of the Five Elements. These conditions, in turn, affected the oracular downpour associated with the Five Colored Clouds. Green indicated that a plague of creeping things was imminent; white represented mourning; red clouds signified warfare and destruction; black presaged floods; and yellow clouds meant that great good fortune and abundance lie ahead.

FIVE BLESSINGS

The *Wu-fu* are symbolized either by the character *fu* (happiness) repeated five times, or else by five bats, also called *fu*. The Five Blessings are long life, riches, tranquility, a love of virtue, and a happy ending.

指畫

魚

釣魚

五氣

五福

中
國
事
物

FIVE-CLAWED DRAGON

EMBROIDERED MEDALLION OF A FIVE-CLAWED DRAGON THOUGHT TO BE FROM AN EMPEROR'S ROBE. EARLY NINETEENTH CENTURY.

An ancient Chinese saying describes the dragon as having the head of a camel, the horns of a stag, the eyes of a demon, the ears of a cow, the neck of a snake, the scales of a carp, and the claws of an eagle. It has a lump on its head that enables it to fly through space. Newborn dragons are tiny, like baby lizards, but the dragons grow at a ferocious rate. For Westerners who are either serious art collectors, or who are simply into counting toes, it will soon become apparent that Chinese dragons will have either five, four, or three claws. This is an iconographic tradition that dates back to the Ming Dynasty.

The five-clawed dragon represented the imperial family, and could only be worn or owned as an art motif by members of the royal family. To be on the safe side, Chinese who owned lacquer or cloisonné pieces with the imperial dragon emblazoned on them would purposely chisel out one entire foot of the beast. Four-clawed dragons were reserved for families of nobility or for high officials, while three-clawed dragons were meant for use by ordinary people. The masses, however, frequently opted for the four-clawed dragon. After all, who didn't have an ancestor somewhere in their family tree who had held some official rank? This subtle form of social climbing was generally tolerated. After the Manchus were overthrown in 1912, the five-clawed dragon became democratized, and began to appear indiscriminately on dishes, robes, and cabinets.

FIVE ELEMENTS

Chinese geomancers, priests, ritual elders, and diviners all had to learn the Five Elements by heart. First mentioned in the classic *Book of Documents* attributed to Confucius, the *wu hsing* are: water, fire, wood, metal, and earth.

These elements are not actually substances, but rather different types of energy that permeate every substance and every process of change and transformation in the universe. Thus water produces wood, but destroys fire; fire produces earth, but destroys metal; metal produces water, but destroys wood; wood produces fire, but destroys earth; earth produces metal, but destroys water.

Since its inception, Chinese civilization has been dominated by a single obsession—that of the possible cosmic disorder caused by the imbalance of the Five Elements. If this were to occur, then the seas might take the place of the mountains, the seasons might no longer follow their natural sequence, and heaven and earth would be confounded. This kind of phenomenalism led to a sort of inverted astrology, the result being that perturbations of the planets' motions, meteors, falling stars, or eclipses could be ascribed to irregularities in the government or the bureaucracy.

When Yang Hsiung was asked whether a sage could make divination, he replied that a sage could certainly make divination about heaven and earth. If that was so, what was the difference between the sage and the astrologer? Yang replied: "The astrologer predicts what the effects of heavenly phenomena will be on man; the sage predicts what the effects of man's actions will be on the heavens."

FIVE GRAINS

The Five Grains were hemp, millet, rice, wheat, and pulse. As with everything that affected the daily life of the Chinese, a virtuous government ensured a bountiful crop. Ecology and enlightenment grew side by side. "When shrubs and trees are in bloom and leaf," wrote Confucian scholar Hsun Tzu during 298-238 B.C., "the ax must not enter the forest....The spring plowing, the summer weeding, the fall harvesting, and the winter storing of the grain: These four things must not be out of season. Then the five grains will not fail, and the people will have an abundance of food."

FIVE METALS

The Five Metals were gold (yellow), silver (white), copper (red), lead (blue), and iron (black). Taoist alchemists were constantly breaking down their properties in order to arrive at a proper elixir of immortality. Their most appetizing concoction was known as the Five Metals Powder, an elixir of stamina.

FIVE PLANETS

Chang Heng (A.D. 78-139) was the grand historiographer during the reign of Han Shun Ti. Chang Heng constructed the first uranosphere, depicting the movements of the Five Planets: Venus, Jupiter, Mercury, Mars, and Saturn. For his contributions to science, he was denounced as a magician and chased into the hills, where he lived a life of distinguished obscurity.

五爪龍　五行　五穀　五金　五星

中國事物

FIVE POISONS

The Five Poisons were derived from the kiss of a centipede, scorpion, spider, toad, and viper. A popular Chinese talisman is a bronze medal with a picture of Chang Tao-ling, a Taoist alchemist, riding a tiger and brandishing the magic sword with which he vanquished the Poisonous Five. He captured them in a box in which he distilled the Elixir of Life.

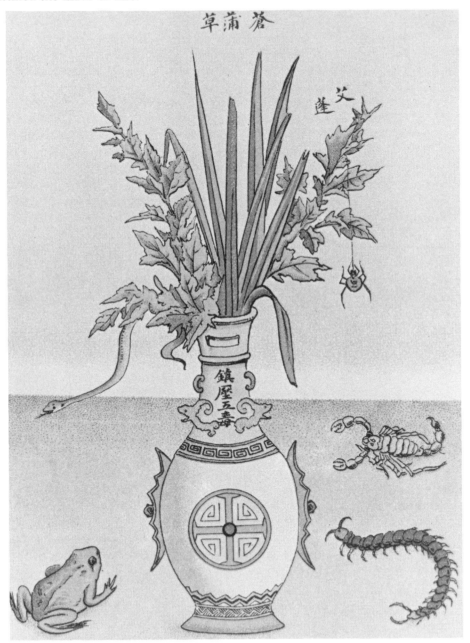

FIVE POISONS, AN OCCASIONAL MOTIF IN CHINESE ART. FROM *Researches into Chinese Superstition* BY HENRI DORÉ.

FIVE PRIMARY COLORS

The Five Primary Colors are black, green, red, white, and yellow. Color co-ordination was popularly used in the art of divination, though sometimes with con-flicting results. When Mo Tzu was traveling North to Ch'i, he met a fortune-teller on the road. The soothsayer warned him: "Today God is going to kill the black dragon of the North. Your complexion, sir, is black, so you must not go North." To which Mo Tzu countered: "If, as you say, Southerners should not go North, then Nor-therners should not go South. For there are some whose complexions are dark and some who are fair. Why shouldn't they be permitted to proceed? If your words are to be followed, that would result in prohibiting all traveling throughout the world." It is important to note that Chinese are rather vague about their colors. *Ch'ing*, for in-stance, may mean green, blue, iridescent, black, gray, or even clear. The Chinese dic-tionary defines *Ch'ing* as the "color of nature." This lack of precision is confusing because there is even an obscure character defining the particular shade of brown-green on a beetle's wing. Otherwise, red is an emblem of joy; yellow is an imperial color; white is the color of mourning; black is the color of bruising, therefore to be avoided; and green is the color of the painted board carried before a criminal on his way to the execution grounds.

FIVE PUNISHMENTS

Under the Chou and Han dynasties, convicted criminals could look forward to either: being branded on the forehead, having their noses cut off, maiming, castra-tion, or death. In later times these pleasantries were amended to: bambooing, bastinadoing, banishment, exile, and the ever-popular death (choice of strangulation or decapitation).

FIVE SACRIFICIAL BEASTS

Victor Hugo once wrote, "China is a museum of embryos." He was referring not to the gastronomical preferences of the Chinese, but to their natural inventiveness, which has led the world in the establishment of such innovations as gunpowder, printing, meteorology, and herbology. Chinese naturalists had museums of their own, and they made five grand divisions of animated nature: the feathered, hairy, naked, shelly, and scaly animals. Of the five classifications, however, the Five Sacri-ficial Beasts ranked at the top of the altar. These were the ox, goat, pig, dog, and fowl.

FIVE TASTES

There was no accounting for them; they could crop up under any suspicious chafing dish or hundred-year-old egg shell. The Five Tastes are: salty, bitter, sour, sweet, and fiery.

FIVE VISCERA

These are, respectively, the liver, heart, lungs, kidneys, and spleen. The liver corre-sponds to love; the heart to propriety; the lungs to righteousness; the kidneys to wisdom; and the spleen to good faith.

FLOWERS

The Chinese are devoted to flowers, and commonly call China the flowery land. Of course, the Chinese have long been famous for their flowers and rock gardens, tradi-

五毒

五色

五刑

五大祭品

五味

五臟

花

中國事物

tionally kept small so as not to monopolize land that could be used for agriculture.

The goddess of flowers is Hua Hsien, and she is represented in the company of attendants who carry baskets of flowers. In certain parts of China a festival of flowers is held on the twelfth day of the second month, to assure an early and fruitful springtime. Chinese women, particularly in the southern provinces, follow the custom of wearing flowers in their hair. In the North, paper, silk, or jeweled flowers serve as house decorations.

In Chinese paintings flowers are highly stylized and conventionalized. Particular flowers are drawn with particular birds, and similar groups of foliage. Bamboo,

CHRYSANTHEMUMS. INK AND COLORS ON SILK BY YUN PING. LATE SEVENTEENTH CENTURY.

prunus, and pine, all evergreen, are frequently grouped together. They are known as the Three Friends. Each month and each season also has a floral representative.

簫
笛

January	Prunus (Plum)
February	Peach
March	Peony
April	Cherry
May	Magnolia
June	Pomegranate
July	Lotus
August	Pear
September	Mallow
October	Chrysanthemum
November	Gardenia
December	Poppy
Spring	Tree peony
Summer	Lotus
Autumn	Chrysanthemum
Winter	Prunus (Plum)

FLUTES AND PIPES

One of the two oldest instruments excavated in China is the *hsuan* (globular flute). Archaeologists place it and the *ch'ing* (sonorous stone) in the Shang Dynasty (c. 1550-c.1030 B.C.). This ancient wind instrument is shaped like a barrel and is about 2½ inches high. Although later *hsuan* are made of earthenware, the Shang example is carved from bone. The player blows into a hole at the top. The *hsuan* has a hollow, muffled tone that resembles the vowel sound *oo*.

Perhaps equally as old as the globular flute are sets of pipes called *p'ai hsiao*. A piece of cane is stopped at the bottom end, and the top edge is notched for easier blowing. The player produces a sound by blowing down into the pipe, just as Westerners make a note by blowing into a soda bottle. Originally, twelve pipes were bound together either in a circle (bundle pipes) or side by side (raft pipes). Later, four shorter pipes were added, bringing the total up to sixteen. The primary function of the pipes apparently was not musical but as a standard of pitch. The Chinese considered musical notes to be masculine and feminine. The first, third, fifth, etc., notes in the series were masculine; the even notes were feminine. The pipes were divided accordingly, and the masculine pipes were placed on one side, the feminine on the other.

A third type of flute was the *ch'ih* (bamboo flute), which was played in unison with the globular flute. "Heaven enlightens the people when the bamboo flute responds to the earthenware whistle," proclaimed an ode of the ninth century B.C. The flute had six finger holes and was stopped at the upper end, rather than the lower one, as the pipes were. The stopped upper end means that the *ch'ih* must have been a cross flute, held horizontally, as the modern Western flute is. The *ch'ih* was probably the world's first cross flute.

Another cross flute is the *ti*, said to have come from Central Asia during the reign of Emperor Wu Ti (141-87 B.C.). The modern *ti* is twenty-four inches long and has nine holes. Six are finger holes. Two are used to tie a long silk tassel to the end of the instrument, purely as an ornament. The ninth hole is just below the mouth opening. It can be covered with rice paper to add a gentle buzzing tone to the notes.

111

中國事物

Among the flutes held vertically, rather than horizontally, are the *hsiao* and the *yueh*. The top of the *hsiao* is closed by a knot in the bamboo, and the notched mouth hole is cut through the knot. The *hsiao* is thus a cross between a whistle and a regular vertical flute.

A flute tuned to the fundamental note of *huang chung* (the "yellow bell") had to be cut the length of an old Chinese foot: 22.99 centimeters or 9.06 inches. This flute is called the *yueh*, which also means "stalk, foot, measure." The distance between holes was determined purely by measurement: The center of the lowest finger hole was three Chinese inches from the bottom. The other holes were all two inches apart, measured from the center of the hole. This method of spacing might be in harmony with the universe and the Bureau of Weights and Measures, but it was hardly musical. The equal spacing could not produce a scale, which requires holes spaced farther apart toward the lower end of the instrument. For proper pitches to be played on a Chinese flute, the size of the holes would have to be varied or the player would have to make adjustments in fingering and breathing.

FOOT BINDING

Yao Niang, concubine of a Chinese prince more than a thousand years ago, walked with such grace that she was said to "skim over the top of golden lilies." At that point

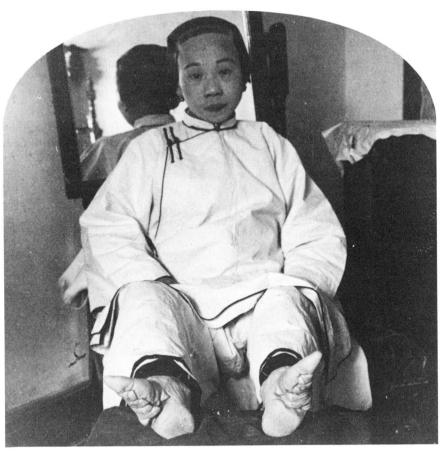

VIEW OF THE "LILY FEET" OF A WOMAN OF HIGH CASTE. SHOES WERE WORN ON GREAT TOE ONLY. C. 1900.

the lily-footed maiden—the woman with bound feet—became the ideal in China.

That is one legend of the origin of the custom of foot binding. Another says that Lady Yao was ordered by her lover to bind her feet so that they would look like new moons. Still a third has it that the practice arose out of sympathy for an Empress with club feet. Some scholars say that it was simply a means by which husbands could keep their wives from straying.

The tiny feet were considered a mark of a respectable woman. The wealthy bound their daughters' feet to demonstrate their gentility, and the poor did it to give their girls a chance to rise to a better situation. In some regions a woman with natural feet was considered immoral. A man who discovered that his promised bride had large feet instead of the small ones he expected had grounds for breaking off the betrothal.

Women with lily feet walk with very short steps, swaying like a willow in a way considered very attractive. Walking on one's heels gives a similar effect.

The foot-binding process began when a girl was between four and eight years old. "Every pair of small feet costs a bath (kang) of tears," goes a Chinese saying. The later the process was begun the truer that became, though opinion differs as to how painful or disabling the bound feet were.

The aim was to stop the growth of the foot, not to make it smaller. The bandages were tightened every week until the desired effect was achieved, and they were never permanently removed. Often they were elaborately embroidered. Tiny handmade silk or satin shoes, only three or four inches long, were worn over the bandaged feet.

Several times in the thousand years that foot binding was practiced in China, edicts forbidding the practice were issued but ignored. Only in the twentieth century has the custom waned.

FORBIDDEN CITY

The noblest examples of Chinese architecture are found in the Forbidden City, the imperial palace and capital built during the Ming Dynasty. It was designed and constructed by the Yung Lo Emperor (A.D. 1402-24), a forceful, brilliant leader who was nicknamed the "Black Dragon." The Forbidden City, or the "Great Within," constructed during a general rebuilding of Beijing, was and is the most lavish royal residence ever created.

It actually consists of four walled cities, one inside another. The outer or Chinese city was walled in 1544. This was a loud, noisy, commercial area, a bustling city of five hundred thousand people. As one headed north on the main avenue, one would pass into the "inner" city, an older section enclosed in 1437.

This, in turn, surrounded the Imperial City. Here the pace was much slower. The official bureaucrats would be at work, surrounded by pagodas, parks, and spacious halls. The public was never allowed through the gates unless on official business. At the northern end was the meridian gate, where the Emperor sometimes received tribute from foreign ambassadors. Beyond the gate lay the Forbidden City.

To make the journey from the outer city into the Forbidden City was like taking a trip out of the world and into an unearthly heaven. After crossing numerous moats and gates, one was confronted with three aligned halls: the Hall of Supreme Harmony, where the Emperor gave audiences; the Hall of Middle Harmony, a waiting chamber; and the Hall of Protecting Harmony, where state banquets were held. Beyond these lay gardens, lakes, palace workshops, and finally the Gate of Heavenly

中國事物

Purity, leading to private quarters, accessible only to the royal family and their eunuchs.

Here, in an atmosphere of solitude, surrounded by magnificent temples and halls, with tiered roofs in brilliantly colored tiles, and wide marble terraces, the Son of Heaven could feel that he was just that. Ironically, the later Ming Emperors who lived here were a particularly undeserving lot, spending their time in a search for earthly pleasures in the midst of this celestial home.

FORTUNE-TELLING

Although the mythological origins of fortune-telling in China stretch back into prehistoric times, the art was formally recognized as a legitimate way to seek knowledge concerning the future during the second century B.C. Most Chinese

FORTUNE-TELLER IN HIS STREET SHOP. C. 1900.

fortune-tellers rely on a system devised by a T'ang Dynasty (A.D. 618-906) imperial censor named Li Hsu-chung, who devised horoscopes using combinations of the Five Elements, the Ten Heavenly Stems, and the Twelve Terrestrial Branches. In order to come up with a person's individual fortune the system required the use of Six Characters denoting the year, month, and day of a person's birth.

Many of the techniques of telling fortunes were published in an official government manual by the Board of Rites in 1683. An updated version was put out in 1741 containing thirty-six books under the title *Hsieh Chi Pien Fang Shu*. In this century the most recognized fortune-telling manual is the two-volume work *Hsuan tse*. It contains all of the essential formulas, regulations, and methods of divination, along with various techniques used in different parts of China.

The most popular fortune-telling practiced is that of Sung Dynasty fortune-teller Su Yen-sheng, who added Two Characters to the Six Characters used by Li Hsu chung. The system of Eight Cyclic Characters is widely known and used by most Chinese to learn their future at key moments in life. After a child is born, the parents present the child's Eight Cyclic Characters for interpretation to a fortune-teller, who prepares a horoscope. Fortunes and compatibilities are again settled by fortune-tellers prior to marriage. The preparation of these horoscopes often involves the cross-referencing of the Eight Cyclic Characters with the animal signs of the zodiac.

Another means of telling a person's fortune that goes back to the most ancient times is the technique used by the physiognomists. They tell fortunes by studying the appearance of their customer's face. According to them, "The ears, eyes, mouth, nose, eyebrows, forehead, cheeks, and the chin correspond to the Five Sacred Mountains, the Four Great Rivers, the Five Planets, and the Six Stars." The senses, hand, fingers, stature, and frame of a person all correspond to various fixed values in the numerological Order of Heaven and Earth. When a physiognomist computes the relations and oppositions of all these factors he can forecast good or bad luck, the length of life, the fortunes of marriage, and whether or not children will ensue from a marriage.

A large number of fortune-tellers encountered in accounts of this art seem to be blind old men led around by a young boy. In a footnote to his chapter on fortune-telling, Father Henri Doré described the fortune-tellers he had seen as recently as 1917: "Some of them have a kind of harp, which they play occasionally as they walk slowly along the street. Others carry a rattle composed of two small pieces of wood. When struck together they indicate the approach or presence of the fortune-teller."

[See ASTROLOGY, DIVINATION, EIGHT CYCLICAL CHARACTERS, and PALMISTRY.]

FOUR SIGNS OF A SCHOLAR

There was a running debate between the Wei and the Chin Neo-Taoists about what actually constituted the four signs of a scholar. The Wei, who were off track, insisted ironically that the telltale signs were: dependence on plagiarism, a wandering mind, overindulgence of spicy foods, and an unnatural affection for little boys. The Chin correctly asserted that the true signs of a scholar were: the lute, the game of cheoo, literature, and painting.

FOUR SUPERNATURAL CREATURES

By examining a bronze mirror from the Han Dynasty (206 B.C.-A.D. 220), it is possible to catch a glimpse of the Chinese conception of the universe. In the center is a plain circle, representing the Great Ultimate Principle. Next you'll find the Four

算命

四維

四靈

中
國
事
物

Supernatural Creatures that preside over the Four Quadrants and the Four Seasons. They are the Azure Dragon (East/Spring); the Somber Warrior, or Divine Tortoise (North/Winter); the Vermilion Bird, or Phoenix (South/Summer); and the White Tiger (West/Autumn).

[See DRAGON, PHOENIX, TORTOISE, and WHITE TIGER.]

FOUR TREASURES

Chinese pedants and poets were united in their veneration of the Four Treasures. These were ink, which when not in use for transcription could be rubbed on the tongue as a cure for convulsions; paper, which when not the object of inspiration was otherwise burned as a charm against infectious diseases; the brush pen, originally made of sable, fox, or rabbit hairs set in a bamboo holder; and the ink slab, made of stone and paste, used to prepare the ink for writing.

FOX

If you think Aesop's foxes are sly you will find the Chinese variety especially cunning. They are able to assume human form and are regarded as the transmigrated souls of deceased Chinese. At the age of fifty the fox can take the form of woman and at one hundred can become a young and beautiful girl, or, if the fox is so inclined, a wizard. The fox was originally a lewd woman named Tzu, who was transformed into a fox for her horrible vices.

In female form the fox causes endless mischief (particularly in love affairs) throughout Chinese literature. Fear of the fox has led the Chinese to offer incense and food to him in order to be on good terms with this crafty animal. Wayside shrines dedicated to the fox and asking his help in curing disease were commonly found in the Chinese countryside.

FUNERAL RITES

> Man at his birth receives his fate,
> And by it each life must be disposed.
> I will calm my heart and pluck up my will;
> What more have I to fear?
> I know that death cannot be refused;
> May I love life no longer!
> This I proclaim to all worthy men:
> I will be an example for you!
>
> —Ch'u Yuan

The ceremonies attached to a Chinese funeral lasted forty-nine days, the period of mourning was three years, and the body might not even be interred by then. The Chinese have a saying that the most important thing in life is to be buried well.

Typically, the coffin would have been purchased long before and left in the hallway near the front door. In form it resembled the trunk of a tree; the boards were three or four inches thick and rounded on top. Three nails were used to seal the coffin and were entwined with hair, since the term for an entwined nail was the same as that for posterity and propagation.

A great deal of what is known of the daily life of the early Chinese comes from sculptures and artifacts buried with the dead. Usually these were symbolic items that represented a man's needs in his afterlife—boats, farm animals, granaries, well heads, dwellings, even jugglers and musicians were all rendered in miniature and placed in the tomb. For the tombs of the royalty, burial practices assumed a grander scale—from the human sacrifices of the Shang to the more humanitarian straw-and-wood figures of the Chou. Perhaps the most intriguing recent find is the spectacular jade burial suits unearthed in 1968 dating from the Han Dynasty.

During the Ming Dynasty a special ceremony was held on the forty-ninth day of mourning in which small bundles of wood, uncooked rice, salt, and oil were offered to the deceased. This indicated to him that the family was going to stop cooking for him. Although quantities of mock money were burned throughout the period of mourning and on numerous festivals honoring the dead, a great quantity was offered at this time, since it was understood that the spirit's expenses would increase. The mock money passed through the smoke to become real money in the world of the dead. The Chinese called it the "World of Shadows," and assumed that life continued there essentially unchanged.

[See ANCESTOR WORSHIP.]

A LONGEVITY GOD, SHOU LAO, WITH MUSHROOM MOTIF.

FUNGUS OF IMMORTALITY

The *ling-chih* is a species of fungus, most likely the *Polyporus lusidus*, that is widely regarded by Chinese mystics and alchemists as being the diet of the immortals. It was believed that the fungus grew on "The Islands of the Blest," just off the coast of China in the "Eastern Sea." Those magical islands became a favorite theme for artists and poets, whose imaginations salivated at the thought of all that magical fungus. Failing to secure passage to the isles, they would settle for eating vast quantities of more terrestrial fungi—such as Devil's Umbrella, Earth's Ears, Thunderballs, or Stone Ears. Fungus was not merely collected; it was quite commonly cultivated on select branches and bits of bark.

中
國
事
物

FURNITURE

Recent excavations of Ming tombs have unearthed complete sets of furniture, including miniature models, made of beechwood. Other favored hardwoods were rosewood, red sandalwood (*tsu tan*), and teak; while walnut, oak, and cedar were used as cheaper substitutes. The earliest forms of Chinese furniture date from the Chou period in the fourth century B.C. The armrests, low tables, and stands indicate that the Chinese at that time had a mat-level culture.

The primary unit of furniture—one that evolved over the centuries—was the *kang*. This was a low platform or dais, which in its various shapes and sizes served for kneeling, sleeping, as a table, or even as an armrest. Sometimes the bed was canopied and closed in on three sides by partitions hung with paintings. There was a double transformation of the wooden dais from a seat with back and arms into a folding chair with a seat of cloth or leather. These were known as "barbarian seats" because they were inspired by models from Central Asia. The chair as we know it today came to China from India in the sixth century.

[See RATTAN and STOVE BED.]

GAMBLING

The Revolution, no doubt, disapproves of gambling, and the Chinese, no doubt, still place a friendly wager. In the old days both men and women from coolie to mandarin would bet on almost anything from the number of seeds in an orange to the names of the scholars who passed the yearly civil service examinations. The New Year's season would be characterized by an orgy of gambling with dice, dominoes, cards, coins, and lotteries.

Confucius called Lao Tzu, author of the classic *Tao-te-ching*, an "ignorant good

GAMBLERS AND MONEY CHANGER AT A GAMING STALL. C. 1920.

man," and blamed the religion he founded, Taoism, for pandering to the Chinese penchant for lucky charms and gambling. A Han Dynasty critic complained that people are in the habit of wastefully cutting up expensive colored silks to make amulets. The Han Dynasty disapproved of gambling in general because it did no social good.

Apparently writing began in China as a means to record predictions made by divination, a form of gambling on the future. For the first thousand years all writing was done on the pieces of tortoiseshell and bone that, when heated, foretold the future by the pattern of cracks that appeared. The next great wave of writing probably involved the writing of talismans or amulets, first on long thin strips of bamboo, and later on silk and wood. One might argue that without gambling and superstition the birth of Chinese literature would have been much delayed.

In the nineteenth century fan-tan was the national game of China. This is a game of extreme simplicity that depends on pure luck. The croupier spills out a heap of coins, and the gamblers bet on what will be left over when the pile is counted by fours. The immortals, in the meantime, played *Liu-po*, a game so complicated that each player was supported by a second.

Today in New China gambling continues. At night under the street lamps of both commune and city, groups of men accompanied by their sons gather to wager on cards or dice. Gambling is very much a part of the social tradition of China's long history.

[See LOTTERIES and MAH-JONGG.]

GARDENS

The Chinese garden is a product of harmonious interactions between the elements and cosmological considerations. In addition to the small private gardens tended by people of means, most Chinese cities boast of larger gardens containing landscaped hills, waterways, bridges, and rockeries. The best-known Chinese garden was the Yuan Ming Yuan outside of Beijing. It was built by the Ch'ing, Kang-Hsi, Yung-Cheng, and Ch'ien-Lung Emperors and destroyed by European soldiers in 1860.

The balance of water and hills is an essential element in the geomantic balance sought when a garden is constructed. The result is most often asymmetrical, with arrangements of rocks and flowing water and pools containing lotus blossoms, as well as rows of potted plants. The lotus growing out of water has religious significance, especially due to the influence of Buddhism. According to Buddhist lore, the Buddha likened the consciousness of men to the lotus growing from mud up through water and into daylight. He vowed to help men arrive at the realization attained by the fully bloomed lotus. The pools and small streams found in Chinese gardens also contain fish, most often carp. The exotic garden beds and streams are embellished with decorative ritual structures such as bridges, pavilions, and arches erected in honor of noteworthy individuals.

GASTRONOMY

The "Seven Necessities" reported by Wu Tzu-mu in the late Southern Sung were: firewood, rice, oil, salt, soy sauce, vinegar, and tea. To this list the more prosperous add *ts'ai* (food to complement the rice) and soup, both mostly of vegetables. The Chinese seem to have more vegetables than other peoples, perhaps because their geography provides such a variety of growing conditions. Beyond the level of bare sustenance, Chinese gastronomy is based on the balanced alternation of the Five

傢具　賭博　花園　美食學

中
國
事
物

Tastes: sweet *(tian)*, sour *(suan)*, fiery *(la)*, salty *(xian)*, and bitter *(ku)*.

Colors and textures of food are also expected to contrast or harmonize, and many foods and colors are imbued with symbolic value as well—the color yellow and the fruit peaches both represent longevity, for instance. Celestial gastronomy distinguishes among textures not only *tender* and *crisp*, but also *gelatinous, spongy, fluffy, chewy, crunchy,* and *gliding.* The textures of foods, as well as their nutritive values, are largely determined by cooking methods.

The question of who invented the wok is unimportant; what matters is that the Chinese mastered its use centuries ago. Among its other virtues, a cast-iron wok will, at the customary high temperatures used for stir frying, part with enough iron to prevent anemia. The Chinese methods of roasting food in clay pots and steaming food in stacked baskets are both fuel-saving and nutritional. From ancient times the Chinese have preserved food by drying, salting, fermenting, and pickling, as well as, in North China, making use of the climate to preserve such prepared foods as dumplings by freezing.

The Chinese were apparently the first to devise the tea cozy, placing large teapots in cotton-lined wooden buckets with a hole through the lid for the spout. But China's most widely appreciated contribution to the art and science of eating may be the little round sweet cakes fried in oil that are described in T'ang manuscripts and are known to us as "doughnuts."

GEESE

Chill wind stirs at horizon's end:
My friend, what news?
When will the geese arrive?
—Tu Fu (A.D. 712-70)

Traditionally, migrating geese in China were associated with messages and airborne letters. This literary image was suggested, no doubt, by the formation of the geese, which did in fact resemble letters written in the air. A wild goose was depicted on the Chinese postal flag, and was a popular design on fancy note paper. The Chinese are convinced that geese never mate for a second time, so the wild goose symbolizes matrimony.

GENGHIS KHAN

"The greatest joy is to conquer one's enemies, to pursue them, to seize their property, to see their families in tears, to ride their horses, and to possess their daughters and wives." Fearful in every aspect, this thirteenth-century Mongol warlord was responsible for some of the greatest carnage and destruction in history. With his cast of thousands of cavalry, Genghis Khan swept across the Chin state to conquer the Middle Kingdom. The Great Wall detained him for a mere two years before he stormed it in a blood-crazed frenzy. His armies finally descended on the Beijing plain, bewildering the Chin forces in much the same way that Mao's Red Army surprised the forces of Chiang Kai-shek in the 1930s. Now that Genghis Khan had one of the world's richest farmlands and most advanced civilizations at his feet, all he could think of was its total destruction. Only when this task was accomplished did he feel the longing to return to the steppes and desert of the Mongol West. There he lived out the rest of his years in tranquility, a doting grandfather and a loving herdsman.

[See KUBLAI KHAN.]

GEOMANCY

鵝

成吉思汗

風水

GEOMANCER'S COMPASS. FROM *Researches into Chinese Superstition* BY HENRI DORÉ.

Feng-shui (wind-water) is the ancient science by which the location of buildings and graves is divined. The purpose for this kind of magical consultation prior to the burial of a relative or the building of a house is based in the belief that heaven and earth reflect each other, and that such critically important earthly activities as burial and building must be done in harmony with the invisible prerequisites of Nature. The science first developed in connection with the selection of burial sites. The Chinese believed that if buried in an auspicious location, the spirit of the dead would benefit from divine favors, and that this would be transmitted to living descendants and their children.

References to the art of "geomancy" in grave selection exist in the Chou Dynasty *Li Chi (Book of Rites),* but the practice was definitively codified by Kuo P'o (A.D. 276-324) in a book of twenty chapters. At first there were two schools of geomancy: (1) the *Fujien,* which stressed the role of the constellations, the Eight Trigrams, the Twelve Branches, and relied more on the geomancer's compass for prognostication than (2) the *Guangxi* school, which used divining sticks, sounding rods, and other instruments to conduct a spiritual evaluation of the contours of the land, the locations of waterways, and the confluence of *yin* and *yang* elements to make a

中
國
事
物

pronouncement about the land being favorable. Eventually the two schools merged, with geomancers using both systems simultaneously. Geomancers and their compasses are also consulted in times of calamity and illness in order to determine exactly which of the gods or spirits of nature must be placated.

GINGER

Ginger is cultivated throughout Asia, Africa, India, and the West Indies, but in China it is appreciated not only as a condiment but also as a vegetable and as a medicinal herb. The best Chinese ginger is grown in Guangdong Province. In Guangzhou, tender young ginger roots are preserved in a syrup and packed in large earthenware jars for export to wealthy foreigners. The Chinese themselves use little syrup ginger, preferring to dry it or pickle it in vinegar or, best of all, use it fresh.

The delicacy of flavoring that is characteristic of Chinese cuisine would be impossible without fresh ginger, which is used to neutralize strongly flavored fish, liver, or chicken. When fresh ginger and fresh garlic are combined in cooking, each neutralizes the other, so that the ginger is not fiery hot and the garlic doesn't linger and linger. Crystallized ginger, which became tremendously popular during the nineteenth century, can be soft and gelatinous like candied orange slices, or hard and crunchy like rock candy.

At the birth of a child the Chinese used to hang up a piece of raw ginger on the front door to ward off evil spirits and the bad influence of strangers. A headache remedy that amazed the early European observers consisted of heating ginger root in a fire, quickly slicing it very thin, and applying it, still very hot, to the temples and forehead of the sufferer. Fresh ginger is easy to grow in a flowerpot or in the garden from a good healthy root. Cooking ginger can be kept fresh for months at a time by keeping the root, peeled, in a jar of dry sherry in the refrigerator.

GINSENG

Second only to tea, said the nineteenth-century sinophiles, ginseng is the most highly regarded plant in the Orient. Ginseng grows wild in eastern Asia from Nepal to Manchuria, and in the American Appalachians. China's ginseng consumption far exceeds the amount she can produce, and she imports the "man root," mostly from Korea, but also from Kentucky. America has exported ginseng since George Washington's time, but American buyers are likely to prefer Korean ginseng as stronger. Both Americans and Chinese value wild ginseng much more highly than the cultivated variety, but there will never be nearly enough of the wild variety to supply the demand.

The oriental ginseng and the occidental mandrake are probably the only medicinal roots of sufficient antiquity and value to be flattered by forgery. Unscrupulous ginseng sellers, unlike the mandrake peddlers who carved their imitations out of other plants, merely increased the age, and therefore the value of their wares. The age of ginseng is determined by the number of rings on the main root, rings that can be induced artificially by binding the fresh root with hair or silk thread. The medicinal properties of the plant are supposed to increase with age, which is also determined by the size of the root and the number of the thin, branching rootlets.

Chang Kuo-Lao, one of the Eight Immortals in Chinese mythology, achieved immortality by eating a ginseng root nearly two feet in length. The reputed aphrodisiac and rejuvenating qualities of ginseng could be side effects of this function. Even the pragmatic Mao Tse-tung is supposed to have taken ginseng for longevity.

Ginseng may be drunk as a tea, mixed in soups, or pickled in rice wine, as well as jellied, candied, and made into syrup or capsules.

薑

人

參

圍

棋

GO (WEI-CH'I)

Just as *t'ai chi ch'uan* is probably the original martial art, *wei-ch'i* is probably the original war game. A Mr. Giles, British consul in China during the 1890s, who wrote two books about *wei-ch'i* (one in eight volumes), informed his readers that the game was invented in the year 2300 B.C. by the "great and excellent Emperor Yao." Certainly *wei-ch'i* appears in Chinese literary works of two thousand years ago. At first it was a game for the nobility. *Wei-ch'i* masters were highly regarded and addressed as *hsien* (holy man) or *shen* (sage).

Wei-ch'i was introduced to Japan in A.D. 735 and there too, at first, only the nobles played it. The Japanese called it *go*, and it took over the country like a long, slow, and steady invasion. After a while, everyone began to play *go*, and everyone took it seriously; until 1600, it was one of the compulsory courses at the military academy of Japan. Despite the fact that *wei-ch'i* is better known in its Japanese incarnation as *go*, it is the most quintessentially Chinese of games.

Europe was not due to receive *wei-ch'i* (as *go*, of course) until the dawn of the twentieth century. *Wei-ch'i* was observed, but not taken seriously by nineteenth-century sinophiles. Perhaps its complex simplicity passed them by, and they saw only two men, a board, and two piles of smooth, round stones. Until about 1920 only a few Westerners had heard of *go*; logically enough, many of these pioneer enthusiasts were chess masters. One, Emanuel Lasker, gave the game cosmic significance, saying, "If on any planet there are rational beings, then they know *go*."

If chess mirrors battles of the age of chivalry, *wei-ch'i*, which is much more ancient, more closely resembles modern warfare. Each player starts out with a theoretically infinite number of stones. In practice, there are 181 black stones and 180 white ones, enough to occupy each intersection point on the board. *Wei-ch'i* boards consist of a grid of nineteen horizontal and vertical lines, which make 361 intersections. Each intersection that a player occupies or controls scores one point; also, each

SPECTATORS AT A *wei-ch'i* (*go*) GAME. FROM THE K'ANG-HSI PERIOD (1662-1723).

中
國
事
物

captured enemy stone scores one point. Chinese boards are often printed on paper and are used both for playing on and for calculating the score; they have wide margins for writing in remarks or comments.

The weaker player generally takes black, and opens play. Each alternates in putting down a stone at any unoccupied point on the board. Territory is occupied by building a chain and enclosing it; *wei* means enclosure or encampment. Enemy stones are taken by cutting off their "breath" (*ch'i*) by filling up the four intersections that surround them. A stone or a chain of stones is captured when it loses its last "breath." Stones on the board's edges begin life with only three breaths; stones on corners have only two. "Then," say the Chinese, unconsciously copying Lewis Carroll, "each one plays in turn until the last move, and then the game stops."

GOD OF FIRE

The mythical deity of fire, Lo Hsuan, once lived as a Taoist adept on the island of Fiery Dragon. He is depicted as wearing a fishtail-shaped headdress. He has three eyes and his face, hair, and beard are all red. He wears a red robe decorated with the Eight Trigrams. His war horse snorts fire, and its hooves radiate fire-kindling sparks. In each hand Lo holds magical weapons, the most impressive of which is the smoke column one thousand *li* in length containing swords of fire.

Another important fire divinity much revered throughout China is one of the three ancient emperors: Chu Jung. It is thought that he was once the legendary Emperor Fu Hsi (b. 2953 B.C.), who taught the people the beneficial uses of fire. According to other traditions Chu Jung became an imperial title for "fire prefect." Various fire prefects are considered spirits harmful or beneficial to the affairs of men. The particular history of a province or of a city often influences which fire gods become the most important for that reason. There is a known case of a seventeenth-century governor of Suzhou throwing himself into the flames after three days of futile fire fighting during a major conflagration in that city. He was subsequently made the god of fire for the city.

It is interesting to note that temples of the fire spirit in China were always built facing north, which is the direction of the rain or water spirit. The Chinese believed that since the south is the fire region, the fire spirit could be most safely kept from devastating the area by making his temple face in the opposite direction or toward the negating direction of water. This was believed to diminish the risk of conflagrations.

GOD OF THE KITCHEN

The kitchen god has been called the center of the Chinese family religion. The cult of Tsao Chun probably originated with the worship of an ancient hearth god. Until recent times Tsao's image was placed in a niche above the stove. He is an important patron of every household, for he sits above the stove determining the length of life of each member of the household, controlling their poverty or wealth, and silently noting their virtues and vices.

During the last month of the Chinese year Tsao Chun takes leave of the house to make his report to the ruler of heaven. Before Tsao's departure around the twenty-fourth of the month, sacrificial meats along with charms and prayers are offered to him. At the end of the ceremony, Tsao's picture is burned. On the thirtieth of the month Tsao returns from his journey to heaven. A new picture of him is installed above the stove amid an offering of vegetables made to content the god for another year.

Tsao is perhaps the most universally worshiped of all Chinese household gods. He has the power to forgive sins and extend the length of life. He is the patron of cooks and has the task of leading the souls of suicides to the first court of hell.

There are dozens of stories describing the origin of the kitchen god. The most popular is that of a wayward husband who was blinded, and upon eating his good wife's porridge bemoaned the fact that he had not eaten so since his marriage. The woman restored his sight, whereupon he was so overcome with shame that he leaped into the stove. The wife placed his tablet over the stove, and so began the worship of the god.

GOD OF LITERATURE

The temples of Wen Ch'ang, the high god of literature, were once located in every major city in China. Wen was long worshiped as the dispenser of official dignities to successful scholars, arbiter of destiny, and patron of literature. His palace is located in the Big Dipper.

Worship of Wen Ch'ang goes back to a T'ang Dynasty scholar named Chang Ya, who was greatly admired for his talent, and who for a while was appointed to the Board of Rites. Upon his mysterious disappearance, or death in battle, the T'ang Emperors canonized him. Subsequent dynasties heaped additional honors on Wen Ch'ang, calling him Diffuser of Renovating Influences.

The god is often accompanied by an ugly individual named K'uei Hsing. Legend has it that he was an ugly examination candidate named Chung K'uei, who scored first in the examinations. It was the custom for the Emperor to award the first-place winner with a golden rose in person, but when the Emperor saw Chung, he refused to hand him the rose. In despair Chung threw himself into a river to die. At the point of drowning, a mysterious sea monster (called *Ao*) came up underneath and brought him to the surface. K'uei was rescued and ascended to the polar regions to become superintendent of literary individuals. K'uei is beseeched by students on the verge of their examinations, and by officials desiring to raise the level of education in their districts.

GOD OF LONGEVITY

The Chinese god of longevity is identified with the polar star Canopus. Emperor Ch'in Shih-Huang-Ti was the first to sacrifice to the star of longevity, which always brought happiness in the wake of its appearance. The spirit of the South Pole was later represented as an old man with an extremely high bald forehead and a long white beard. Shou Hsing is often depicted riding on a spotted stag and holding a staff, a gourd, and a scroll, as well as a golden peach from the magical tree that blooms only once every three thousand years and then bears fruit only three thousand years later. Sometimes he is shown with a bat flying over his head.

The god of longevity is one of five characters honored by Chinese on New Year's. Beginning during the Southern Sung Dynasty (A.D.1127-1279), the practice of pasting up five strips of paper over the door on New Year's became widespread and has continued to modern times. The five characters are: happiness, honors, longevity, joy, and wealth.

GOD OF THE PIGSTY

Chu-Chuan Shen is considered god of the pigsty. Historically he was an officer named Chu Tzu-chen. In the middle of a battle he changed himself into a giant pig and

火神
灶神
文昌
壽星公
豬圈神

125

中
國
事
物

swallowed a hero named Yang Chien. Upon returning Yang to his general, Chu-Chuan was slain and reappeared in human form. According to legend, "He had a black face, short beard, long lips, and large ears. He wore a silk waist belt to tie his black garments, and armed with a sword always fought on foot. His body was formed of coagulated air."

Chu-Chuan Shen is worshiped extensively by pork dealers. He is invoked in the hope of keeping pigs free of disease. Farmers paste up numerous paper charms dedicated to Chu-Chuan and other animal patrons around their pens.

GOD OF THUNDER

"Thunder is the great voice of heaven," say the Chinese. It combines the three highly respected elements of terror, power, and the rapidity of action. According to popular tradition, thunder results from a collision between *yin* and *yang*, the two primal eternal opposites.

Lei-tsu is often found enthroned on the main altar in both Buddhist and Taoist temples. His name is frequently written on the lintels of houses for protection. *Lei-tsu*'s birthday is celebrated on the twenty-fourth day of the sixth month. He is worshiped by innkeepers, millers, grain dealers, and candy-store owners, who set off firecrackers and burn incense in his honor. Farmers and those who handle grains and cereals are especially respectful of *Lei-tsu* because part of his function is to distribute rain for the crops. *Lei-tsu* punishes those who waste grain or trample it. He is capable of unleashing a deadly thunderbolt from a third eye in the middle of his forehead, which can either strike a man down or level a field of crops. *Lei-tsu*, which means literally "Thundering Ancestor," is one of the most powerful of all traditional Chinese gods.

GOD OF WAR

With over sixteen hundred temples built throughout China in his honor, the god of war, Kuan Yu, is among the most popular of all Chinese gods. The ruler of war was once a great military hero named Kuan Kung (Kuan Yu). Kuan, together with Liu-pei and Chang-fei, embarked on a Three Musketeers-like pact to restore order and rid the country of brigands and invaders. In A.D. 217 Kuan was captured and killed by an enemy general who forwarded his head to his traditional enemy Ts'ao-Ts'ao. Kuan was fifty-eight at the time of his death. Almost immediately he became a cult figure. His reputation for courage and loyalty spread rapidly. In 1594, Emperor Wan-Li of the Ming Dynasty named Kuan Kung a god.

Kuan's popularity continued to increase beyond the military affairs he originally presided over. He is considered the guardian of Buddhist temples, and he led the heavenly hosts who preside over the Five Sacred Mountains. He is also a literary god and a god of wealth. Kuan, it seems, was so popular that he became nearly all things to all people. In A.D. 1856 a Manchu Emperor named him "Sage or Great Teacher" for his assistance in suppressing the T'ai-p'ing rebellion.

GOD OF WEALTH

The Celestial Ministry of Finance is populated by a great number of gods and spirits, all of them responsible for the wealth of their human devotees. First among them is Ts'ai Shen—the god of wealth, the most widely worshiped god in all China. Although there are various historical characters thought to have been deified as Ts'ai, the oldest is a warrior named Chao Kung-ming. Chao was reputed to ride a black tiger and hurl pearls that exploded like bombs. He was killed by an opposing general through witchcraft, and was later raised to the presidency of the Ministry of Riches.

Various other gods and spirits of wealth are worshiped throughout China, including Wu Lu Ts'ai Shen, or Five Roads god of wealth, who controls the wealth of scholars, farmers, artisans, merchants, and soldiers. Some other favorites are named call riches, enter wealth, fairy ruler of favorable markets, heavenly ruler bestowing happiness, god of affluence, lord of fortune, god of wealth, giver of joyful opulence, and precious treasure of happiness god.

Whatever name he happens to be going under, the god of wealth has pictures in every shop and house. His birthday is on the fifth day of the first month, and elaborate feasts are prepared in his honor on the fourth day. One curious custom is the hanging of live fish over the offerings. The fish are then returned to the water they were taken from in order to spawn and grow rich. The word *yu* for fish is pronounced the same as the word *yu* for abundance. On the god of wealth's birthday, employers invite their workers to the feast if they intend to continue them on the payroll for the coming year. Likewise, the employee attends only if he intends to keep his job. Farmers and rural villagers believe that the god of wealth controls the wealth of the world, distributing it to each family once a year. It is in the hope of getting a larger portion during the coming year that each family worships him so devoutly.

雷神 關羽 財神 送子觀音

SHRINE DEVOTED TO THE GOD OF WEALTH. C. 1900.

GODDESS OF FERTILITY

The perpetuation of the family was possibly the most important task facing any traditional young Chinese couple. Without children the cult of ancestors was doomed to fall by the wayside. For this reason a wide range of gods and spirits were invoked to

中國事物

guarantee the birth of healthy children.

The first of these is the beneficent Kuan-Yin, goddess of mercy and giver of sons. Father Henri Doré noted in 1914 that every temple in China contained statues of Kuan-Yin with small shoes dangling beneath them. A woman desiring a child places a borrowed single baby shoe at Kuan-Yin's feet. When the child is born, the shoe is removed and replaced by a pair of brand-new baby shoes in thanks to the goddess for her help.

Besides Kuan-Yin, the goddess *T'ien-hsien Sung-tzu*, the celestial Immortal who brings children, is commonly prayed to for children. She is the first Princess Pi-hsia Yuan-chun of azure clouds, and is attended by a number of minor goddesses, all of them having to do with some aspect of fertility, or the childbearing process. The goddess is also worshiped because it is she who receives the recently purified souls from the Buddhist hell, and decides into which bodies they are to be reborn on earth.

Another of the gods involved in birth is Chang Hsien, the purveyor of children. A picture of Chang with his bow and peachwood arrows hangs in Chinese bedrooms everywhere to ward off the dog that devours newborn children. The dog is the dog star, and if the fate of the family falls under this star, there will be no children born, or those born will be short-lived. Chang is always depicted as a warrior protecting children from the dog with his bow.

GODDESS OF LIGHTNING

The *I Ching* proposes that lightning comes from the earth, which is the domain of the female principle *yin*. Another theory holds that lightning was born when the King of the Immortals, Tung Wang-kung, missed a shot while playing the "pitch-pot" game. The heavens grinned and a stream of light escaped from its open mouth. The goddess or mother of lightning, Tien-Mu (literally "Electric Mother"), is represented dressed in brilliant blue, green, red, and white. In each hand she holds a hand mirror from which two flashes of light pour downward to earth.

Tien-Mu is often called the mirror of the god of thunder, because the lightning bolts coming from the twin mirrors she holds help the god of thunder punish his victims. Because lightning frequently causes uncontrollable fires, Tien-Mu is closely related to the minor fire gods who reside in the Fifth Celestial Ministry of Fire.

GODDESS OF MARRIAGE

Marriage is for uniting two persons of different families,
the object of which is to serve their ancestors in the temple and to perpetuate the coming generation.
—Book of Rites

Traditionally, Chinese marriages were arranged by a go-between, rather than by the couple. One of the principal deities worshiped in the marriage celebration was Nu-Kua, the goddess of go-betweens. She is often depicted with a human head and a snake's body. She is also referred to as Snail Maid, and is shown with long horns protruding from her head and a snail body. The twin gods of peace and union are sometimes represented by two little boys, and sometimes by two T'ang Dynasty monks, one of whom holds a lotus, the other a casket. They are called Ho Ho, because the words *ho* for peace and *ho* for lotus sound the same as the words *ho* for union and *ho* for casket. Pictures and emblems of all these divinities were carried in nuptial processions.

GODDESS OF MERCY

Until recent times Kuan-Yin was the most widely worshiped goddess in all China. She is the most important of all Chinese and Japanese Buddhist divinities due at least partially to the very meaning of her name: "one who hears the prayers of the world." She is known as the goddess of mercy, she is at once savior and deliverer, a sea goddess prayed to by sailors in a storm, the bestower of male and female children, and the idealization of all that is considered gentle, graceful, and compassionate in women. Ever since Westerners have come in contact with Chinese religion, scholars have compared the cult of Kuan-Yin to that of the role of the Virgin Mary in Christianity.

It is generally thought that Kuan-Yin is a sinified manifestation of the Buddhist male god of mercy, Avalokitesvara the compassionate, who became known in China around the fifth century A.D. How the god became popular in female form is thought to be the result of the romantic legend of Miao-shen, a Chou Dynasty princess whose father reigned 696-681 B.C. Miao-shen refused to marry and entered White Bird Monastery, where her father continued to persecute her. He tried to burn the nunnery down, but the god of rain interceded. Her father ordered her beheaded, but the sword splintered into a thousand pieces. Finally he had her strangled, but when Miao-shen arrived in Hades it turned into paradise. Yama, the god of death, ordered her back to life and she ministered to the sick of P'u-t'o Island. To this day all the temples on the island have her image in the place of honor. Her birthday is celebrated on the nineteenth of the second month, and is attended by thousands of pilgrims to the island from throughout China.

Images of Kuan-Yin are to be found everywhere in China. She is considered to be the only deity really loved by the people. Worshiped as mother and protector, she is sought out in times of trouble. In her role as the ship of salvation, Kuan-Yin delivers the souls of the dead to the Buddhist heaven of Amitabha. She is also known as the universal protectress and mistress of the Southern Seas.

GONGS

According to Chinese tradition, gongs came from the western region of China, between Tibet and Burma. Writings refer to them during the early sixth century. In 1841, two kinds of gongs were described: a large, flat one for prayers; and a smaller gong, with a cylindrical edge, for other uses.

Good-quality gongs are made of bronze that contains about 80 per cent copper and 20 per cent tin. Lower-quality ones drop to a 70 per cent copper content, with the addition of 10 per cent lead. There are six steps in making a gong. The metal must be poured, hammered, and smoothed. Then the gong is tuned, polished, and ornamented.

Richard Strauss scored five large Chinese gongs in "Die Frau ohne Schatten" in 1919. The gongs, however, were to be tuned to definite Western pitches.

GOURDS

The double gourd (Lagenaria siceraria), otherwise known as the gourd bottle, has a long and distinguished use in Chinese history and folklore. It is not fragrant, although it is prized for its many different shapes. Its fruit is generally elongated and constricted in the middle. Other varieties have large rounded fruit, and make ideal containers for wine, medicines, and flowers. Some are shaped like flat disks, or are club-shaped, dumbbell-shaped, or even goosenecked. Colors range from green to tan; occasionally they are striped, mottled, knobby, or ridged.

電母

月老

慈悲觀音

鑼

葫蘆

中國事物

Gourds were a necessary accessory for most of the Immortals. Li T'ieh-kuei is depicted as holding one in his hand, white spirals of smoke pouring out from it, symbolizing his power of being able to set his spirit free from his body. Gourds were worn as charms for longevity, and paper lanterns made in the shape of gourds used to ward off persistent demons.

GOVERNMENT

China's governmental structure was closely aligned with the ideas of Confucius, the "uncrowned ruler of China." Confucius was a product of the anarchic, intolerable world of the Chou Dynasty and in many respects was a political rather than a religious leader. On one occasion a student asked him what was the most important quality for the government of a state. He replied, "the rectification of names." This sounds strange to our ears but it belied a simple and honest concept—that names should reflect actual relationships. Just as a father should embody paternalism, so the Emperor should truly act as the Son of Heaven. This idea was furthered by the Confucian term *li*, which came from the word for sacrifice and denoted proper conduct in all phases of life. By encouraging filial piety Confucius tried to encourage proper conduct at all levels, and to develop a government that ruled by positive example rather than by force. "To rule," he once said, "truly is to serve."

These ideas were further enforced by belief in legalism. In political terms it might be said that legalism instructs one to go beyond the spirit of the law in one's behavior. For example, it was not considered enough merely to obey laws, such as refraining from murder or robbery, but one also was held accountable for the behavior of his family and neighbors. It was one's responsibility to prevent the conditions that lead to crime and social disharmony. This idea is far different from the Western condition of justice, where mere individual adherence to the letter of the law is required. The courts in China operated with few of the legal safeguards known in the West, and sought solely to re-establish proper conduct by all parties as quickly as possible.

In practice, each governmental official was like a father, with a domain over which he wielded power. Just as a father was ultimately responsible for all acts committed in the family, so a viceroy would be ultimately responsible for all acts committed in his province. The multiple obligations of each person in government—to his family, his neighbors, his provincial government, and his Emperor—made every person aware of his social responsibilities. This extremely successful form of government lasted longer than any other before or since.

In many ways the structure of central government in the People's Republic of China is a continuation of China's past. The government is still responsive to the broad concepts that govern human behavior, while it is inextricably tied to the current economic goals of "modernization." Therefore, ideologies such as communism, capitalism, democracy, and socialism are being culled for the development of an ideal community.

[See COURTS, DYNASTIES, and TAXATION.]

GRAND CANAL

The Grand Canal, dug during the Yuan Dynasty (A.D. 1260-1368) and extended by the Ming Dynasty (A.D. 1368-1644), was designed to connect Beijing, the capital, with the Yangtze Valley, which had been the seat of power during the Sung and many previous dynasties.

Canal building in China, however, goes back to the third century B.C., when the Cheng Kuo Canal was dug. This facility irrigated a large segment of land, and gave the Ch'in Emperor a military advantage over the other warring states of the Chou Dynasty.

The most important canal built was probably the New Pien Canal, sometimes called the First Grand Canal. Built by Sui-Yang Ti in 616, this canal linked the productive southern half of China to the northern half and paved the way for the reunification of China under the T'ang Dynasty. Ironically, the severe authoritarianism of the Sui Emperor, necessary for undertaking such a public-works project, helped lead to the downfall of the Sui Dynasty.

The Grand Canal was reconstructed in 1958 during the Great Leap Forward to handle six-hundred-ton barges. Today, it is one of China's most important inland waterways.

政府

大運河

蚱蜢

LIFE ALONG THE GRAND CANAL. C. 1900.

GRASSHOPPERS

Crickets and grasshoppers provide a unique gambling sport in China. Two of them are placed in a bowl and agitated until a fight ensues, invariably ending in the loss of life and limb for one of the contestants. Tubsful of them are sold on the streets in autumn, and great sums are bet on the matches. Because of its fighting prowess the grasshopper is an emblem of courage, and it is symbolic of summer.

中
國
事
物

GREAT ULTIMATE PRINCIPLE

According to the philosopher Chu Hsi (A.D. 1130-1200), "The Great Ultimate is the principle of heaven and earth and the myriad of things....It is the principle that through movement generates the *yang* (the active principle). It is also the principle that through tranquillity generates the *yin* (the passive principle)." Chu continues by explaining, "There is only one Great Ultimate, yet each of the myriad things has been endowed with it and each in itself possesses the Great Ultimate in its entirety. This is similar to the fact that there is only one moon in the sky but when its light is scattered upon rivers and lakes, it can be seen everywhere."

The Great Ultimate is an all-encompassing Chinese philosophical concept for substance, containing everything, and also the source of all things, beginning with the primal duality of *yin* and *yang*—the eternal opposites. From *yin* and *yang* spring the Five Elements or Forces: water, fire, wood, metal, and earth, from which all things result.

The *t'ai chi* or Great Ultimate symbol is one of the most powerful mystical forces known. When combined with the Eight Trigrams of the *I Ching*, it is called *pa kua*, one of the strongest good-luck charms available.

[See EIGHT TRIGRAMS, FIVE ELEMENTS, and YIN AND YANG.]

GREAT WALL

The distinction of the Great Wall of China truly lies with the men who built it. Probably over a million workers died while slaving at the task, while it took a constant labor force of over 300,000 to work on the project. Most impressively, the Great Wall is the one man-made work on earth visible from the moon to the naked eye.

Basically the Great Wall was built as a wall between civilization and barbarism. To the west were the nearly inaccessible Altaic Mountains, to the east was the ocean, and to the south were peoples who were easily assimilated. But the constant threat to China came from the Mongols and other nomads on the northern steppes.

Construction of the wall began in 214 B.C. during the reign of Ch'in Shih-Huang-Ti. General Meng-Tien, who held the title of conqueror of the Tartars, directed the construction of the wall, which runs for 1,500 miles from Mongolia to the sea. In addition to his 300,000 workers, he often had a great number of soldiers along to prevent attacks by Mongols even as they worked. Along the path of the wall were 34 supply headquarters, each with its own farm. Each day convoys of women would carry food to the workers; the women walked as much as 20 miles in a single direction. Of course, all building materials were transported by hand as well, and in steeper places goats pulled the stones uphill.

The construction itself, though massive, used a fairly simple technique. Furrows were dug, approximately 25 feet apart, and then foundations 4½ feet wide and 6 to 12 feet high were laid. The outer walls were hard-baked brick with limestone mortar. The inner roadway was compacted clay. Legend has it that when a workman died he was pounded into the clay as human building material.

The most interesting features of the wall are the defense towers. Standing between 100 and 500 yards apart, there were over 10,000 of them. Each was 40 feet high and 40 feet square, and they present a most impressive sight. Today thousands of the towers still stand. When Ch'in Shih-Huang-Ti began the wall he said it would last for 10,000 generations. He may have been right.

[See MAPS.]

VIEW OF THE GREAT WALL. C. 1900.

太
極

萬
里
長
城

火
藥

GUNPOWDER

Although firecrackers are mentioned in Chinese sources long before gunpowder, it seems that the earliest firecrackers were, in fact, produced by putting fresh bamboo into a fire, where it would burst with a loud noise due to the vaporization of the water it contained. At the beginning of the seventh century there are references to a "fire drug," which seems to be some sort of firework used in theatrical performances. Although there is no clear indication of what materials were used to produce the effects of the "fire-drug plays," the phrase "fire drug" is the one that is later used for gunpowder itself.

Gunpowder is a mixture of sulphur, saltpeter, and charcoal. In the third century A.D., saltpeter and sulphur were being mixed by alchemists in the same proportions as they are in gunpowder. The mixture was then exposed to fairly intense heat, making the discovery of gunpowder rather likely.

By the time of the Sung Dynasty, which began in A.D. 960, military manuals begin to discuss gunpowder and describe how it is made and used. There are also a number of accounts of disasters caused by carelessness in making or storing gunpowder. The first uses of gunpowder in weaponry were to make more effective fire arrows, some of which carried a charge of gunpowder, and some of which were actually projected by it. By the middle of the tenth century, gunpowder was definitely being used for military purposes. Land mines were also in use.

The catapult, which had long been used for hurling stones at enemy fortifications, was easily adapted to hurling explosives, firebombs, and various chemical-warfare devices that generated clouds of poisonous, or at least noxious, smoke. By

中國事物

the twelfth century, these weapons were being used not only by the Chinese, but also by their Tartar enemies.

In 1233, the use of a "fire gun" by the Chin Tartars is recorded, but this instrument seems to have been a sort of flame thrower. By 1259 an actual gun barrel is recorded, though made of bamboo reinforced with fiber wrappings; the first metal gun barrel is recorded in 1275. For some time after their introduction, however, metal gun and cannon barrels were made ribbed, as though in imitation of the bamboo they replaced.

EARLY USE OF FIREARMS, AND FIRECRACKER MOTIF. FROM THE *T'ien Kung K'ai Wu* AND *Kissho zuan Kaidai.*

HAIRDRESSING

Heavily oiled or pomaded, a Chinese woman's hair was elegantly arranged in buns and twists. The more extravagant hairdos resembled teapot handles or the wings of bats and butterflies. The woman decorated her coiffure with flowers—fresh ones were sometimes placed in a tubule hidden in the hair—or with pins and combs of gold, silver, ivory, jade, or pearl. Butterflies might grace her head or a large phoenix almost hide her hair. A great quantity of hair was desirable, so she may have added false hair to make the real appear thicker.

The Chinese man's queue was originally a symbol of subjugation, imposed by the conquering Manchus in the mid-1600s. To the Manchus, it resembled a horse's tail and was a tribute to that animal, whose speed and endurance they admired. Since criminals were forbidden to wear the queue, the men who did wear it came to consider it a badge of honor, and eventually it became the coiffure of choice for Chinese men. The front of the head was shaved and a long braid hung down the back. Like the women, the men were vain of thick hair and added false hair or a black braid to make their queues longer. Laborers often pinned their queues around their heads when they were working, but good manners required them to let the hair down again when a superior came by.

Missionary E.J. Hardy once described the wondrous uses to which a queue can be put:

> In a street fight the combatants hang on to each other's queues. A *raconteur* supplements manual gesture with his queue. A queue is sometimes plied as a tawse upon the backs of refractory boys. It serves as a noose in which a suicide can strangle himself and a handle for pulling taut the neck of a man being decapitated. Does a Chinaman wish to explain foreign astronomy? He fastens a weight to his queue and whirls it around his head to illustrate the revolutions of the planets around the sun.

Chinese men did not grow mustaches or beards until they were past forty years old. A man with a long beard, because he must be of great age, was highly respected. A man kept his beard neat by grooming it with a special comb and by placing a bag over it each night.

Chinese parents had no problem with getting their youngsters to stand still while the snarls were brushed from their hair. The heads of the little ones were shaved, except for a small tuft on top of a boy's head or over a girl's ears. Baby's first shave, when he was about a month old, was celebrated with a feast and gifts for the child.

Hair in New China is considerably more practical: Most women sport braids or tie their hair back. Men wear their hair short in Western-style cuts.

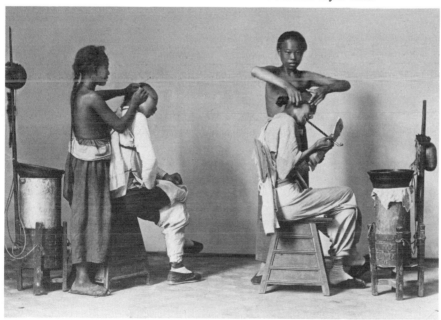

BARBER SHOP. SHANGHAI. C. 1908.

HATS

Huang Ti, Emperor of China 47 centuries ago, had a marvelous headdress, decorated with 288 jewels. A curtain of gems could be lowered in front of his eyes so that the Emperor wouldn't have to look at anything unpleasant or ugly. The sides of the headdress covered his ears to prevent him from hearing slanderous talk.

Most Chinese wear headgear considerably less exotic. The soft cotton brimmed cap worn by Mao Tse-tung is most familiar. Another common hat is a black silk or cotton skullcap, often worn by merchants or craftsmen. The lower classes sometimes sport felt hats with turned-up brims, edged in gold thread in the fancier versions. At times turbans have been popular—in the twelfth and thirteenth centuries one could tell the wearer's occupation by his turban's color and shape. Official hats were constructed of lacquered gauze and worn by scholars. Fur-trimmed hats are favored in winter in the northern regions. In the summer workers are shielded from rain and sun by round hats woven of straw or bamboo. Some of these are nearly a yard in diameter and act like an umbrella, with the wearer serving as the handle. A child with such a hat has been described as a "walking mushroom."

Bamboo is a durable material for hats, protecting the wearer from more than the weather. Soldiers and policemen once wore small, conical bamboo hats to deflect blows dealt by various miscreants.

H E M P

The neolithic Chinese venerated hemp as a gift of the gods, having been given to them by the Divine Cultivator Shen Nung to provide for most of their needs. From this hearty-growing plant they were able to derive clothing, rope, fish nets, foodstuffs, oil for their lamps, and a miracle drug for their aches and brains. The classic *Book of Songs* makes an early reference to it in the third century B.C.: *"I pluck the holy hemp and jasper blooms/To bestow on those who live far from home./As creeping old age draws nigh to an end,/Not to be close together is to drift apart."* Later when *huo ma* (hemp) became a general term for fiber plants, *cannabis sativa* was called *ta-ma* (great hemp). During the Han period (206 B.C.-A.D. 220), the *Shen Nung* pharmacopoeia classifies *ta-ma* as being among the "superior" immortality elixirs.

H E R B O L O G Y

In China, little distinction is traditionally made between food and medicine: Foods are medicines, and are taken like medicines, to cure some illness, or to forestall a threatened illness. Both foods and herbs are classified according to the theories of *yin* and *yang*, and of the Five Elements. There are, for example, Five Seasons: spring, summer, Indian summer, fall, and winter. Each one is characterized by a particular balance of *yin* and *yang*, and thus by appropriate and inappropriate foods.

This attention to diet made the cure of deficiency diseases an important aspect of traditional Chinese medicine, and one at which it was quite effective. For example, beri-beri, a vitamin B-deficiency disease, has for centuries been treated by dietary supplements that provide a substantial increase in vitamin B intake.

Western physicians have become interested recently in the pharmacology of Chinese herbs and herbal treatments, and at the same time, three hundred researchers at the Institute of Materia Medica in Beijing are currently engaged in isolating and identifying the active ingredients in traditional herbal medications. Chinese herbology is regarded as the oldest and most advanced in the world.

H O R S E

Chang Kuo, one of the Taoist Eight Immortals, used to keep his magic white horse inside a gourd. The steed would carry him thousands of miles in a day, and needed no food. When Chang halted, he would fold his horse up and return it to his pocket-sized stable. When he required its use again, he would squirt it with water, and off they would gallop.

The Mongolian pony was indigenous to China. As early as the second century B.C., stronger horse species from Central Asia were imported. Their physical superiority caused the Chinese to refer to them as *T'ien ma* (heavenly horses). They became the favorites of a Han Emperor who filled the stalls of the imperial stables with them, believing they could transport him to heaven.

According to the *Pen Ts'ao*, the great Chinese *Book of Medicine* published in 1596, the horse could travel at night because it had eyes on its knees. These "eyes" were actually warts, and physicians would prescribe them as a remedy against toothache. Horsehair was also used as dental floss.

HOUSEBOATS

It is thought that the general strength of Chinese junks contributed to the fact that for a thousand years or more, every city of any importance contained a large population of "boat people" or houseboat dwellers. The most notable of these is Hong Kong, but houseboats are common along China's great rivers as well. One advantage is that the houseboat dweller does not traditionally pay rent, although the restrictions of space in modern times have required berthing and registration fees—even in Hong Kong.

FISHING BOATS AND JUNKS ALONG THE RIVER. C. 1907.

中國事物

While some Chinese houseboats are permanently anchored, others house families of fishermen, or traders who regularly ply the waters with cargoes of various manufactured goods or raw materials. There is no accurate estimate of how many Chinese live aboard the countless houseboats floating in China's crowded waters, but in Hong Kong alone there are some 250,000.

HUNDRED ANTIQUES

The Hundred Antiques form a miscellaneous collection of emblems that are popularly used in Chinese graphic art. These include the Eight Treasures, various musical instruments, sacrificial vessels, flowers, and animals, as well as any small decorative motifs that might be squeezed into any one painting.

HUNDRED-FAMILY LOCK

Chinese parents customarily created the Hundred-family Lock as a charm for their offspring. One hundred persons would be asked to contribute three or four coins each, which would be strung together around the child's neck to insure a hundred generations' worth of longevity for the little one.

HUNDRED-FAMILY TASSEL

Chinese children were frequently given the name of an animal, and provided with a silver dog collar when taken out for walks. This was in order to fool the greedy grabbing spirits into thinking that the infant was actually a quadruped and not worth their attention. Otherwise, in a pinch, the Hundred-family Tassel proved to be an effective remedy against person-snatching. The parents would beg a bit of thread from door to door. These multicolored threads would be woven into a tassel and hung from the child's dress in hopes of confusing the spirits.

HUNDRED INFANTS

A piece of porcelain or most commonly a silk bedspread decorated in various colors with the pleasing design of the Hundred Infants would be presented to married couples eager to have children. The message was unmistakable.

HYPNOSIS

The primitive folk religion of prehistoric China, as well as the shamanistic practices of neighboring tribes created a tradition of self-hypnosis. From ancient times there were Chinese shamans (*wu*) and magicians (*fang-shih*) working as spirit mediums. Emperor Wu Ti (second century B.C.) kept hundreds of Taoist magicians around him at all times. Upon losing his favorite concubine to death he re-established contact with her through a medium. The technique was tried by Emperors down to the fifteenth century, but there is no corroboration of its success beyond Wu Ti.

The autohypnotic shamanic trances were also components of the fanatical secret societies that regularly rose out of the Taoist religion over thousands of years. The nineteenth-century Boxer rebels reputedly used a form of hypnosis on their members to inspire their enthusiasm and desensitize them to pain.

Hypnosis was traditionally considered to be part and parcel of the Taoist adepts' bag of tricks. The alchemist used simple hypnosis to impress the imperial court, as well as to accomplish his own goal of ascension to *hsien* (immortality). Evidence that magicians used hypnosis to impress groups as well as individuals with their powers is abundant. Perhaps the most notorious sorcerer/alchemist known to have practiced hypnosis was Wang Chieh (A.D. 980-1020), who ran an "artificial gold factory" under Emperor Chen Tsung (A.D. 997-1022). It was said that Wang "could make people see anything that he chose to think about, so that many were astounded and perplexed."

INK

What we call "India ink" the French more accurately term *encre de Chine*, for this rich, black nonfading ink was developed in China toward the end of the remarkable Han Dynasty. Ink and paper appear to have developed somewhat concurrently, although the brush had been perfected many centuries earlier. The first writing fluid of the Chinese was a sort of black lacquer, in use from the late Chou Dynasty for marking on bamboo, wood, and silk. The viscosity and stickiness of lacquer became liabilities as paper came into wider use, and an ink based on soot came to replace it.

China's first professional ink maker was Liu Ch'ao of the T'ang Dynasty. In the *Mo Ching*, or *Ink Classic*, written in the twelfth century by Chao Kuan-chih, Han inks based on coal or charcoal are mentioned, but the very best inks are said to be made from pine soot mixed with glue made from carp skins, deer horns, or horse, ox, or donkey hides. Good ink depends on good pigment, good glue (which imparts texture and longevity), and long grinding.

The earliest molds for forming ink sticks were all boat-shaped, and ancient inventories sometimes refer to "so many boats of ink." The most common shape for ink sticks now is rectangular, but ovals, squares, lozenges, and irregular shapes outlining fungus, clouds, bamboo groves, or dragons are sometimes made. Rectangular sticks are often modeled in relief with landscapes, flowers, or calligraphy, and highlighted with red and gold.

Perfumes are sometimes added to Chinese inks (the West went the other way and scented its papers), and other additions are often made for texture or tone. Vinegar and pomegranate peel are said to lend a cold tone to ink, and Li T'ing-kuei, the famous inkmaker of the Southern T'ang, used twelve ingredients in his inks, including gamboge, rhinoceros horn, and powdered pearls.

INK STONES

Of the *Wen-Fang-Szu-Pao (Four Treasures of the Room of Literature)* only one has any degree of permanency. Paper is used but once, ink sticks are ground down to nothing, and even well-cared-for brushes eventually wear out, but ink stones are treated as heirlooms in China. The earliest ink stone we know of belonged to one Wang Ch'in, who lived around 500 B.C.

Prior to the T'ang Dynasty, most ink stones were made from bricks, tiles, clay, or earthenware. Ink stones today are commonly made from two kinds of stone. *Tuan* stones from the Ling-yang Gorge in Tuan District were first mined in T'ang times. These stones are mostly purplish in color, with random streaks and lines and sometimes spots. The spots, called "eyes," increase the value of the stone according to whether the eyes are "lively," "tearful," or "dead." The second sort of stones are *Hsi* stones mined in the Lung-wei Mountains of Hsi District. These stones are very hard and dense, and distinctively banded and streaked.

All ink stones have in common a flat, smooth surface for grinding the ink stick and a well for water. The schoolchild's version is apt to be a dull black rectangle, but Chinese artist-scholars took delight in carving ink stones, sometimes with covers, in the shapes of geese, dragons, fungus, parrots, melons, and tigers. Even a plain ovoid or rectangular shape could be adorned with inspirational calligraphy.

百寶　百家鎖　百家纓縒　白子　催眠術　墨　墨硯

中國事物

烟 清 掃 燃

LAMPBLACK FACTORY. FROM THE *T'ien Kung K'ai Wu.*

昆
蟲
樂
師

Bad stones are "slippery" and do not "grip" the ink. A stone gets slippery from exhaustion, by being used too much, or by excessive contact with the grease normally found on human fingertips. Good stones neither repel nor absorb ink. Repellent stones produce "shallow" inks, and absorbent stones allow inks to dry up too fast. Stones are tested by hanging from metal hooks and tapping with the knuckles for a certain tone.

INSECT MUSICIANS

Young insect hunter with cage. C. 1900.

Insect musicians are very well received in China. They make their debut in the spring, give their best performances in the summer, then retire to thunderous applause when autumn storms dampen their enthusiasm.

From Shandong, especially in the southern part of the province, come the chirping grasshoppers. These are kept in polished bamboo cages about four inches square. Owners who prefer a "double strength" chirp from their crickets will keep them in pairs, a slight partition separating the two soloists in order to stimulate musical competition. Another favorite, the grass lark, sings in the key of G; the pine insect in E or F. The Yama cricket, named after the King of the Dead because of its large protruding eyes, sings with a trill in tremolo, with a somewhat slower tempo than other insects.

From Suzhou comes the bell insect. This is the violinist of the insect world; its tune is a *sforzando piano*, a delicate *liin-liin-liin*. Also known as the "golden bell," it

中國事物

is the aristocrat among insects. None is larger than a housefly, and they are sold in paper boxes with a glass top, each containing a pair. Their cages are made of horn or bone with glass tops. They are fed diced pumpkin, pears, and apples. The concerned owners take special pains to keep the cages clean of leftover fruit juice, lest ants that are attracted by the sweetness prey on the tiny singers. Insect *aficionados* will frequently place their cages near their pillows at night so as not to miss a single note.

[See CICADA.]

IRRIGATION

There is evidence of Chinese irrigation in the form of upstream reservoirs as far back as the eighth century B.C., but the greatest feats of hydraulic engineering to benefit the agricultural process resulted from early attempts to control China's great rivers, many of which fluctuate annually by over 100 feet. China's dependence on a complex wet-rice economy was aided over the past 25 centuries by engineering accomplishments of immense scale. The Yellow River was first dammed in the seventh century B.C., and from the fifth century B.C. the complex tasks of embanking and diverting the Yellow, the Yangtze, and their tributaries became a regular task. Lateral irrigation canals were built off each of these rivers, with thousands of branches further subdivided and channeled to the needs of each community and plot. The third century B.C. saw construction of the hugely sophisticated Kuanxien system as well as the Ninghsia desert reclamation.

The Kuanxien system, which is still in use, made it possible for an area of 40 by 50 miles to support an agriculturally based population of 5 million without danger of flood or drought. The 2,200-year-old system constructed by an engineer named Li Ping consisted of feeder canals and subsidiary conduits with a total length of 730 miles and irrigating over half a million acres. Li Ping's original conception and execu-

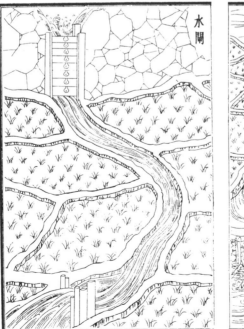

EXAMPLES OF EARLY IRRIGATION METHODS. FROM THE *T'ien Kung K'ai Wu.*

tion involved hundreds of small dams, and spillways, and required annual maintenance during low-water periods, which is still carried out according to the original formula.

The engineering accomplishments in water management extend throughout China and throughout its history. Through a continuity of centralized governments, each period was able to field enormous contingents of organized labor to construct dams and levees, engage in draining and tunneling, and carry on the important work of river control. It is still done in the same way in many of China's water-management districts. Thousands of highly disciplined laborers participate in the ongoing work of harnessing the country's rivers, as they have for centuries.

The Chinese were great innovators in the placement and use of damming materials. Levees were frequently restored by the lowering into place of enormous straw bales measuring 20 to 30 yards on a side. Dams were built by laying gabions (bamboo baskets holding rocks) in several layers along the stream or riverbed. The most impressive items in water management are the sluice and flood gates as well as the spillways used to control the conduits, channels, and irrigation ditches throughout the country. Flash-lock gates and double slipways were used to assist navigation as well. Throughout these systems, waterwheels and wheel-drive buckets moved and pumped water down to the smallest trickle needed to moisten a furrow.

Maintenance rules of the Kuanxien irrigation system were inscribed in stone in what has been called the "Trimetrical System," from the name of an instruction manual dating from A.D. 1290.

> Dig the channel deep
> And keep the spillways low
> This six-character teaching
> Holds good for a thousand autumns.
> Dredge out the river's stones
> And pile them on the embankments. . . .

[See CANAL LOCK and WATERWHEEL.]

ISLANDS OF THE BLEST

The first known reference to these fabulous three islands in the Eastern China Sea is in the work of Taoist philosopher Lieh Tzu. The islands, especially Peng-lai, were the home of divine spirits and apotheosized immortals (*hsien*) who had discovered the secret of immortality and become perfect in their earthly lives. One of the most important goals of every Taoist adept was to discover some secret access to the isles. Inhabitants lived in glorious mansions, drank from the jade fountain of life, and ate the fabled *Ling-chih* (fungus of immortality).

Han Dynasty historian Ssu-ma Ch'ien considered the islands accessible by distance, but protected by strong winds, which drove the ships of mortals away. Emperor Ch'in Shih-Huang-Ti (who built the Great Wall and unified China) dispatched an expedition to the isles in 219 B.C. under the leadership of a Taoist mystic named Hsu Shih, but they encountered the unfriendly winds and were driven home.

IVORY

There is an old Chinese saying, "Ivory doesn't grow in a dog's mouth," suggesting that the Chinese were quite relentless in their search for the tusk of the *Elephas maximus*, especially after having decimated their numbers in the wild expanses of Central

143

中國事物

China. By Han times, in fact, the elephant in China was just a poor memory.

Marco Polo relates how five thousand elephants of the Great Khan were exhibited in a procession at New Year's, covered with gay saddle clothes and carrying plates and furniture upon their backs. During the reign of the Ming Yung Lo Emperor, the eunuch Admiral Cheng was dispatched to Africa to procure ivory for the court and the ladies of the imperial harem. His overseas shopping excursion was looked down upon by the Confucian literati, who felt that such extravagance was deplorable. Nevertheless, the Chinese were soon importing great quantities of tusks not only from Africa, but also from Annam, Cambodia, Siam, Burma, and India. In general, Indian ivory was softer in texture, whiter in tone, and smaller in size than African ivory, which was considered inferior. Siamese ivory was thought to be the best quality. Because of its close-grained texture, its lack of brittleness, and it smooth, even surface, ivory presented a wonderful face to the Chinese carver.

For over two centuries Guangzhou supplied Western markets with carved ivories. These included fans, brushes, glove boxes, and gambling counters. Interesting offshoots of the export trade were the little ecclesiastical figurines made by the Chinese of Macao for the churches of Portugal and Spain. During the past hundred years the Chinese were mass-carving models of palaces and pagodas, figurines from an inch to two feet high, incense burners, vases, animals, birds, and an endless supply of snuff bottles.

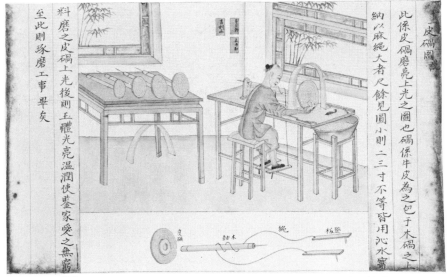

METHOD OF OPENWORK CARVING WITH EQUIPMENT DETAILS.

J A D E

Confucius praised it, saying that jade shines like benevolence; that it is strong and dependable like wisdom; that, like justice, its edges are sharp but do not cut; that, like truth, it does not hide its flaws. Chinese connoisseurs likened a finished work in white jade to liquescent mutton fat, or to congealed lard, shaped, as it were, by the fire. They would carry ancient or tomb jade in a silk bag filled with bran, so as to stimulate the colors of the stone with ongoing friction. At every opportunity they would bring the piece out to give it an extra bit of loving polish.

The Chinese believe that jade is imbued with spirit. It has even been known to glow with the vitality of the owner, or for its colors to become tarnished when

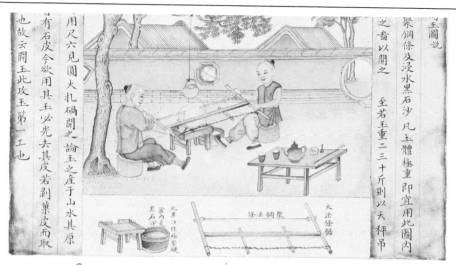

玉 茉 莉

SAWING OPEN CRUDE JADE IN THE FACTORY COURTYARD.

serious illness sets in. In ancient times it was valued so highly that one prince would offer another several populous cities for a *pi*, a piece of circular jade. Rare jade pieces conformed to certain thicknesses—and visitors at royal audiences would present their jade identification cards through a slot in the palace door before being given admission.

During the eighteenth century, techniques of jade carving attained new heights as a result of the patronage of the jade-loving Ch'ien-lung Emperor (1736-95). Workshops flourished throughout the empire. It was not unheard of for a master carver to spend an entire lifetime working on a single piece. It was a slow, painstaking process, involving grinding the stone with various abrasives, including quartz crystals ("yellow sand"); garnets or almandin ("red sand"), used with a circular saw; a kind of emery ("black sand"), used with a lap wheel; and ruby crystals ("jewel dust"), with which the leather wheel was smeared in order to give the final polish to the jade. The largest collection of Chinese jade in the United States can be found in the Asian Art Museum in San Francisco.

[See PI.]

JASMINE

> Picking fragrant plants,
> their fragrance brings no forgetting....
> —Hsieh Ling-yun (A.D. 385-433)

Of all the exotic plants and flowers that were brought into China during the Han Dynasty by Persian, Arabian, and other Western Asian traders, the single best-smelling flower was the jasmine. Known to the Chinese as the *Mi li hua*, it was possibly related to the Latin *moly*, the magic plant with a white flower and a black root that Hermes gave to Ulysses as a charm against the sorcery of Circe. It is also called the *Yeh-hsi-ming*, a transliteration of the English "jasmine."

The largest center of production was Fuzhou in Fujian Province, where over three million pounds of jasmine flower buds were produced annually for the famous scented jasmine tea. According to the eighteenth-century *Account of Interesting Objects in Guangdong Province* by Li T'iao-yuan, there were thousands of workers

145

中國事物

employed to string flowers into headdresses, lampshades, and other ornamental articles. The cultivation and production of jasmine goods were considered as artistic as the "carvings of jade and ice." Perfumes and fragrant oils were in great demand. Jasmine was also used to scent food, wine, and other drinks. At the height of the season the city of Guangzhou was so enveloped in jasmine that it resembled "snow in the night." A much-appreciated attribute of jasmine was its ability to reduce heat. During the hot summer months blossoms would be presented to visitors, and strung around beds. At feasts jasmine balls would be passed around to relieve hangovers.

JEWELRY

"Virtue is man's only jewel," says a Chinese proverb, but the Chinese don't really believe it. Both men and women are fond of elaborate jewelry. More than just decoration, it is a form of investment and a medium of exchange.

Jewelry jade, symbol of purity and excellence, is the most highly prized stone. As it is expensive, the poorer women make do with imitations. Pearls have been used in Chinese jewelry since ancient times, and it was in Fuzhou, in the thirteenth century, that the art of creating cultured pearls was discovered. Coral, symbol of longevity, and amber, said to be made from the souls of tigers, are popular in jewelry, along with many semiprecious stones.

Kingfisher feathers, brilliantly colored in blues and turquoise, are finely cut and appliquéd to silver or copper, creating delicate hair ornaments, combs, and brooches. The feathers are sometimes combined with pearls or semiprecious stones. In some regions brides wear crowns of kingfisherwork.

The Chinese wore ornaments to help keep diseases and demons at bay. Children were given jewelry to place them under the protective influence of silver or gold. For instance, a silver padlock, inscribed with wishes for happiness and long life, was hung around a child's neck to lock him symbolically to life and to prevent death from stealing him.

JOSS STICKS

There was either "good joss" or "bad joss," depending on luck, money, and how fiercely the mosquitoes were biting. *Shih ch'en hsiang* ("hour" or "time" incense) was widely used in all Chinese religious ceremonies and festivities. It was made from sandalwood, aloeswood, or other fragrant woods, and mixed with cedar or fir, with just enough clay for the mixture to stick together. Occasionally nutmeg shavings were also used. Chinese would make joss sticks that were sometimes twelve to eighteen feet long in coil form. These would be burned in shops, not only for their fragrance but also to mark time. In wealthy homes and at court, essences and incense would be burned to freshen the atmosphere, especially when guests were being entertained. Cheaper joss was sold under the name of "mosquito smoke" and, in fact, was used to drive the pests away.

JUGGLERS

Jugglers, along with musicians, gymnasts, puppet shows, animal acts, dancers, and story-tellers have toured China since prehistory, bringing not only entertainment, but often news as well. Juggling may have derived from war dancing, much as ballet stems from fencing. Celestial jugglers don't juggle balls or clubs but long knives and swords, with which they also do conjuring tricks, apparently running their assistants through or cutting off their heads. Infants of tender years sometimes perform atop long poles balanced by the adults, who also round out the act by swallowing swords and, infrequently, snakes.

JUJUBE

The jujube has been considered from ancient times to be one of the Five Celebrated Fruits. Li Shih-chen lists the other four as being the plum, the apricot, the peach, and the chestnut. A favorite Chinese delicacy known as the "red date" is really the fruit of the jujube tree.

JUMP ROPE

Chinese children play a kicking game with a regular jump rope that is a variation of the English game "high water-low water." Two players hold the rope about waist high to start with, and everyone takes it in turn to kick the rope, first forward, then backward. The rope gets raised a little higher on each go-round, and anyone who misses a kick has to drop out. The winner is the last one left.

A Chinese jump rope is another thing altogether. It is a large elastic loop like a giant rubber band between six and twelve feet in diameter. These loops can still be found in variety stores and toy stores, but most kids make their own colorful and easily repairable Chinese jump ropes by looping rubber bands together. The game requires at least three players. Two stretch the loop out into a rectangle, beginning at ankle height. The rest take turns jumping in to the rectangle and out the other side without touching the rope. The rope loop is raised until all the players but one are out; the one remaining is the winner.

Contemporary Chinese teens play the rope-kicking game as a part of their dance or martial-arts training. Hitting the rope accurately at head level or above takes a surprising amount of strength, balance, and precision.

KINGFISHER

The metamorphosis from creature of natural beauty to that of feathered art object, appliquéd on silver or copper, is the fate of this majestic bird. The kingfisher is found all over China, the most common variety being the black-capped and pied species. Inlaid kingfisherware is chiefly produced in Guangzhou and Beijing. Headdresses, combs, and brooches are created by alternating azure, ultramarine, and sapphire blues with filigree flowers and dragons interspersed with pearls and enamel on a metal foundation. Since the Chinese are willing to go to any expense to acquire kingfisher feathers, this definitely cannot be regarded as "pauper's art."

> Kingfishers nest on South Sea islands,
> Male and female in vermilion-colored groves.
> How would they know the minds of fair ladies
> Who cherish them far more than gold?
> Their bodies slain in the land of the burning sun;
> Their feathers cast in a dark corner in a jade hall.
> Resplendent, they glitter as hair ornaments;
> Lush, they decorate the embroidered quilt.
> It isn't that you can't keep your distance;
> A forest official's net will suddenly seek you out.
> To be born with talents is to invite disaster:
> I heave a sigh at this fabulous bird.
> —Ch'en Tzu-ang, T'ang Dynasty (A.D. 661-702)

中國事物

青雲得路 一二八

DECORATIVE MOTIF OF KITE FLYING. FROM *Kissho zuan Kaidai.*

KITES

Kites did not reach Europe until the eighteenth century, although Marco Polo reported seeing them on his travels through the Middle Kingdom. Kites may have evolved from banners and were used as scarecrows, observation posts, and divining instruments. From the tenth century on they were flown for fun, especially on Kite Day, which falls on the ninth day of the ninth month.

The basic kite-building materials are bamboo and paper, although silk is sometimes used as a prodigiously strong and light but very expensive covering. Nature must have intended bamboo for making kite frames. It is modular, and each module is structured like a bird's bone, it is probably stronger than steel for its weight, and it is very easily worked. Bamboo soaked and split can be bent into circles without much trouble—hence that exclusively Chinese kite, the caterpillar, with its several circular segments and leglike stabilizers.

Circular kites shaped like spectacles or coins have been spotted in Chinese skies along with other kites in the likenesses of lizards, butterflies, and men. Kites shaped like hawks are flown like hawks, with deceptive swoopings and dives. A hovering flock of birds turns out to be a group of kites tethered to a single cable and worked like a marionette. A kite shaped, shall we say, like a goat, is used as a sort of scapegoat, and when its string is cut it carries away a whole cartload of man's misfortunes.

Kites are native to the Chinese countryside, but city dwellers somehow manage to fly kites off their flat roofs. City kites are often hexagonal or octagonal, and have no tails, although tassel stabilizers are often attached at each intersection. These tailless kites twirl and tumble as they fly, like giant Yo-Yos. Sometimes bamboo whistles or bullroarers are built onto these kites, so that they hum in flight.

Country dwellers have two kite games that are worth mention. Groups of a half dozen or so men will sometimes get together to fly a single giant kite with a main string like a tug-of-war rope. The other game is kite-fighting. Any kite can fight, although hawks, octopi, and serpents seem obvious choices.

To prepare a kite for combat the last part of the string (the part nearest the kite) is soaked in starch or glue and dusted with powdered glass. This makes the string both stiff and extremely sharp. Two fliers will each try to sever the other's string by crossing over it and giving a sharp snap.

KOWTOW

A full-fledged kowtow was executed by kneeling three separate times and each time knocking one's forehead against the floor three times. This most elaborate form was reserved for the Emperor, who was thought to be the representative of heaven on earth. Less dramatic gradations of the kowtow involved fewer kneelings and fewer bumps. These were accorded to the other gods and lesser officials of the court, and they honored the spirits of dead ancestors.

The kowtow dates back to remote history. Confucius offered instruction on proper behavior when entering the room during a funeral—whether to kowtow to one's ancestor first, or to bow to one's living relations.

[See Bowing.]

KUBLAI KHAN

Unlike his savage grandfather, Genghis, whose sole dream was to raze China to the ground, Kublai Khan was determined to return the Middle Kingdom to its original glory. In 1271 he officially proclaimed a new Chinese dynasty, Yuan, meaning the first, and became Emperor, not only of China, but also of almost the entire Asian continent. He rebuilt Beijing as Ta-tu, the Great Capital. Once again the east-west, west-east caravan traffic began its flow, bringing with it rare treasures and new ideas. Marco Polo arrived with his yet unwritten diary. From the Tibetan mountains

中國事物

to the China Seas, from Manchuria to Guangzhou and the Burma borders, the Great Khan's empire spread in its enormity. Kublai introduced the Mongol postal system, which was to serve China in such good stead in centuries to come. It consisted of relays of post horses that traveled the roads between stations at twenty-five-mile intervals. Mongol officials, being inadequate to the task of administering the giant bureaucracy, were gradually supplanted by Chinese. Ultimately, the alchemy of China worked its spell on Kublai Khan. Soon he was issuing his edicts like a T'ang Son of Heaven and preparing the empire for his heirs to the throne.

KUBLAI KHAN DIRECTING A BATTLE FOUGHT WITH 860,000 COMBATANTS.

LACQUER

When Chuang Tzu was preaching his doctrine of uselessness, he selected the lacquer tree as a prime example, saying that it invites damage to its body because it produces the coveted lac resin. This sap from the *Rhus vernicifera* has been applied not only as a preservative but also for decorative purposes since prehistoric times. Evidence of lacquerwork has been found in Shang tombs dating back as early as the tenth century B.C.

Lacquer has been used to coat the surface of almost any type of material—

fabrics, bronze, porcelain, basketwork, pewter, and, of course, wood. A lacquerer could choose from any number of different colors: white, yellow, green, black, red, brown, silver, gold, and turquoise blue. Sometimes the lacquer is embellished with precious stones, metals, and mother-of-pearl, as well as carved designs. The best pieces require many hundreds of layers, and can sometimes take over ten years to complete.

During the past three hundred years, the export of Chinese lacquered goods to the West reached crisis proportions. The demand was so great that Western cabinet-makers were reduced to taking apart oversized panels and screens and turning them into chests and commodes. They took a lot of shortcuts in their work. Antique vermilion lacquer vases, screens, and panels are now very rare, and command astronomical prices.

LANGUAGE

Chinese is at the same time the simplest and the most difficult language in the world to learn. It is simple because of its almost entire absence of grammatical inflection. It is difficult because of the combination of different sublanguages or dialects that fall under the heading of being "Chinese." There is a written language, in its two or three different forms; and there is a spoken language, with its innumerable dialects and subtle variations in pitch. (Some Chinese words are actually derived from sounds in nature—of noises of falling objects; of calls and cries of animals, birds, and insects; and of actions by man himself.)

Mandarin is now spoken in all of the eighteen provinces. But even Mandarin has its northern and southern divisions, the principal one being Pekingese. Of the other major dialects, Cantonese is more like the ancient language of China; while Hakka is practically aboriginal in origin. A simple walk outside the gates of any major city in China would bring a traveler within earshot of numerous linguistic variations.

More people on earth speak the Mandarin dialect than any other language, and Chinese is the world's oldest continuously spoken language. The Beijing dialect of Mandarin is considered the common language and is referred to as *p'u-t'ung-hua*. Since 1950 the Chinese have been developing a system of romanization in their written language to aid in their goals of modernization and effective mass communication.

[See DICTIONARY and PUNS.]

LANTERNS

If an orbiting satellite had passed over the city of Hangzhou during the Festival of Lanterns in 1274, it might have recorded a miraculous sight of glowing, ever-shifting lights. For this agrarian celebration of spring, held in the second month, anything that was a lantern—or, for that matter, any lantern that resembled anything—would be illuminated into service. The finest lanterns were from Suzhou. They were circular in shape, and made of glass in five different colors, with paintings of people, landscapes, birds, beasts, and insects. Fuzhou lanterns were a close second, made of glittering white jade. There were lanterns that revolved to the trickle of miniature fountains; roundabout lanterns with determined horsemen galloping around and around; and lanterns that were decorated in gold, silver, and pearls. There were "night butterflies," which were huge cicadas made of white paper that the dandies of the town favored. And after the intensity of the celebrations dimmed, just before the dawn, enterprising citizens would comb the streets with small utilitarian lanterns searching for lost treasures—gilt hairpins, ornaments, or necklaces that had been

漆器　言語　燈籠

中國事物

dropped on the ground by revelers. This practice was known as "sweeping the streets." These simple lanterns were made from split bamboo frames covered with waxed paper colored black, red, or yellow. They were bell-shaped, square, oblong, or octagonal. The Chinese regarded their lanterns as *yang*, the light principle. No festival or wedding was complete without them.

SHOP WHERE LANTERNS ARE MANUFACTURED AND SOLD. C. 1830.

LAW

Imperial governments in China have never solely relied on codified laws. Whether to insure effective authority or to maintain the rights of citizens, the Chinese have generally distrusted systematic legal codes or constitutions. This is perhaps due to the severe penal code established in the third century B.C. by Li Kuei, an adviser to Emperor Ch'in Shih-Huang-Ti. Li codified tha law into 436 sections, spanning 40 volumes. Rather than prison terms, it provided punishments such as death or mutilation for many crimes. This penal code was behind the emergence of slavery—for certain crimes, offenders were not only punished personally, but also their relatives were forfeited to the state. When the government had an excess of slaves, they were sold to the public. These laws were frequently revised by later dynasties, and were often overlooked by more human provincial authorities.

In practice Chinese law was guided by what has been called the Doctrine of Mutual Responsibility. Officers in the government and military were held accountable for the actions of their inferiors and were expected never to shift the blame to others. In the same way, families and neighbors were often held accountable for the actions of one another. A member of society was expected to know what happened in his family or neighborhood and to help people with problems before a crime was committed. So strong was this doctrine that a person could be beheaded if he knew of a capital crime and did not report it to legal or social authorities.

Existing alongside the formal legal system in China today is an informal but organized system of *ad hoc* mediation, investigation, and sanction. The Communist Party is the link between both systems, since it has access to detailed personal information on Party members.

[See COURTS and CRIMINAL PUNISHMENT.]

LEOPARD

DRAWING OF A LEOPARD SIGNIFYING COURAGE IN BATTLE.

The Chinese regard the leopard as a symbol of bravery and martial ferocity. Leopard emblems were embroidered on the robes of military officials of the third rank. The animal is most commonly found in southern China around Fujian, and in the northern provinces bordering on Manchuria. Leopards are not known to be social, although it is reputed that Wang Yuan, a Taoist astrologer during the Han Dynasty, had one in his service. Wang had been commissioned by the spirit of Lao Tzu to supervise fifteen thousand genii. Their lamps had to be filled every day, and in this task he was assisted by a lame tiger and a leopard.

LITCHI NUTS

Litchi, lichee, or *li chih* nuts are not nuts, but a fruit about the size and color of a large, round strawberry. There are several different varieties of *li chih* grown; the one considered the best has a very small stone. *Li chih* stones are oval and dark brown, surrounded by a moist, translucent, edible pulp with a sweet taste. The outer skin is rough and red, almost like a shell. *Li chih* are indigenous to Guangzhou Province, and are exported either tinned in syrup of some sort, or dried. Neither version gives much of an idea of the exquisite taste of the fresh fruit.

LOCKS

The prints of the door gods and the goddess of mercy may have been replaced by portraits of the current Chairman or of members of the Communist Party Central Committee, but beyond the doorways of houses the spirit screens are still there pro-

153

中
國
事
物

tecting the peace. There has never been much need for locks in China. Even as far back as the Sung Dynasty, when many Chinese lived in crowded buildings, their wash hanging out over the babble of the street, front doors were generally not locked. Since families consisted of members from several generations, it hardly ever happened that everyone would be out at the same time. On the other hand, it was considered prudent to secure personal belongings in chests and individual rooms against the prying eyes and pilfering fingers of loved ones. Even the poorest Chinese who couldn't afford a chest would make a point of maintaining an extra set of clothing in the local pawnshop for safekeeping.

There was quite a variety of padlock shapes, but the principle was always the same: A set of springs was compressed by pushing a key into the lock so that it would be released. Padlocks were invariably made of wrought iron. Fixed-door locks that were placed on garden gates, sheds, workshops, and places of storage were locked from the outside. They were constructed entirely of wood, and consisted of casing, bolt, and inside tumblers. A wooden key would turn the pegs and raise the tumblers that rested on notches in the bolt.

LONGEVITY

In the Chinese pantheon of gods, the god of longevity ranks alongside the gods of happiness and wealth. Chinese artists sometimes visualized the god of longevity riding a stag and carrying a peach. He had a high-domed forehead and always wore a gentle smile.

Not long after the book *Tao-te-ching* appeared in China around 300 B.C., it became the backbone of an entire religion designed to prolong life. The *tao* (way) is considered synonymous with Nature, and is the fundamental formula underlying reality. The Taoist masters saw no distinction between matter and spirit, so the immortality they sought to achieve was literal.

The Taoist canon embraces a number of closely linked traditions, each practicing a different art to rejuvenate the body. Taoist meditation teaches that one can find bliss and eternal life by relaxing the body and mind and allowing the vital forces of Nature to take over.

Taoist meditation techniques and internal exercises are designed to combine the vital breath of the universe with the vital breath (*ch'i*) of the body. Thus regulation of breathing is the other crucial technique employed in the search for long life. To derive the greatest benefit from your breath, you must learn breath retention, with the ultimate goal of immortality accessible only when you can hold your breath for a period equal to one thousand respirations! Breath control also involves guiding the breath to parts of the body not normally reached by air, particularly the lower abdomen. There the divine *ch'i* mingles with the male essence *ching*, and a man is close to perfection.

For best results, Taoist breathing and meditation should be practiced in conjunction with dietary, gymnastic, and sexual techniques. The chief function of Taoist gymnastics is to aid in carrying out the respiratory and sexual techniques, although two, *wu shu* and *t'ai chi ch'uan*, have become popular as martial arts in America.

The final branch of Taoist prolongevity is dietary. Even before the Taoists emerged, the Chinese had an extremely sophisticated knowledge of foods and herbs, but the new religion, dedicated to finding the fastest route to immortality, codified and expanded this field to the point where Chinese herbology is without doubt the most respected in the world.

長
壽

TUNG FANG-SO STEALING THE PEACHES OF LONGEVITY. MING DYNASTY SILK TAPESTRY.

中國事物

LOTTERIES

The Chinese go in for lotteries in a big way. Besides the defunct *Wei Hsing* (the yearly lottery based on government civil-service exams, district by district), there are the *Pa Ko Piao* lottery (twenty winning characters from the eighty characters that are printed on the fly leaf of the *One Thousand Character Essay* and the *Tzu Hua* lottery (rhyming clues leading to which of the thirty-six historical figures is the winning name). Women, who were not often educated, just guessed at the answer.

A less literary lottery uses thirty-six animals instead of men, and the winners get thirty times what they have staked. Butchers will run daily lotteries for cuts of meat, bakers will wager cakes for cash, and a fruit dealer will open an orange very carefully, section by section, so as to satisfy those who have bet on the number of seeds it will contain. Orange lottery winners get triple their stakes, and the two runners-up get double theirs.

LOTUS

In the Imperial Park of the Forbidden City in Beijing there are three magnificent lakes, each one many acres across. They become transformed into vast seas of

LOTUS. INK AND COLORS ON SILK BY YUN PING. LATE SEVENTEENTH CENTURY.

lotuses during the summer. The huge green leaves grow up to six or seven feet above the water, and are topped by even higher flower buds. Waterways are cleared through the jungle to permit small boats to pass. This is a familiar scene in the ponds and lakes of public gardens all over China.

The sacred or Indian lotus (*Nelumbo nucifera*) is the Chinese emblem of summer and fruitfulness. Venerated by Buddhists and Taoists alike, it represents the spirit of the perfect man. It epitomizes purity because it grows out of the mud but remains undefiled. "Though the lotus tube is broken, the silks are still connected," goes an old Chinese proverb that describes an affair that can't be easily terminated by the parties involved. Emperor Tung-hun Hou of the Southern Ch'i Dynasty in A.D. 498 had water lilies made of gold leaf strewn over the ground for his concubine Pan Fei to dance upon. "Every step makes a lotus grow!" he cried out ecstatically. The terms "golden lilies" and "lotus hook" later came to signify the erotic proportions of women's bound feet.

Every part of the lotus has a definite purpose for the Chinese. The root and leaves are staples in the diet; the dried yellow stamens are applied as an astringent, or as a cosmetic. The seeds make a delicious dessert. The kernels are boiled in soup, roasted, or eaten raw. The stems are also thrown into the pot; and the leaves are used by grocers to wrap merchandise.

LUCKY AND UNLUCKY DAYS

An early system for selecting lucky and unlucky days was designed by a Taoist wizard named Hsu-sun (A.D. 240-374), and was based on the Ten Celestial Stems and Twelve Terrestrial Branches used in the computation of the Cycle of Sixty. Until the end of imperial times every Chinese purchased the Imperial Chinese Almanac at the beginning of every year. The almanac was an official government publication providing information on the effects of every day in the year, as well as listing prohibited and recommended activities for the days.

The table listing the specific effects of each day on a variety of activities was consulted whenever anything important, such as marriage, beginning construction of a house, or burial of a relative was contemplated. The charts were also consulted regularly to settle the details of domestic life, such as keeping or not keeping pets, when to make clothes, or getting a haircut.

LUMINOUS INSECTS

> Bamboo's chill creeps into the chamber,
> A wilderness moon floods the garden nook.
> Heavy dew trickles in little drops,
> Scattered stars appear and disappear
> In dark flight, a glowworm lights itself. . . .
> —Tu Fu (A.D. 712-70)

The Chinese firefly averages some twenty-six light pulsations per minute. The light of the insect may be of protective value, not unlike the warning colors of some caterpillars and butterflies. This seems to be substantiated by the fact that birds find the firefly unpalatable on account of its bitter taste. Frogs, however, do not mind the taste at all, and will fill their bellies with fireflies until the light shines through them.

The firefly, however, is not nearly as common in China as the beetle *Lampyris nocticula*, otherwise known as the glowworm. The female is wingless and emits light

抽獎

蓮花

好壞時辰

螢火蟲

中
國
事
物

from certain cells in its ventral region, apparently to attract the flying male.

The most remarkable of the luminous insects in China is the lanternfly. It is quite large, has a pretty green color, is banded with yellow, its underwings being yellow tipped with black, and its abdomen being yellow barred with black so as to resemble an oil-paper lantern. Its head is drawn out into a long hornlike snout, and its tip is distinctly luminous.

Ask a Chinese about the morphology of these light-giving insects, and he will more than likely shake his head and refer you instead to the legend of Chu Yin. Chu Yin was an impoverished scholar who lived during the Chin Dynasty. He was so poor that he could not afford a lamp to study by. But being a bright fellow, he filled a bag full of glowworms and passed his examinations with flying colors. He subsequently arose to a high position in government. The glowworm is therefore not only a symbol of beauty, but also of hard work and perseverance.

MAGIC

Perhaps the most powerful force in traditional Chinese popular religion is that of magic. The fact that the Chinese never developed a strong sense of the boundary between heaven and earth (spiritual and material realities) helped sustain the popular

TAOIST MAGICIAN HOLDING CEREMONIAL SWORD AND *pa kua* OR THE EIGHT TRIGRAMS. FROM *Researches into Chinese Superstition* BY HENRI DORÉ.

notions concerning the constant interaction between human life and spiritual agencies. The activities and help of the heavenly (invisible) forces could be controlled somewhat through the use of magic. Magic can be used to solicit divine assistance, fight off evil influences, and coax the processes of Nature to serve human purposes. From the earliest times, the Chinese employed shamans and magicians, known as *wu* and *fang-shih*, to perform rituals in order to influence the non-material forces.

Magic became a truly formal element of Chinese religion during the rule of the first Ch'in Emperor, Shih-Huang-Ti, who first unified China in 221 B.C. The *fang-shih* who had become specialists in immortality flocked to his receptive court and expanded the corpus of magical lore. This renaissance constitutes the creation of the popular Taoist religion, which abounds with magical devices and practices and has little relation to the philosophy of Lao Tzu or Chuang Tzu. The magicians who surrounded Shih-Huang-Ti persuaded him to search for the Islands of the Blest and to conceal himself from evil spirits. As a result the Emperor ordered his 270 palaces to have covered walkways. The famous magicians of his rule were the Taoist wizards Hsu-fu and Master Lu.

During the Han Dynasty Emperor Wu Ti also came under the influence of magicians. Among the magicians in his court was an alchemist, Li Shao-chun, who conducted alchemical experiments in search of the "elixir of immortality." By this time the Taoist "church" was completely dominated by the magical practices of the sages searching for immortality. Chang Tao-ling, the first Taoist "Pope," became a *hsien* (immortal) and was called "Heavenly Father." Images of Chang Tao-ling are used in magical ceremonies to this day. The widespread use of charms and the frequent employment of sorcerers and witches to conduct exorcisms lasted well into this century. In China, magical practice was more a part of tradition than the secret illegitimate activity it became in Western countries.

[See ALCHEMY.]

M A G N O L I A

The wanderer was in love with the spring of the year
And the spring was in love with the wanderer.
—Shen Yueh (A.D. 441-512)

The magnolia is beyond doubt the most gorgeous and striking of the early spring-flowering trees. When the trees are in full bloom they are laden with huge white or purplish-pink flowers. The Chinese *Magnolia yulan* is called *Ying-ch'un-hua*, the Flower that Welcomes the Spring. It grows up to fifty feet high, with leaves that are seven inches long. The *Magnolia fuscata* is known to the Chinese as *Han-hsiao-hua*, or the Secretly Smiling Flower, because it recalls the smile of a winsome maiden. It represents feminine sweetness and beauty. Yu-lan (Magnolia) is a common name for women in China.

The magnolia has been cultivated in China since the T'ang Dynasty (A.D. 618-906) in gardens and temple grounds everywhere. It has always been a popular motif in paintings, ceramics, and embroidery. The Chinese have a fragrant tooth for it. The petals are dipped in flour, fried in oil, and eaten as a delicacy.

M A G P I E S A N D C R O W S

According to conflicting testimony, the Chinese claim the magpie's "voice is good, but its heart is bad," while the crow's "voice is bad, but its heart is good." To further

159

中
國
事
物

confuse matters, the magpie is a bird of good omen, and should it build its nest near a home, the people dwelling there can expect great good fortune. The crow, on the other hand, is considered to be a malevolent bird. Its cry *"ka"* is a common Chinese word for "bite." The crow is said to be the propagator of bad omens.

MAH-JONGG

Mah-jongg is a big gambling game in the Chinatowns of New York and San Francisco, and, after a short period of ellipse due to revolutionary disapproval, it is once again a popular game in China. Like playing cards, mah-jongg tiles developed from dominoes. Different versions of the game have been played in North China and in South China since antiquity. Enthusiasts claim that mah-jongg is some thirty centuries old, and that it was popular in the time of Confucius, who no doubt disapproved of it.

Part of the appeal of the game was romantic, and part, intellectual. Without attempting to explain it (the rules of play are much too complex for this brief section), mah-jongg combines the subtlety of bridge with the virility of poker. Good players augment the vagaries of chance with their skill and daring. Bluff and foresight are both important weapons in the mah-jongg player's arsenal.

The curious admixture of romance and aggression have shaped the physical characteristic of the mah-jongg set itself. Once this was a game of Mandarins, and the 152 tiles, invariably of ivory, were engraved with symbols of the Chinese Army: spears, targets, and vans (loaded with booty). In time, the civilian version modified these suits of tiles and added four more. The spears became bamboos (called "bams"), the targets turned into circles (called "dots"), and the vans were represented by characters (called "craks"). The other tile suits that developed were the "honors" (winds and dragons), and the flower and joker suits.

Chinese mah-jongg tiles, like dominoes, have no Arabic numerals, but in the reduced space for decoration elaborate portraits of mythical heroes and historic warriors, a few famous women, and trees, flowers, or shrubs appear.

MAPS

The first maps in China were icons of the religious cosmic system: These easily became maps of the imperial world system, which was the earthly embodiment of the sacred order. Since the Chinese felt the human world, when well governed, is a reflection of heaven, it made sense to apply the regular divisions of the heavens to the surface of the earth. Once this had been done, the practical advantages of a grid system became clear, and map-making became a valued instrument of government.

The first historical reference to maps in China occurs as part of the story of an assassination plot. An agent of the Prince of Yen attempted to approach the King Cheng by offering a map of a particular district as a sign of its availability to the King. When he took the map out of its case, he also took out a dagger and made an unsuccessful attempt on the life of the man who later became the first Ch'in Emperor.

By this time maps were valued, both as emblems of imperial power and as tools of imperial conquest and consolidation. No specimens of these maps survive, however, and little is known about them. They could not have been too much like modern maps, since a practical grid system was not introduced until some time toward the end of the first century A.D., by Chang Heng. The grid system was combined with a decimal numbering system by P'ei Hsiu in the third century A.D.

P'ei Hsiu laid down various principles of mapmaking, including the use of grids

麻將　地圖

將　結婚

to keep relations between features constant, the use of measured divisions to insure a constant scale, the use of careful measurement to insure accurate portrayal of variations in terrain, and the use of right triangles to estimate distances that could not be traversed.

By the eighth century A.D., it was possible for the Emperor to order Chia Tan, a cartographer, to produce a map of the empire and get, only sixteen years later, a detailed map of some thirty feet long and thirty-three feet high, on a scale of one inch equaling one hundred *li*, or Chinese miles.

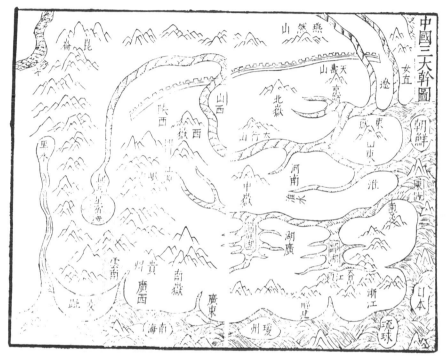

ANCIENT MAP OF EARLY CHINA SHOWING MAJOR RIVERS AND THE GREAT WALL. FROM THE *San Ts'ai T'u Hui*. C. 1607.

MARRIAGE

If a man died unmarried, he was buried without ceremony. His spirit would not be admitted into the ancestral hall unless he married and had, or had adopted, a son. A girl had no status at all within her own family, since it was understood that she was destined to become a member of another family as a wife and daughter-in-law. So marriage was extremely important business.

Marriages were arranged by the boy's mother through the medium of a matchmaker, who was usually a female relative or friend of the family. The economic conditions of the boy's family concerned the girl's mother. When both families were satisfied, the boy's family sent presents and a letter to the girl's parents, requesting the engagement. Bride and groom might have been very young at the time of betrothal, so that the actual wedding occurred many years later.

The end of the year was considered a good time to bring a new daughter-in-law into the family. At this time, during New Year's, the household gods were making their annual visit to the heavens and wouldn't be upset by the new arrival.

The bride was brought to the groom's home in an enclosed chair and wore a red

中國事物

veil over her face until after the couple paid homage to his ancestors. When they retired to their new room and the groom lifted her veil, it was supposed to be the first time the two had set eyes on each other. This form of marriage, according to legend, was codified by Fu Hsi, who reigned between 2953 and 2838 B.C.

Although bride and groom, throughout China's history, were usually very young, New China initiated a recent campaign to encourage later marriages. This new policy exists for two reasons: first, to reduce the population growth in China, and second, to alter the status of women, allowing them to join the work force, become educated, and fulfill themselves socially. Arranged marriages have been illegal since 1950.

BRIDE AND GROOM, WEDDING PORTRAIT. GUANGZHOU. C. 1900.

METEOROLOGY

As far as the development of weather lore in China was concerned, *Chu Kho-Chen* paints an accurate picture: "Prediction never advanced beyond the stage of peasant proverbs." Indeed, the *Tao-te-ching* states, "A hurricane never lasts a whole morning, and a sudden rainstorm will never go on for the whole day." According to the *I Ching* halos will forecast storms, and eastward-traveling clouds (going in the opposite direction of the monsoon rains) means happy traveling. If there ever was a severe meteorological disturbance in the empire—such as hailstones in August, or smog during the T'ang Dynasty—it was regarded as being indicative of some deficiency on

氣
象
學

鏡

寺
廟

the part of the Emperor or his administration. It was chiefly for astrological reasons that any weather records were kept at all. However, for all their reliance on fortune-telling and on almanacs, the Chinese are noted for having invented the first rain-measuring gauge, the *ts'e-yu-ch'i*, in the early part of the thirteenth century. These stood on "cloud-watching platforms." Skiers might be interested to learn that the first snow measuring gauges were made of bamboo, in the shape of large baskets, and placed beside strategic mountain passes.

In China today the Central Meteorological Bureau supplies information on weather and climatic conditions. It administers weather stations, provides weather reports to agricultural production units, and collects data from both modern forecasting technologies and traditional folk sources.

MIRRORS

The mirrors of early China, usually round in shape, are decorated on the back with curious magical symbols. These include the animals of the zodiac, the Four Supernatural Beasts, and various Taoist patterns. These metal mirrors were thought to confer good fortune upon the owner, and some of the mirrors were believed to have magical properties. The Ch'in Dynasty Emperor Shih-Huang-Ti was said to possess a mirror that reflected the inner parts of those who gazed into it.

These unusual mirrors are also called "light-penetration mirrors." When the mirror is exposed to the sun, the characters on the back seem to "pass through" and be reflected on any convenient surface. This effect puzzled scientists from the eleventh century A.D. right through the nineteenth century. The effect is caused by minute inequalities in the surface of the mirror. The inequalities are due to differences in the curve of the surface that arise during the polishing process in the places where the characters occur on its back.

The oldest mirror yet discovered came from the tomb of a Shang Dynasty lady warrior, who was known as Fu Hao. She was a well-known concubine of King Wu-ting, who reigned 1324-1265 B.C.

MONASTERIES

> Dark and dim, the Bamboo Grove Monastery,
> Faint and faraway, the sound of bells at dusk.
> Your bamboo hat carrying home the evening sun,
> Alone you return to the distant green hills.
> —Liu Ch'ang-ch'ing (A.D. 709-80)

At about four or five every morning, after the bells of the Buddhist and Taoist monasteries had been rung, monks would come down from the hills and enter the streets of the town beating their strips of iron or knocking on their wooden-fish sound boxes. They would announce to the general population that it was indeed dawn, and what the weather was like: "It is cloudy," or "It is raining," or "The sky is clear." They would also state what court receptions would be held that day. Following these public-service announcements they would observe a few hours of silence as they canvassed the town collecting alms. Although this was a daily ritual in Hangzhou during the Southern Sung period, it is nevertheless representative of the close ties maintained between the monasteries and their congregations.

Taoism modeled its sacred texts, its gods, its liturgy, and its monasteries after its more affluent cousin, but ever since Buddhism was introduced to China from India in

中
國
事
物

the first century A.D., it reigned supreme. Buddhist monasteries were as numerous as lotus blossoms in the summer lakes at the imperial palace. The number of monks at each one varied from one or two to three hundred, depending on the size of the institution.

Although it is reported that some two hundred thousand Buddhist monasteries were active before 1949, the Cultural Revolution began a program to deinstitutionalize religions and return persons with religious occupations back to the work force. Nevertheless, religious customs, cult beliefs, superstition, and magic are alive in New China. And, although the actual doctrines of Buddhism and Taoism are studied at universities, a recently reopened Buddhist temple eagerly accepted one hundred new members.

[See CELIBACY.]

BUDDHIST MONASTERY. PHOTOGRAPHED BY JOHN THOMPSON, C. 1870.

MONKEY

Ch'iu-p'u teems with white gibbons:
They leap and bounce like flying snow.
They tug and pull their young hanging from the branches,
Come down to drink and play with moon in water.
—Li Po (A.D. 701-62)

The rise and fall of gibbons is a popular theme in Chinese art and literature. But while these long-armed, stubby-tailed, short-faced creatures are considered to be the most active and intelligent of the species, the golden-brown monkeys of Sichuan and Gansu also figure prominently in Chinese lore.

It is said that when long-tailed monkeys find distances too great for leaping that they would form monkey chains by which they could swing themselves from great heights across wide chasms. Not infrequently, the last monkey in this living pendulum would come to grief, hence the Chinese proverb "The last monkey is sure to be drowned." Actual structures across gorges came to be known as "monkey bridges."

Monkeys are inordinately fond of the moon. They are depicted as reaching up for it, or else pawing after its reflection in the water, not because of any unconscious love of beauty but because of their covetousness. Once again, Chinese monkeys invariably drown in the process. That is why they are included among the list of the "Three Senseless Creatures": the tiger, who is always angry; the deer, who is always lovesick; and the monkey, who is forever grabbing at things.

The monkey has been worshiped in China since T'ang times. Their skin was considered especially valuable, and only members of the imperial family were permitted to wear it. One monkey, Sun Wu K'ung, was awarded the title "Great Sage Equal to Heaven" by the Emperor for services rendered to a Buddhist priest, Yuan Chuang. This famous tale, translated by Arthur Waley into English (*Monkey*, Grove Press), tells how Sun Wu K'ung, the King of All Monkeys, accompanied the priest on a 17-year journey to India, where they collected 657 volumes of sacred Buddhist scripture, which they brought back to China. Sun was definitely no ordinary monkey. He knew 72 different forms of magic, could assume 9,000 transformations, ride clouds, turn somersaults of 6,000 miles, and peer into the ends of the universe with closed eyes.

Since the monkey symbolically is also supposed to bestow health, protection, and prosperity on mankind by controlling the demon population, Chinese who were ill or who were unsuccessful in their ventures would select monkey charms in order to drive away evil influences.

MOON CAKES

Moon cakes (*yueh bing*) are eaten to celebrate the autumnal Moon Festival, celebrated on the fifteenth day of the eighth lunar month. These are small round pies baked out of "moon colored" grayish-white flour, heavy as a Western fruitcake with stuffing. In North China moon cakes are stuffed with either white sugar paste or brown date paste, but in the South a variety of fillings abound, utilizing nuts, fruits, lard, spices, eggs, preserves, and watermelon or lotus seeds.

Today most people buy moon cakes from a baker, but for many years it was a matter of pride to bake one's own, because of the part they played in Chinese history. In the fourteenth century Mongolian conquerors ruled China with a heavy hand, and had spies planted in nearly every noble household. One year, as was usual, the noblewomen baked moon cakes and exchanged them with other households, but with a difference: Small pieces of paper bearing the time and location to meet were baked into the cakes sent to loyal souls, and the resulting rebellion that successfully overthrew the Mongols' Beijing garrison began the great and bloody war that rid the country of her invaders from the North.

MOSQUITO

An emblem of wickedness and rebellion, the mosquito is common throughout China. In the past, mosquito nets, wire windows, and the burning of specially prepared incense were used to combat the malaria-carrying anopheles mosquito.

In New China pesticides control the mosquito population. In the early 1950s the Patriotic Health Movement named mosquitos as one of the Four Pests to be eradicated; the other three were flies, rats, and bedbugs. As a result, the death rate for malaria (thirty million in 1949) was negligible in 1960.

中
國
事
物

MOUTH ORGAN

Sweet and delicate, the sound of the mouth organ or *sheng* is said to resemble the cry of the phoenix. The instrument itself is crafted to imitate a phoenix with folded wings: Seventeen bamboo pipes are arranged in a circle and held in a gourdlike wind chest. This type of mouth organ is very ancient—characters on bone from the Shang Dynasty (c. 1550-c. 1030 B.C.) refer to it.

The pipes contain reeds, thin vibrating membranes, which are cut to the diameter of the pipe so that they are free, unattached to the side of the pipe. Each pipe also contains a finger hole. When the hole is closed, air is forced over the reed, causing it to vibrate and produce a note. The *sheng* works on the same principle as the reed organ and is the earliest instrument known to use that principle.

In the eighteenth century, a Chinese *sheng* found its way to St. Petersburg in Russia. A German organ builder studied it there and then introduced the free reed to Europe. By the start of the next century, Western instrumentmakers had applied the principle to develop the harmonica and the accordion.

MULBERRY

MULBERRY FARM FOR SILK PRODUCTION. C. 1900.

Mulberry leaves are the principal diet of the silkworm. The mulberry tree represents industry and the comforts of hard work. When the philosopher Mencius was discoursing on the real meaning of peace, he declared that only with such understanding could one then properly address himself to pruning the mulberry tree.

In the 1930s, with the development of synthetic fabrics around the world, silk production fell off. However, in recent years exports have grown tremendously, and the mulberry is once again of great importance to the agricultural community in China. Mulberry wood is also an important source of paper.

[See SILK.]

笙
桑
音
樂

MUSIC

Music was probably with the Chinese from prehistoric times, but it played an especially prominent role in three aspects of life during the Chou Dynasty (c. 1030-256 B.C.): court ritual, religious ceremonies, and the agricultural festivals that had been held since remote antiquity. Knowledge of music was a sign of good breeding, as well. The *I Li* or *Book of Etiquette* enumerates the attributes a gentleman was expected to possess. The first was knowledge of ceremonial practice. "The practice of music and the knowledge of significance of tunes come next."

The place of music in early Taoism, conceived by Lao Tzu (604-517 B.C.), is not well recorded. However, a basic Taoist concept is comparison of the individual human essence with a musical tone. Confucius (551-479 B.C.) developed his philosophy during the Chou Dynasty. He considered music an essential ingredient in the order of the state. The philosopher Mencius also linked music to the well-being of a country. When told that a certain King loved music, he responded, "If the King's love of music were very great, the kingdom of Ts'e would approach a state of good government."

Music was not enough to keep order in the kingdom. The Chou Dynasty and rulers of neighboring feudal states succumbed to the onslaught of the Ch'in Kingdom. Then music itself fell victim. Shih-Huang-Ti, King of Ch'in, ordered the destruction of all books, music manuscripts, and instruments. A few were hidden and saved, however.

The idea of court music persisted and was revived during the Han Dynasty (206 B.C.-A.D. 220). Under the Han, the court orchestra employed some eight hundred musicians in four sections. The actual number of participants in the orchestra for a particular banquet or ritual—and the number of dancers—were determined by Confucian numerology.

From A.D. 200-600, Buddhism exerted a strong influence on China and its music. The Buddhist rite was chanted, with intonations and responses, accompanied by the percussion instruments (drum, bell, gong, cymbals, triangle, and "wooden fish") that were traditionally prominent in Chinese music. The Buddhists also incorporated the *ch'in* (zither) into the ceremony.

To the basic distinctions of court music and common music, the T'ang Dynasty (A.D. 618-906) added foreign music (*hu yueh*). Plucked lutes, the Assyrian angle harp, the Persian harp, cymbals, and some new types of drums were introduced. The Chinese invented their own new instruments as well: Sixteen iron slabs were hung and struck like chimes; bell sets came into use.

Under the Sung Dynasty (A.D. 960-1279), music entered a golden age. Confucian ritual music sometimes reached elaborate proportions, governed only by how much a shrine or temple could afford to pay. One ritual called for 240 *ch'in* and *se* (two types of zithers), 200 mouth organs (*sheng*), and twenty oboes, plus drums, bells, chimes, and voices. Unlike the Buddhist sacred music, with its elaborate rhythms,

中
國
事
物

the Confucian ritual hymns were performed in strictly measured notes.

During the Sung Dynasty, vocal music—to the accompaniment of lute or zither—was emphasized. Advances in instrumental solo music that emerged in the Sung period and the following Ming (1368-1644) have lasted through the present. Chinese music, however, was not again to reach the heights of the Sung Dynasty. It slipped into a gradual decline, which was accelerated by the destruction of the imperial tradition in 1911 and the Communist Party's utilitarian view of the arts. While performance music declined, fresh approaches and musical innovations moved from court ceremony and religious rite to the theater.

A general interest in music has begun to flourish again in New China. The music of Western composers was stilled in China from 1966 to 1976 during the Cultural Revolution. However, in the years after Mao Tse-tung's death in 1976, several guest conductors from the Western world have been invited to lead the Chinese Central Philharmonic Orchestra. In 1979 violinist Yehudi Menuhin was invited to play with the Orchestra in Beijing.

[See MUSICAL SCALE.]

MUSICAL INSTRUMENT SHOP. C. 1830.

MUSICAL SCALE

A single note lies at the base of Chinese musical theory. This fundamental tone was originally felt to be an eternal note and the cornerstone of good government. The note is called *huang chung* (yellow bell). According to legend, the mythical Emperor Huang Ti in the third millennium B.C. assigned Ling Lung (the "music ruler") the task of determining correct pitch. One version of the myth holds that Ling went to the westernmost part of the kindgom, where he cut a piece of bamboo and blew into it. The note was the pitch of a man's voice when he spoke without passion. Ling then created the scale by cutting pipes in sizes proportional to the first one. When they

樂
譜

Young musicians. C. 1910.

assumed power, later Emperors traditionally ordered musicians and astrologers to work together to recalculate the proper length of the imperial pipe and thus keep the Emperor in harmony with the universe.

Beginning with a pipe the length of the fundamental note (traditionally considered to be F above middle C), Chinese musical theory uses a rather complex method of cutting shorter pipes to produce a series of twelve notes, called *lus*. They are the same twelve notes used in Western music. Only the first five in the series (beginning with F, they would be FGACD) are used to produce the Chinese scale of five notes, the pentatonic scale. Texts from the fourth and third centuries B.C. call the notes: *kung, shang, chiao, chih,* and *yu*. The five-note scale could begin on any of the twelve notes. The choice of the starting note depended on the time and date. Ritual assigned a correct pitch to each hour and month.

The five tones were also associated with nonmusical relations, such as the Five Directions and the Five Elements. The full twelve notes were sometimes divided into two six-note groups: Those generated by going up a fifth were designated *yin* (female), and those generated by going down a fourth were considered *yang* (male). Legends say the male phoenix sang the notes of the lower series, and the female sang those of the upper. The extensive symbolism associated with music, however, was matched by extensive and accurate theory. Two thousand years ago, the Chinese

中
國
事
物

knew as much about the laws of vibration and tuning as Western theoreticians knew at the turn of this century.

Theory did not always influence practice, though. In order for music to be more easily sung, the notes can be tempered, slightly altered in pitch so that they sound in tune to the ear. Because they are determined by mathematical proportions, the notes of the Chinese scale are untempered. In 1596, scholar Prince Tsai-Yu worked out a system of equal temperament. He was well ahead of the West, where the same formulas were arrived at a century later. Tsai-Yu's work, however, generated little enthusiasm in China, and Chinese music remains untempered, in contrast to Western music.

NAMES

The Chinese surname, spoken and written first, comes from among fewer than five hundred clan names. Most of them are only a single syllable.

A baby is unnamed for the first month. Then it's given a name, customarily of two syllables, which may come from anywhere in the Chinese language. When he goes to school the boy picks up another name, and another when he marries (although a wife does not adopt any of his names). If he gets a degree or official rank, he gets still another name. After death, he will be known by his posthumous name in the Hall of Ancestors.

As if this wasn't a sufficient collection of names, very often the most common name used will be a flowery name, similar to a nickname. These names customarily take note of some personal defect or characteristic; a girl might be called Earthquake Meter, a boy might be called Leatherbag Bones or Dwarfy. *Chin-shih* described one who passed the highest exam under the imperial examination system. When used as a flowery name, however *Chin-shih* referred not to intelligence, but to bad eyesight.

[See ONE HUNDRED NAMES.]

NARCISSUS

The *Shui hsien* (water immortal) or *Narcissus tazetta* brings in the Chinese New Year, flowering exactly at the stroke of the zodiac. It is grown from bulbs in bowls filled with pebbles and water, and is very easy to culture. In place of pebbles sometimes fancy miniature rockwork is used. In order to compensate for its relatively few variations—its general appearance is that of a great cluster of snow-white fragrant blossoms—the Chinese will induce what is known as a "carving." The result of this operation is that the narcissus will assume a new form consisting of curved and crooked leaves. This type of carving produces the crab's claw narcissus. Other techniques will invoke a tiger shape, a fairy shape, or more fantastic narcissistic phantasmagoria. The narcissus was introduced to China a thousand years ago by Arab traders through a southern port in Fujian. Ever since then it's been blooming right on time.

NEW YEAR

This is by far the most important festival in the Chinese calendar, and it lasts a full month. The feast prepared for the Lantern Festival on the fifteenth of the first lunar month finishes off the last of the New Year leftovers.

Legend explains that an offended household deity went to heaven and asked the Jade Emperor to destroy the world, but before the Jade Emperor could act, the other gods followed to intercede for humanity and urge the gods to visit earth and judge for

姓
名

水
仙

新
年

PAPERCUT DEPICTING FIREWORKS AND NEW YEAR'S FESTIVITIES.

themselves. Informed of the threatened destruction, the people stopped work and threw a great feast, which lasted several weeks until the people were certain the gods had called off the end. And that began the New Year celebration. So still, the week prior to New Year the household gods are sent to heaven, and while they're gone everything in the house is cleaned, repaired, and rearranged.

After elaborate preparations, when it's dark on New Year's Eve, the father and the oldest son go to the ancestral graveyard to invite the spirits home. Then a ceremony is performed at the front door to welcome the gods back along with the spirits of unknown ancestors.

Very early New Year morning, the candles and incense are lit and all the male members of the family worship before the ancestors' scroll. When this solemn ceremony is concluded, the head of the family lets off a long string of firecrackers and the celebrating begins. Fireworks were originally supposed to scare away evil spirits. Conversely, an evil spirit betrays its presence by his discomfort when they explode.

The feast will be concluded while it's still dark. One tradition held that the later the children went to bed, the longer their parents would live. At sunrise the men, even young sons, go visiting to extend best wishes to relatives and friends.

Early in the morning of the third day, another ceremony bids farewell to the ancestors' spirits as they leave the home. After this, the clothing returns to normal,

中
國
事
物

although the extravagant feasting continues.

Chinese New Year celebrations can be enjoyed in most major American cities, provided you like firecrackers. It is the only holiday based on the old lunar calendar that is still celebrated in mainland China, although it is now called a spring festival.

NINE TRIPODS

The Nine Tripods were bronze ritual vessels that were given in tribute to the Great Sage Emperor Yu, who supposedly ascended the Dragon Throne in 2202 B.C. The tripods actually represented the nine provinces of China at the time, and each one bore a map of the province, along with statistics on the population, and the division of properties and fiefs.

NOODLES

Scholars confess themselves puzzled over the origin of noodles. Certainly the Italians were avid pasta eaters long before Marco Polo; certain, too, is the archaeological evidence provided by fossil "pot stickers" (similar to ravioli) found in T'ang Dynasty tombs. Although egg noodles seem definitely Chinese, noodles of some sort appear to be a cultural universal throughout most of the world. Chinese today make noodles out of bean paste, corn, and peas, in addition to the more usual wheat and rice flours.

NOODLE BREAK AT A PORTABLE RESTAURANT. GUANGZHOU. C. 1910.

Noodles can vary in shape from thread-fine, almost translucent vermicelli (cellophane noodles or *kua-mien* or Fukien fine dried noodles) to the sturdy flat wrappers for won ton and other dumplings. There are, the experts say, noodles and noodles. There are handmade noodles and machine-made noodles. The difficulty of making noodles by hand explains the popularity of machine-made noodles, but they are not the same at all. Handmade noodles can be cut with a knife or swung. Swinging noodles is a skill not unlike spinning a pizza. One begins by grabbing the dough with both hands and stretching it out as far as possible. Then taking both ends of the dough in one hand and the middle in the other hand, one swings the dough outward some five or six feet. Keep on doubling it over and swinging it outward until, by geometric progression, the correct number and thinness of noodles are obtained. The stretching of the dough gives it a texture that cut noodles lack.

"If you don't have that swing," several choices remain. Ordinary egg noodles are suitable for many Chinese dishes. Chinese grocery stores, of course, carry a variety of Chinese noodles, and often stock refrigerated or frozen won-ton and egg-roll wrappings. Italian delicatessens sometimes stock homemade noodles and shiny hand-cranked pasta machines for making square noodles at home. The one time that foot-long store-bought noodles absolutely won't do is on a birthday, when one eats the longest possible noodles to wish longevity to the celebrant.

NOVELS

The novel is a relatively late development in the literary history of China, dating back only as far as the Yuan (Mongol) Dynasty and reaching its zenith in the Ming (A.D. 1368-1644). Three out of China's four best-known novels came out of the Ming, and while the fourth, *Hung Lou Meng (Dream of the Red Chamber)*, was written during the first century of the Ch'ing (Manchu) Dynasty, it is set back in the "good old days" of the late Ming. A fifth novel, contemporary to the *Hung Lou Meng*, might be added to this list. *Hu Chen Chu (Marriage as Retribution)* was not published until 1870, 155 years after its author's death. His identity as P'u Sung-ling was not considered certain until quite recently (1953). His is an extreme example, but although greatly admired by foreigners, the Chinese novel flourished in what Pearl S. Buck called "blessed obscurity" from its inception.

Chinese scholars snubbed the novel because of its common birth and low companions. Although Chinese novels derive from poetry, their more immediate ancestors were the short stories told by story-tellers in *pai-hua* (simple talk), the vernacular of the common people. Scholars wrote in *wen-li*, the ancient and stately language of the classics, which cannot be easily understood when it is read out loud to the common people. Prose fiction was simply not literature; stories were called *hsiao-shuo* (something slight and useless), and novels were called *ts'ang-p'ien hsiuo-shuo* (a longer something slight and useless). It is not surprising that Chinese novelists have long preferred to remain anonymous.

It is also no wonder that Chinese novels are full of jokes about scholars, especially scholars reading novels and pretending they don't. An intensely comic scene occurs in *Hung Lou Meng* when the sweetheart of the hero, Pao-yu, catches him reading an improper novel (he is pretending to read Confucius). Written by the impoverished son of an out-of-favor Manchu bureaucrat, *Hung Lou Meng* is a huge novel with over four hundred characters, telling the story of the decline of an aristocratic family, and of the tragic romance of Pao-yu and Black Jade.

Among the important Chinese novels are *Shui Hu Chuan (Water Margins, or*

九鼎 麵 長篇小說

173

中國事物

All Men Are Brothers), based on stories about the Chinese Robin Hood, Sung Chiang, and his thirty-five brother bandits; *San Kuo-chih Yen-yi (Three Kingdoms)*, is a historical novel of intrigue and statesmanship set mostly in the Han Dynasty; and *Hsi Yu Chi (Monkey or Travels in the Western Regions)*, a series of supernatural fantasies circulated during the Sung and Yuan (Mongol) Dynasties, and organized into a novel during the Ming.

Only in the twentieth century have the Chinese discovered the respectability of fiction in other countries. Chinese government bookstores are filled with interested crowds lined up to buy whatever new books become available. China has a long history of literary purges, but in New China fiction has become as popular in the home as television is in the West.

[See SHORT STORIES.]

DRAWINGS FROM AN EARLY EDITION OF THE NOVEL, *Dream of the Red Chamber* (*Hung Lou Meng*).

OAK

As with many Western cultures, the oak is a symbol of masculine strength. There are more than forty species of *Quercus* in China. The *Chu-tzu* (evergreen oak) is commonly used for making pillars for houses and for coffins because its wood does not decay easily. All parts of the oak are used by the Chinese. Wild silkworms feed upon oak leaves to produce a light brown silk. The nutgalls of the *Hsiang-shih* are used in making inks and dyes. The bark is used in tanning, and the acorn in medicinal concoctions. The acorns of some oak are also ground up into a form of edible curd.

OBSERVATORIES

Chinese observatories were huge astronomical instruments. They emerged from smaller devices used to measure the length of the solar shadow, and in fact, that was their primary function.

The increase in the size of instruments that led to the building of observatories came from an attempt to make more precise measurements of the solar shadow. There is a technological limit to the accuracy of the measuring scales on small instruments. The only option of these early astronomers was to increase the scale of the instruments to a point where precise measurements could be made.

In 1276, Kuo Shou-ching erected an observatory that still stands some fifty miles south of Luoyang, though it no longer has the 40-foot gnomon it was built to house. The observation platform is some 28 feet above the graduated scale that stretches for over 120 feet on the north side of the tower. At the top of the tower was the star-observation platform, where measurements of meridian transits were made.

The need for large-scale observatories of this type vanished with the emergence of more reliable and precise craft techniques from the fifteenth century on. Although the detailed records of observations made by Kuo and his assistants have been lost, the results that remain have led to his work being called "perhaps the most accurate ...ever done on solstice shadows."

ONE HUNDRED NAMES

The One Hundred Names are listed much like a telephone directory as part of the Chinese almanac. Practically all Chinese families can be classified under one of these names. They originally correspond with the *hsien* (counties), where in each district everyone had the same clan name. Even when names don't correspond, it is customary to address a man by what is equivalent to his Christian name being tacked onto the name of a town. Thus *Wang Tso-ming* of *T'ai Yuan Chi* becomes *T'ai Yuan Tso-ming.*

ONE-THOUSAND-CHARACTER ESSAY

This was a Chinese composition that contained exactly one thousand characters, arranged four to a line, each sentence complete in itself but in general having no connection with the rest of the text. The story goes that Chou Hsing-ssu, a great scholar of the T'ang Dynasty, incurred the displeasure of the Son of Heaven (the Emperor). Chou was sent to prison and ordered to make a composition of one thousand characters that would be jumbled together and supplied to him. Chou completed this essay in a single night, but the effort turned his hair white. His work was later referred to as *pai-t'ou-wen* (white-haired essay).

OPIUM

A Chinese legend ascribes the first opium pipe as having been presented to the legendary Yellow Emperor Huang Ti by a six-armed, vermilion-faced god who created it by blowing on the earth. The first breath produced a bamboo cane, the second a poppy, and the third a flame—the three essentials of opium smoking.

The opium poppy (*Papaver somniferum*) has been known since ancient times. Originating in Asia Minor, it was first mentioned in Sumerian tablets as early as the fourth or third century B.C. The Chinese term for it is *ya p'ien*, a corruption of the Arabic *afiyun*. It was introduced to China by Arab traders during the T'ang Dynasty (A.D. 618-906) and was used for its medicinal purposes, especially as a cure against dysentery.

By the sixteenth century, imports of opium were increased by the Portuguese, who were operating from their island base of Macao, off the coast of China. The actual smoking of the drug developed as an offshoot of tobacco smoking, which

橡樹

氣象台

百家姓

千字文

鴉片

175

中國事物

SMOKING OPIUM IN THE AFTERNOON. C. 1908.

reached China in the seventeenth century. At this time, too, East-West commerce was dominated by the fact that the West wanted Chinese tea, porcelain, and silk, but the Chinese had little interest in Western products. The British alone were consuming fifteen million pounds of Chinese tea each year. Needing to restore the balance of trade, the British stepped up opium imports despite strict edicts against it. It took two opium wars, a great deal of suffering, and several generations of addicts before the British Parliament put an end to opium shipments to China in 1911. That was the year the Manchu Dynasty collapsed, a victim of the credo "So long as there is opium, there will be no revolution."

In the early twentieth century, China resolved to eradicate the poppy, which was by then an illicit agricultural crop. The *Ying Su* or "jar seed," as poppies were called (because of the shape of their capsules) no longer exists in Central China. Southeast Asia and the southern hills of China, however, continue to find the poppy a very profitable crop.

ORCHIDS

蘭
貓
頭
鷹

八
卦

> The dark orchids release glorious fragrance,
> The lotus radiates a red glow.
> A hundred birds, how they flap and flutter,
> With winged tumult the flocks chase each other.
> —Ts'ao P'i (A.D. 187-226)

The Chinese orchid, or *Lan Hua*, actually has very little in common with its tropical cousins or with the Western hothouse varieties. Known in the West as the miniature *Cymbidium*, it is small or medium in size, yellowish-green in appearance, and fragrant. Confucius regarded the orchid's fragrance as being its greatest virtue, and held it as an example of true friendship, since its delicate scent could permeate any association without the slightest hint of self-consciousness. On the other hand, it was not unheard of for an orchid to inspire great jealousy or even enmity between close friends—especially if an orchid fancier would refuse to provide his blossom pal with an offshoot of a rare or unusual variety. When the orchid gatherers would come in from the Yangtze Valley, a fancier might buy an entire boatload of flowers in the hopes of discovering a novelty.

Needless to say, raising orchids was a popular pastime of scholars and retired officials who could afford the time and patience required for their care. Different types of orchids would be named after their original cultivators, such as "Judge Li" or "Magistrate Wang." Medically speaking, orchids were limited in their application as general tonics and as remedies against ear mites.

OWL

> Owls mimic human speech. . . .
> —Meng Chiao (A.D. 751-817)

> Ghosts wailed at night when the ancients invented words. . . .
> —Kung Tzu-chen (A.D. 1792-1841)

Known to the Chinese as the *hsiao*, the owl was considered to be an ill-omened bird because of its association with bats, serpents, toads on dark cliffs, and its soft, noiseless flight. The Chinese believe its cry sounds like the digging of a grave, and they regard it as a harbinger of death. This belief caused the owl to be counted among the Ten Kings of Hell. There was nothing noble about this characterization, since like the cuckoo, the owl is reputed to kill and eat its own mother. Naughty children in China were referred to as "little owls" by their mothers.

PA KUA

Myth has it that the longevity exercise *pa kua* was originally learned in a dream by a nameless immortal over a thousand years ago. Ordinary mortals might never have had a chance to learn *pa kua* if it weren't for a young martial-arts student who managed to penetrate this immortal master's mountain retreat. The ancient master whipped the student so thoroughly that the master had to nurse him back to health. Once the student recuperated from his first lesson, the anonymous immortal finally transmitted the art of *pa kua*.

中國事物

Circularity is the basis of all Taoist systems, and *pa kua* may be the one art most devoted to the principle of circular movement. The movements are all based on turning, pivoting, circling, and spiraling. The *sifu* (teacher) sometimes chants an old *pa kua* song while students walk the circle: "Walk like a dragon, turn like a monkey, change like an eagle." The students walk around in a circle in a specific manner, performing the eight "palm changes" that constitute the basic hand movements. As a fighting art, *pa kua* is highly effective, since the primary strategy is to remain behind your opponent's back at all times.

Pa kua, like *t'ai chi ch'uan*, is based on the circulation of the *ch'i*. The repeated exercises of the eight palm changes—each of which is linked to a trigram of the *I Ching*—is designed to awaken and circulate the *ch'i* energy through the blood and bone marrow. *Pa kua* is known as the "bone changing" method, because the movements are supposed to heat and cool the bones systematically to produce an esoteric substance that keeps the bones supple and promotes long life.

PAGODA

A pagoda is a rectangular tower consisting of an uneven number of tiers—usually between three and nine. Each tier is narrower than the one beneath it. Pagodas began to appear in China along with Buddhism, both being imports from India. In time, thousands were built, and there are still over 2,000 important pagodas in China today. While most pagodas are under 200 feet in height, the great pagoda of Nanjing measures over 260 feet.

The structures are most often hexagonal or octagonal, and are to be found on hillsides providing spectacular views to and from the cities they overlook. While the pagodas were originally associated with Buddhism, they became important in *feng-shui* (geomancy), and it was thought that a well-kept pagoda insured the good fortunes of the neighborhood around it.

Most pagodas were built of brick, but a variety of materials were used as well. There is even an "iron" pagoda in Henan. Another peculiarity of many pagodas is the absence of stairs or any means of ascent—rendering them externally ornamental, although they do house religious relics and are functional in that respect.

Pagodas were never employed for other than religious, ornamental, or geomantic purposes. They were not used like the more than ten thousand towers of the Great Wall for defense, nor were they like the many great bell towers of medieval and Renaissance Europe—used for observation and bell ringing. As many have noted, the pagoda is a series of Indian shrines atop a Chinese tower.

The oldest existing pagoda is at Sung-Yueh Ssu on Sung Shan (Mountain) in Henan. It is a twelve-sided, fifteen-story structure built in A.D. 523.

PAINTING

Among the earliest Chinese paintings were funeral shrouds, tomb decorations, and portraits of historical figures in didactic poses. During the early period Chinese artists were mainly employed as interior decorators or illustrators, doing murals and frescoes for the court. Their less-fortunate cousins were subsisting on rice-and-pickle commissions from Buddhist temples.

Landscapes were still in their infancy, little bitty horizons and immature hills serving strictly as backgrounds for other subjects. It was only during the T'ang Dynasty, that most inspired period of Chinese art, that landscapes emerged as an independent art form that would soon overshadow all other categories. The landscapes

塔
畫

Marble pagoda near Beijing with precious stone pagoda in the background.

中國事物

appeared formal and stylized at first, protraying the usual Taoist hangouts above the high-rising jagged peaks, painted in misty watercolors.

By the late Sung period, illusions of cosmic grandeur were gradually scaled down to present a more humanized, gentler view of nature. The Sung Emperors, although atrocious administrators, were not half bad as painters and calligraphers. They opened up the range of acceptable subject matter. Nothing was considered too significant or insignificant: birds, buds, bees, bamboos.

Painters could take imperial examinations in order to become painters-in-residence. At the same time, there were those who shied away from the academic school of painting. These were the wild-eyed Zen and Taoist philosophers who preferred to render a few sparrows on a branch expressionistically than to depict the feathered chest of a kingfisher meticulously.

By the time of the Ch'ing Dynasty, these iconoclasts had a history of their own eccentric making. One such painter was Chu Ta. He wouldn't paint for money, he wouldn't paint for art's sake. He would paint only if he was in the mood, which meant being adequately wined and dined. One night, feeling annoyed by his host's insistence, he picked up a brush and drew a nondescript shape. Then he threw away the brush, lifted the inkstone, and hurled it onto the paper. After Chu Ta stalked out of the party, his chagrined host surveyed the mess. There it was—a perfect picture of an eagle perched on a big rock, ready to fly.

After the turmoil of the early part of this century painting took an interesting turn in New China. Peasant paintings employing themes of everyday life—harvests, tractors, planting, construction—rendered in bold, lively colors have become a serious new art form. Recently eighty of these paintings toured the United States and Europe, giving Western audiences their first view of contemporary Chinese art.

[See CALLIGRAPHY, DRAWING, and FINGERPAINTING.]

"HALL OF GREEN WILDERNESS" BY YUAN YAO. AN EXQUISITE EXAMPLE OF LANDSCAPE PAINTING. DATED 1770.

皇宮　掌相學

PALACES

The building of palaces is a fine art in China, stretching back as far as recorded civilization itself. During the reign of Ch'in Dynasty Emperor Shih-Huang-Ti (221-210 B.C.), a gigantic imperial palace was built. One terrace was so large that it could hold ten thousand persons. Over seven hundred thousand conscripted laborers worked on its construction.

During later dynasties palace construction was expanded and refined. Han Dynasty palaces (206 B.C.-A.D. 220) were built more elegantly than the Ch'in. The Han Dynasty palace walls and pillars were inlaid with jade, gold, and semiprecious stones. They had not yet perfected floor tiles, so the floors of their palaces were of beaten earth painted in brilliant colors.

During the T'ang Dynasty (A.D. 618-906) and later during the Sung Dynasty multistoried buildings were constructed. These were artful constructions with highly decorated pitched roofs. This period, considered the apogee of Chinese architecture, also spawned special winter quarters in the palaces, equipped with fire screens and cozy wrappings, and the Pure Cool Quarters, freshened by fans and ice in the summer.

Though these palaces must have contrasted with most of the buildings of the cities, they were actually constructed along similar lines. For centuries the typical Chinese building was a rectangular one-story (and later, two-story) structure with a pitched roof. As since prehistoric times, the buildings faced south; and like most modern skyscrapers, both inner and outer walls had no structural significance, since pillars provided the support. The roofs, particularly of the later palaces, and the Forbidden City buildings were resplendent with glazed tiles. The ridgepoles were decorated at each end with mythical fish-tailed creatures charged with warding off calamities, while smaller animals and decorative motifs were carved into the eaves. The areas around the palace buildings were magnificent with artificial lakes, exotic plants and animals, ornamental towers, and astrological observatories.

The most famous, and certainly the largest imperial compound was the Forbidden City of the Ming Dynasty. Enclosed by a wall nearly fifteen miles long, it contains many palaces, servant quarters, recreation areas, temples, halls, barracks, stables, theaters, and sports grounds.

[See COURT LIFE and FORBIDDEN CITY.]

PALMISTRY

A very popular form of fortune-telling in China used to be the *Ta-shih* because of its simplicity. The system involves the inscription of six possible prearranged phrases on the two upper joints of the three middle fingers of the left hand. The order in which the phrases are written is determined by the numerical order of the month, day, and hour in which the event one is asking about has or will take place. By correlating the time, the correct numbered finger joint, and the sentence inscribed on it, a person can arrive at an answer.

The six phrases are as follows:
1. Grand peace and luck.
2. A little patience.
3. Prompt joy.
4. Disappointment and quarrels.
5. Scanty luck.
6. Loss and death.

中
國
事
物

Each phrase has detailed commentaries devoted to its explanation, but by understanding the general drift of the formula and relating to the object of inquiry, a person can get a quick answer without involving the expense or time of seeking out a professional fortune-teller.

P ' A N K U

Out of the formation of heaven and earth came the first man, P'an Ku (meaning "solid"). His role in the Chinese creation myth is as architect of the features of the world. He is depicted as being covered with hair, with horns growing out of his head, and teeth projecting from his mouth. He knew how to transform *yin* and *yang*, and out of the primordial chaos he began to create mountains, rivers, and even the sun and moon. P'an Ku is most often depicted with a hammer and chisel, but occasionally with an ax in the act of separating heaven and earth. The Taoists claim he lived eighteen thousand years, and upon his death, his breath became what we call winds and clouds, his voice became thunder, his eyes the moon and sun, his four limbs became the cardinal points, his blood the rivers, and his muscles the crust of the earth. His flesh turned into fields, his beard into stars, his hair into trees and grass, his teeth and bones into rocks and metals, his marrow into precious stones, and his sweat into rain. The parasites infesting his body were carried off by the wind and became the ancestors of men.

This creation myth is considered to date from the fourth century A.D. This makes the P'an Ku story a relatively recent creation myth, at least for the Chinese, many of whose myths date back thousands of years.

P A N D A

MODERN PAPERCUT OF PANDA FROM FUSHUN, CHINA.

The Chinese word for panda is *bai-hsiung* (white bear). It is not a bear at all, however, but a member of the raccoon family. Although the Chinese have known about pandas for four thousand years, the giant panda was not introduced to the Western world until 1869 when a Jesuit missionary, Père Armand David, reported their existence. The first live giant panda taken out of China was Su-Lin, a male, who was purchased for the Brookfield Zoo in Chicago in 1937.

Giant pandas live in the central-northern parts of Sichuan Province and the southern end of Jiangsu Province in dense bamboo forests at altitudes from five thousand to ten thousand feet. The mountains are shrouded in heavy clouds, and there are torrential rains and dense mists all year round. The pandas are considered rare, but not necessarily in danger of extinction. They have no predators and never run out of food, since they eat bamboo. Exact population figures are unknown, since the pandas elect to live solitary lives.

The only giant pandas in the United States today are Ling-Ling and Hsing-Hsing at the Washington National Zoo. All attempts at breeding pandas have failed except in China, where 16 cubs have been born, most recently, with the aid of artificial insemination.

PANGOLIN

When the Chinese pangolin feels it is being threatened, it will roll its body up into a ball till it resembles nothing more than a very large pine cone. Otherwise, in its normal state, with its elongated form, scaly covering, and awkward gait, this Chinese anteater is more reptilian in appearance than its South American relations, the armadillo or the sloth. The pangolin's scales are broad and heavy plates, like shingles on a roof, although they are actually modified from hairs.

Originally native to Taiwan, the pangolin ranges across southern China to Hainan Island, Indochina, Thailand, and Burma. At mealtimes it will ascend the banks of streams, and lying down, open its scales wide and play dead. As soon as the swarms of unsuspecting ants have checked in, the pangolin will close its scales and return to the water to open them. The ants float out dazed, and the pangolin devours them at his leisure.

PAPAYA

The papaya or papaw is the same fruit that is native to Central America. It is now successfully grown in the South of China, and in other tropical parts of the Far East. The *Mu Kua* (tree melon) is considered to be a longevity fruit, and the Chinese have learned to appreciate its qualities as a meat tenderizer.

PAPER

The Chinese wrote (and painted) on silk since the third century B.C., and the first papers they made were probably silk based or silk reinforced. Paper and silk alike were used to make fans, parasols, and screens. A Han eunuch named Ts'ai Lun is generally credited with making the first batch of pulp paper, out of a mixture of hemp, the inner bark of trees, old rags, and fish nets. He is supposed to have presented his paper to Emperor Ho-ti in A.D. 105, and paper from about that time was found by an archaeologist named Bergman at Kharakhoto in 1942.

Sir Aurel Stein found the marvelous caves of Tun-huang on the Turkestan border in 1907, where priests had stored more than ten thousand manuscripts, some on silk, but most on paper, dating from about A.D. 406-996. In the ninth century the courtesan Hsieh T'ao made paper in double sheets four feet wide and six feet long. Li Hou-chu of the Southern T'ang Dynasty (A.D. 923-34) invented a superlative paper called *ch'eng hsin t'ang* that was thin, fine, and extremely smooth. The great artists of the Sung and Yuan dynasties preferred this paper over any other.

So much paper and silk were made in the Sung Dynasty that it was common well into the Ming Dynasty for artists to use Sung materials. Artists often choose old papers for their "mellowness," although this practice adds considerably to the dif-

盤古

熊貓

穿山甲

木瓜

紙

中國事物

蕩 料 入 簾

VIEW OF AN EARLY PAPER FACTORY. FROM THE *T'ien Kung K'ai Wu.*

剪
紙

鸚
鵡

ficulty of authenticating the dates of works of art. Fine papers today are often made from hemp fiber, mulberry bark, or bamboo pulp. What foreigners call rice paper has nothing to do with rice, but is made from the pith of a fellow marsh dweller named *Tetrapanax*, a plant closely allied to the common ivy. Known as *T'ung-ts'ao*, this paper is used not only by painters but also in the construction of artificial flowers.

PAPERCUTS

For the first several centuries after its invention in China, paper was too rare and valuable to be diverted to the frivolous use of mere decoration, but by the T'ang Dynasty (A.D. 618-906), papercuts of colored paper had begun to appear. Tu Fu, a renowned poet of this period, mentions the art of paper folding, and China was exporting artisan paper makers to Baghdad and Samarkand. Despite its antiquity, paper cutting and folding was considered "folk art" and not taken terribly seriously until the 1950s.

Papercuts were used as guides for cutting out wood blocks for printing, and as stencils on lacquerware and pottery. Tacked onto cloth, they served to guide embroiderers in their craft. During the T'ang Dynasty, gold and silver papercuts called spring flags, in the shape of auspicious calligraphy and flowers, were sewn onto silk flags, tied to flowering bushes, and pinned in women's hair. Papercuts are the Chinese equivalent of stained glass, glowing happily in night-lit windows and the traditional lantern of cane or split bamboo and stretched paper.

Traditional subjects for papercutters include the mythical unicorn, the lotus, pomegranate, and pig, and chrysanthemums, plum blossoms, pine trees, and bamboo to symbolize courage, as well as tigers and lions. Cranes, peaches, and pines were used to symbolize longevity. Sometimes the character itself for longevity, happiness, or whatever would be used as a papercut, and sometimes elaborate puns were made in which the character is read for its sound (for example, the character for fish, pronounced *yu*, is then read as abundance, also pronounced *yu*).

PARROT

Parrots dwell in the west country.
Foresters catch them with nets, to bring them to us.
Lovely women toy with them, morning and evening.
As they go to and from their courtyard pavilions.
—Han-Shan, T'ang Dynasty

Parrots are mainly found in the southern parts of China, although various *psittaci* such as macaws, cockatoos, and parakeets are imported from the Malay archipelago. Oddly enough, the best bargain in parrots from China today is the African or Congo gray parrot. The Chinese obtain these birds in great numbers from their African allies and import them into the United States at greatly reduced prices, often undercutting the regular wholesalers by half.

There is no easy trick to teaching a parrot to talk, although Chinese parrots have been known to spout everything from Confucius' *Analects* to inadvertently recorded sighs of passion. A story tells of a pearl merchant in Jiangxi Province who was on the verge of being ruined by the intrigues of his promiscuous wife when the true state of affairs was revealed to him by his pet parrot. The parrot in China is therefore looked upon as a warning to women to be faithful to their husbands.

中
國
事
物

PAWNSHOPS

Imperial China produced what might be called four distinct types of financial institutions. The largest were the central banks, which grew to huge size from the twelfth century on. Next were the small native banks, which existed in every town and served the needs of small businesses. Below them were the moneychangers, working out of tiny stalls in the major cities; and finally, the pawnshops.

Pawnshops were probably more respected than their Western counterparts, and like other institutions in China, depended heavily on long-standing reputations. They lent money, like the banks, at interest rates from 15 to 25 per cent and, like modern pawnshops, lent money on clothing, jewelry, and other goods.

Pawnshops were introduced along with poor houses and hospitals by the Buddhists in the sixth century A.D. Pawnshops first existed to provide revenues for the new Buddhist movement. Pawnshops apparently served some of China's financial needs for fourteen centuries until 1952, when the new government closed them down.

PEACH

The peach is most plentiful in China and originated there. It is most important as an emblem of marriage and as a symbol of longevity and springtime. The peach tree of

PEACH LONGEVITY CHARM.

the gods was said to blossom once in three thousand years and to bear the fruit of eternal life. The god of longevity is therefore often pictured emerging from within a peach.

For these reasons peach charms are used to ward off evil influences, and February (when peach trees blossom) is considered the most propitious time for marriage. The branches of the peach trees were used to beat fevered patients, in hopes of expelling the fever.

PEACOCK

The Chinese referred to the peacock as *k'ung-chueh* (large sparrow), and for all its bright plumage it was regarded as being the symbol of the spirit of fire. It was introduced to the Middle Kingdom from the Malay Peninsula, and according to T'ang records, "Many thousand districts paid tribute in peacocks, their feathers being required for the state not only as decorations for imperial processions, but [also] for designation of official rank." The beautiful daughter of Tou I—a military commander in A.D. 562—painted a peacock on a screen and offered herself in marriage to the man who could hit it twice in a row with an arrow. The first T'ang Emperor put out both its eyes. The term "hitting the bird screen" therefore came to mean selecting a husband in China.

PEANUTS

Hua-sheng have been cultivated for centuries in southern China, although peanuts are now being grown successfully everywhere from Central Manchuria to Henan. The original Chinese peanut was diminutive in size compared with the Western variety. Actually, this larger-sized peanut, so familiar to beer drinkers in the West, was introduced to the Chinese by foreign missionaries. Peanuts are a major crop in New China and are used primarily for cooking oil.

PEAR

Pear wood is very hard and is favored for Chinese wood-block prints. Only a few varieties of the Chinese pear are considered edible by Western standards. Most of them are in fact rather pulpy and tasteless. The oil pear could be kept for a year without spoiling, though not many people would be willing to attest to the fact. The Chify pear was originally imported into China from America, and closely resembles the Bartlett pear. The Duke of Shao (1053 B.C.) held court and dispensed justice underneath a wild pear tree, so pears have come to represent wise and benevolent administration to the Chinese.

PEARL DIVING

> Why should you look
> for treasure abroad?
> Within yourself you
> have a bright pearl!
> —Pao-chih (A.D. 418-514)

The earliest Chinese pearl fisheries were located near Leizhoy in southern Guangdong, somewhat north of Hainan Island. Natural pearls were first discovered there in A.D. 716, and demand soon outstripped supply. Pearls were valued as ornaments, as cosmetics, and as immortality elixirs. The method of pearl diving was primitive in

押店 桃 孔雀 花生 梨 採珠

中
國
事
物

the extreme, and resulted in an unwarranted loss of life. A diver weighted with a stone was simply tossed over the side of a sampan while attached to a rope, and hauled up whenever his cohorts saw fit. According to records, most of them "found a tomb in the bellies of fish." In order to relieve the hardship, a Sung inventor devised a kind of weighted dragnet with iron prongs like a plow, and a hempen bag that was held open to receive the oysters so that the pearl fishermen could tow their catch while their boats were under sail. By this time divers could descend as much as 70 to 120 feet with a long rope that was secured to their waists and lowered by means of a winch. They breathed through a pipe that was reinforced by rings of tin, and fastened over their face with a leather mask.

Pearl diving was halted for a while during the T'ang Dynasty when Emperor Wen Tsung had a religious experience at his dinner table. He was addicted to oysters, and fishermen were forced to supply the palace with enormous quantities of oysters every day without any payment. One day an oyster of phenomenal size was served at the imperial table. His Majesty could hardly wait for what he thought was going to be a gastronomic treat. But the oyster could not be opened. Finally, it did open on its own, revealing a perfectly formed mother-of-pearl image of the goddess of mercy, which chided the Emperor for his greed and selfishness.

PEKING MAN

In 1927 the remains of forty-five hominids were found in the village of Chou-k'ou-tien, not far from Beijing. These were the bones of *Homo erectus Sinanthropus*, or Peking Man, who lived five hundred thousand years ago.

Like the members of *Homo erectus* family found in Africa and Europe, Peking Man was a hunter of large game. The bones of extinct species of deer, bear, hyena, and buffalo were also found at the site. Since the human skulls were cracked open at the base, possibly for extracting the brain, Peking Man may have hunted humans as well.

Though *Homo erectus* brains are slightly more than half the size of modern man's, *Homo erectus* was able to make fire, to shape quartz into primitive tools, and to communicate in words. Because Peking Man shared certain characteristics with modern Mongoloid populations, such as lacking a third molar and shovel-shaped incisors, it is likely that Confucius, Lao Tzu, and Mao Tse-tung were all descended from him.

In 1963-64 an earlier form of Peking Man was discovered in Shaanxi Province. Known as Hantian Man, he lived approximately six hundred thousand years ago. An even earlier man with similar primitive physical features is Yuan-mou Man, who lived about a million years ago.

PEONY

Such radiance of green,
  so casual and composed;
The tint of her dress
  blends crimson with pink.
The heart of a flower
  is nearly torn with grief:
Will spring's brilliance
  ever know her heart?
    —Wang Wei (A.D. 701-61)

没水採珠船

北京人 牡丹

DIVING FOR PEARLS WITH BREATHING TUBE. FROM THE *T'ien Kung K'ai Wu.*

中國事物

PEONIES. INK AND COLORS ON SILK BY YUN PING. LATE SEVENTEENTH CENTURY.

Although Marco Polo wrote home about seeing roses that were as large as cabbages, he was most likely confusing them with the Chinese "King of Flowers," the peony. The peony has the greatest romantic history of any flower in the floral annals of the Celestial Kingdom. There are two cultivated species: the tree peony (*Mu-tan*), and the herbaceous peony (*Shao-yao*). The *Shao-yao* has been grown since prehistoric times, and is mentioned in the *Book of Songs* (5 B.C.). The *Mu-tan* has a relatively shorter history, growing back to the T'ang Dynasty in the seventh century. It became the most popular flower during the Sung, when there was a *Mu-tan* craze and over thirty varieties were developed. Its large, showy blossoms and rich colors inspired a number of florid pseudonyms, such as "A Hundred Ounces of Gold," "Color of Nature and Scent of Earth," and "Flower of Wealth and Rank." It grows most readily in North China and in the Yangtze Valley, and is planted in terraces on raised beds, protected by mat awnings during the hottest part of the day. The Chinese regard it as a symbol of feminine beauty, as an emblem of love, and as a sign of spring. They also value it for its special action on the spleen, liver, stomach, and intestines. Physicians would prescribe essence of peony for nosebleeds and feminine disorders.

Once the wicked Empress Wu, during the T'ang Dynasty, ordered all the flowers in the royal garden to bloom in midwinter. They all did, with the exception of the peonies. Enraged, the Empress ordered all the *Mu-tan* to be dug up and burned. The peonies that survived the purge were banished to Luoyang, where they eventually gained the support of artists and poets and were able to plot their return to power.

PERSIMMON

The Chinese persimmon or *shih-tsu* is grown in orchards at the foot of the hills in northern China. The trees can grow up to sixty or eighty feet high, and the fruit can weigh over a pound. There are many varieties of this plumlike fruit, though the best type is the millstone-persimmon. Because of its bright, festive color, it is regarded as an emblem of joy. It is also used as a popular design on bowls and dishes, most often depicted as a deep-orange-colored fruit supported on a twig that is buckling under its own weight.

PHEASANT

Chinese pheasants have been oppressed by greedy landowners and merciless chefs for centuries. As Marco Polo made his gastronomical observation, "Pheasants are found there twice as big as ours, indeed, nearly as big as a peacock, and having tails of seven to ten palms in length." The English ultimately imported the Chinese ring-necked pheasant into their own preserves, where it had no difficulty interbreeding successfully with the local varieties.

PHILOSOPHERS

Chinese philosophy consists of an astonishing array of advanced conceptualized thinking and early scientific explanations concerning existence. The civilization of China is one of the oldest continuing cultures on earth, and the written language has remained relatively unchanged since its beginning. Consequently the ancient classics could be read and fully understood by many successive generations of scholars and philosophers. Chinese philosophy, then, is unusually well recorded, cross-referenced, and expanded.

There are hundreds of prominent Chinese scholars who, over the past twenty-five hundred years, advanced the philosophy of this unique culture. Among the most well-known philosophers are:

Fu Hsi (2953-2838 B.C.)—Fu Hsi is the legendary father of industry and religion. He is said to have been born miraculously after a twelve-year pregnancy. He taught mankind to hunt, fish, and tend livestock. He invented tools for splitting wood, and was the first to twist silk into strings for the making of musical instruments. He supposedly received his name, which means "Hidden Victims," because of the snares and nets he introduced for fishing and trapping animals.

Fu Hsi's most significant innovation was that of the Eight Trigrams consisting of a series of straight full and broken lines arranged in a circle. The Eight Trigrams represent the primary forces of Nature. The trigrams are said to be at the root of organized religious divination in China, and their arrangements to be the source of modern calculus. Fu Hsi arrived at the trigrams by interpreting the patterns on the shell of a tortoise. His arrangements and subsequent commentaries by Wen Wang and the Duke of Chou became the Chou Dynasty work known as the *I Ching (Book of Changes)*, in which the Eight Trigrams were combined into Sixty-four Hexagrams

中國事物

and used for a more sophisticated kind of divination involving moral and political considerations.

The Duke of Chou (1231-1135 B.C.)—The Duke of Chou was the son of the founder of the Chou Dynasty, Wen Wang. He is reputed to have rescued his father from a dungeon where he had been imprisoned by the last Shang Dynasty emperor, Chou Hsin. The Duke of Chou, together with his father, wrote commentaries on the Eight Trigrams and Sixty-four Hexagrams of Emperor Fu Hsi (2953-2838 B.C.). Their work constitutes the bulk of what is known as the *I Ching* or *Book of Changes*. The Duke of Chou is also credited with the invention of a primitive compass called the "south-pointing chariot."

Lao Tzu (b. 604 B.C.)—Also known as Laocius, Lao Chun, Lao Tan, and Li Erh, this possibly mythic philosopher is reputed to be the founder of Taoism, perhaps the most influential popular religion ever to exist in China, and certainly one of the most compelling of philosophies.

According to legend, Lao Tzu was born in 604 B.C. in Henan. Various tales about a miraculous birth after 64 and even 80 years of pregnancy are given as a reason for the fact that he was born with white hair and a beard, and thereafter was referred to as "The Old Boy." He was keeper of imperial archives at Luoyang.

At the age of 160 Lao Tzu decided to retire to the mountains beyond Han-ku Pass. The keeper of the pass, Yin Hsi, begged him to compose a book before retiring from public life. It was then that Lao Tzu wrote the 5,000 characters that have survived as the *Tao-te-ching*, the most enigmatic and most frequently translated work (excepting the Bible) in history. Lao Tzu then disappeared into the mountains.

Lao Tzu was canonized by Kao Tsung in A.D. 666 as "The Great Supreme Emperor of the Dark First Cause." In A.D. 743 Lao Tzu was given the title "The Venerable Prince of the Great Supreme." He is worshiped by Taoists as the first of their great Trinity, which also includes Buddha and Confucius.

Confucius—K'ung Fu-Tzu (551-479 B.C.)—Confucius is considered to be China's most renowned sage. He was born in the state of Lu and earned a reputation for honesty and integrity through a series of official jobs. He then took up a life of teaching and wandering, occasionally acting as a diplomat and adviser to numerous princes. He propounded an ethical philosophy based on respect for traditions, and the careful observation of religious obligatory rituals. He projected an ideal moral man whose primary virtues were self-restraint, goodheartedness, and the setting up of good examples to others. He taught that the key to good government was the education of the princely class, and the perpetuation of values in each ruler that are desirable in his subjects.

Confucius wrote and edited numerous works, including the *Book of Songs*, the *Canon of History*, and the *Spring and Autumn Annals*, a history of the state of Lu from 722-484 B.C. His major philosophical prescripts were collected and written by a series of disciples. Collectively these are called the *Analects* of Confucius, although it is certain that a good part represents the concerns of different schools of his followers.

Confucius and the values he tried to convey to his followers have fluctuated wildly through the changes of Chinese history. His reputation has changed along with that of the scholar class as they took turns dominating and losing control of the government and control of religious institutions. In 195 B.C. Emperor Kao Tsu of the Han Dynasty sacrificed to Confucius. In A.D. 629 Emperor T'ang T'ai-tsung decreed that temples be erected to Confucius in every city in the empire.

While the masses of Chinese people were not exposed to the written work of

哲學家

像教行子孔師先

德侔天地道冠古今
刪述六經垂憲萬世

THE WISE SAGE, CONFUCIUS, SHOWN IN A STONE RUBBING.

中國事物

Confucius, they came to know him through his pictures and temples. Hundreds of legends and tales are attached to his life and death. One curious note is that the descendants of Confucius have traced a line to the present day, making them one of the longest unbroken lineages in the world, a fact that would please the Master—who was so dedicated to reverence for ancestors.

Chuang Tzu (399-320 B.C.)—One of the greatest Taoist philosophers, Chuang Tzu was a disciple of Lao Tzu, and elaborated the way of Nature and skepticism first introduced in the *Tao-te-ching*. His book is called the *Nan-hua chen-ching (Pure Classic of Nan-hua)*, but he is the confirmed author of only the first seven chapters.

His philosophy was written in highly readable anecdotes and conversations between sages. Much of what he had to say ridiculed the Confucian values of social propriety, ancestor worship, and veneration of the past. Chuang advocated instead the path of noninterference and inactivity, which he claimed put a man in greater harmony with the evolutionary processes of Nature. He professed to know nothing about the mysteries of heaven and earth, claiming they were unknowable.

Chuang Tzu's ideas were repulsive to later philosophers such as Chu Hsi (A.D. 1130-1200), who accused him of not propounding anything useful to men or rulers. His thinking and work have, however, enjoyed continuous popularity. Much of his philosophy contributed to the development of Zen Buddhism. His insights also became absorbed into medieval Chinese Neo-Confucianism.

Mencius (371-289 B.C.)—The life of Mencius parallels that of Confucius to an amazing degree. Mencius was a member of the ruling class of Lu State, and spent much of his life as an itinerant teacher. He held a few official posts and retired from public life a disillusioned man. His teachings were derived from those of Confucius, and many of them formed an extremely sensitive and perceptive analysis of the motives of men. Mencius held onto and solidified the Confucian belief in the inherent goodness of man. Upon this he constructed what has been called an "idealistic" philosophy advocating the pursuit of "recovery of our original nature" by developing our innate abilities. He elevated the virtues of humanity and righteousness above all else, and proposed a system by which "humane government" could replace "the way of the despot."

Mencius maintained the traditional Confucian values of reverence for tradition and respect for ancestors. His concept of humanity began with the performance of duties to the family. Morality was located in every individual, making the people the most important elements of government, and therefore giving them the right to revolt against injustice.

The *Book of Mencius* is divided into seven books, and subdivided further, each into two parts. The sage Chu Hsi (A.D. 1130-1200) named it one of the "Four Classics" along with the *Analects*, the *Great Learning*, and the *Doctrine of the Mean*.

Chu Hsi (A.D. 1130-1200)—Chu Hsi is considered to be the greatest Chinese philosopher to follow the classical age of Confucius, Mencius, Lao Tzu and Chuang Tzu. Chu Hsi is known as the greatest Neo-Confucianist "synthesizer," and his influence dominated Chinese thought well into the seventeenth century.

Chu Hsi reworked all the great themes of Chinese philosophy, applying rigorous standards of rational investigation and analysis. He extracted the essence of a humanistic tradition in Confucianism, ridding it of the more mystical Buddhist and Taoist influences that had infiltrated over the centuries. Chu Hsi re-examined the classics and selected a group of them; the *Analects*, the *Book of Mencius*, the *Great Learning*, and the *Doctrine of the Mean*, writing commentaries in which the main tenets of his ethical and social philosophy are formulated. The "Four Classics" became the basis for the civil-service examinations in China in 1313 and remained so until the examinations were abolished in 1905, a fact that illustrates the extent of Chu Hsi's influence.

鳳
凰

PHOENIX

The mythical phoenix bird is the second of the four supernatural animals, the others being the dragon, the unicorn, and the tortoise. The phoenix was associated with summer and the sun, and regarded as a sacred creature ruling the southern quadrant of the heavens. The Chinese phoenix is a combination of *feng* (pheasant) and *huang* (peacock). In art and literature it has become an emblem of everlasting love.

The Chinese phoenix, like the other sacred animals, is the most beautiful in its realm—that of birds. It symbolizes beauty, and is often used as a motif in clothing

"WATCHING THE PHOENIX." MING DYNASTY PAINTING (A.D. 1280-1367).

中
國
事
物

and head ornaments by prominent women following styles set by the women of the imperial household.

In legendary times the phoenix appeared frequently to bestow its blessing on the reign of the great founding Emperors of China. It was believed that the phoenix shows itself only in times of peace and prosperity, when the rule of reason prevails in the country. Therefore, an Emperor who hears of a phoenix visiting the land during his rule is sure to gain the good will of his people. The phoenix is also associated with longevity. It is said that the immortals eat the eggs of the phoenix in order to achieve eternal life.

P I

JADE PI DISC SYMBOLIZING THE UNIVERSE. FROM THE HAN DYNASTY (206 B.C.-A.D. 220).

The *pi* is one of the Eight Precious Treasures. It is also one of the most popular objects of Chinese jadework, symbolizing heaven and earth. It has the shape of a flat disc with a hole in the center. Most probably the *pi* was responsible for affecting the traditional shape of Chinese coins—and, in fact, coins for warding off evil spirits are known as *pi-hsieh-ch'ien*. The *pi* is a *yang*, or male principle. Some *pi* were adorned with one, two, or four projections in a pointed representation. These were used in performing sacrifices to heaven, the sun, the moon, and the stars.

PILLOW

Traditionally, Chinese pillows are neck rests made of stone, wood, or pottery. More comfortable pillows were made of stalks of plants, leaves, and flowers that were rolled up. Most Chinese looked down on these because they felt that softness resulted in a loss of vitality. Some of the more unusual types of pillows included the medicinal pillow, which was filled with twenty-four herbs; and the book pillow, favored by the legendary Yao, who took three scrolls and piled them one on top of the other. He believed that sleeping on the *Heavenly Chart*, the *Book of Long Life*, and the *Register of the Immortals*, would inspire pure and elegant dreams. Perhaps the most bizarre pillow was the "necropillow." There was an old woman who was paralyzed from the neck down. Sung physician Hsu Ssu-po diagnosed her illness as "corpse sickness." He prescribed a dead man's pillow, boiled, and administered orally as a medicine.

PINE

The pine, an evergreen, is regarded by the Chinese as a symbol of longevity, and used as a metaphor for constant friends. They are planted around cemeteries, since they are distasteful to Wang-Hsiang, a demon that devours the brains of the dead.

PIPES

RICE FARMER RELAXING WITH HIS PIPE. C. 1900.

璧
枕
頭
松
簫

中國事物

Chinese commonly used two kinds of pipes: the dry pipe and the water pipe. The water pipe was a copy of the Indian hookah. It consisted of a receptacle for water in which a tubelike piece about the size of a small finger was inserted. The upper end of this tube contained a small cavity into which tobacco was put. The smoke was inhaled through the water, up a foot-long tube, and gradually out the mouthpiece. The dry pipes were made of copper and silver, although coolies smoked their own bamboo variety. Chinese pipes would scarcely hold a thimbleful of tobacco. A few puffs would exhaust them, and the owners, too, who had arduously to replenish the bowl. This apparently was less troublesome if one was smoking opium.

PLANTAIN

A great food producer, the plantain is popular for its aesthetics, fruit, and shade. The tree is emblematic of self-education due to a legendary student who wrote on plantain leaves for want of writing paper. The plantain tree grows to a height of fifteen or twenty feet and is quite common in southern China.

PLUMS

I pluck plum blossoms....
Let me present you with a twigful of spring.
—Lu K'ai (A.D. 3)

The finest Chinese plums are grown in Shandong, where the unusual hybrid apricot-plum is also found. The *prunus* is noted for both its fruit and its blossoms, and is a symbol of winter and longevity since its flowers will continue to bloom on apparently withered branches. Lao Tzu was said to have been born under a plum tree, which may explain some of the tartness of his teaching. Pupils are sometimes referred to as plums, being unripe and receiving cultivated instruction from their teacher. Ch'ing Dynasty potters favored the plum motif on their porcelain, the reticulated deep azure providing a background for the white plum blossoms. In fact, the plum blossom has been a favored motif with many artists since the fourteenth century—some even became specialists, painting only plum blossoms all of their lives.

POETRY

Sixth-century scholar Yen Chi-t'ui wrote in a book on family instruction that the function of poetry was "to develop one's native sensibility." Almost as an afterthought, he added, "or to give others unembarrassed advice." Poetry has been a part of everyday life in China for over three thousand years. Although considered a scholarly art, it was venerated by all classes of people. During the Sung Dynasty, even before the spread of printing, copies of poems by the most famous poets of the day were circulated in markets and sometimes used as means of payment for wine and tea. The term *shih* is used by the Chinese as a generic label to describe most types of poetry.

The earliest anthology of Chinese poetry was the *Shih Ching (Book of Songs)*, a collection of songs dating back to the twelfth century B.C. If there is any thread that unites the amazing diversity of styles, themes, and modes, it is the commonality of music and painting to Chinese poetry. Even when the original musical or shamanistic context of the lyrics had been forgotten, poems would still be written to be chanted, not merely read aloud. Similarly, there is no defined boundary between Chinese poetry and the pictorial arts. A painting was often accompanied by a poem that provided a clue as to the subject, expressing the same idea in a different medium.

Chinese poetry has always been impressionistic in character, naturally concise in its expression, arriving at its meaning not by means of logic but through juxtaposition of image and sensibility. Calligraphy plays a large part in this concept. Since the words are written in "pictograms," poetry can be animated through various calligraphic styles.

[See BOOK OF SONGS.]

POMEGRANATE

When peaches are unobtainable, Taoists will make use of pomegranates in temple functions. But it is the Buddhists who find the pomegranate filled with meanings as numerous as its seeds. To them the fruit represents the essence of favorable influences. The brilliant red fruit is said to resemble a tumor; an open pomegranate is said to resemble a grinning mouth.

The pomegranate is not native to China, being imported first during the Han Dynasty. It has since been widely cultivated in China.

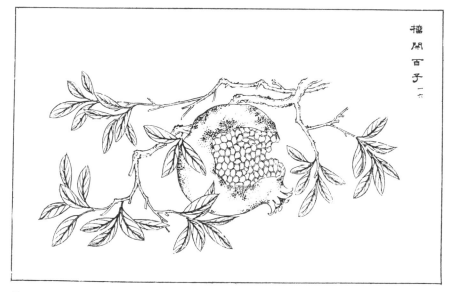

DRAWING OF POMEGRANATE REPRESENTING FERTILITY. FROM *Kissho zung Kaidai.*

PORCELAIN

The discovery of porcelain has been attributed to the alchemists of the Han Dynasty, who stumbled across the properties of clay and glaze in their relentless search for the philosopher's stone. Chinese porcelain consists essentially of two elements: the white clay, or *kaolin*, which gives plasticity to the body; and the felspathic stone, or *petuntse*, which upon being fired gives the form its translucency. The glaze *yu* is made of the same stone, the best pieces of *petuntse* being reserved for the glaze. The glaze always contains lime. It is the lime that gives it a characteristic tinge of green or blue. At the beginning of the T'ang Dynasty, a number of pieces were presented to the Emperor as "imitation jade."

The *Ch'a Ching*, a classical book of tea, describes the different kinds of bowls preferred by the tea drinkers, classifying them according to the color of their glaze in

中
國
事
物

enhancing the tint of the liquid. The poets of the time likened their wine cups to "disks of thinnest ice," or to "tilted lotus leaves floating down a stream." Later on, Emperor Shi Tsung (A.D. 954-99) ordered his porcelain to be "as blue as the sky, as clear as a mirror, as thin as paper, and as resonant as a musical stone of jade." This eclipsed in its delicacy all that preceded it and soon became so rare that it was described as sheer invention.

The different classifications of Chinese porcelain, the glazes and subglazes, and the styles of decoration of the pieces are as ephemeral in their complexity as Shi Tsung's cups. Cracked, eggshell, five-colored flambé, green soufflé, Ming, rose, Ting—these are only a few of the better-known types of porcelain that exist.

MUFFLE STOVES USED FOR FIRING PORCELAIN IN A GUANGZHOU WORKSHOP. NINETEENTH CENTURY WATERCOLOR.

POTTERY

A Chinese might spend his entire day inside a teahouse, doing business, discoursing on matters of empire, or arguing with his friends. Regular customers would frequently bring their own teapots, and sometimes even their own tea leaves, requesting only that the management provide them with boiling water. Teacups were superfluous appendages, since spouts on the pots were designed for sipping. As a man sipped, he would constantly be rubbing the teapot with his hand. After years of such convivial contact, the pots would acquire a smooth, oily sheen, much prized by their owners. Upon returning home at night from the teahouse, the Chinese would invariably rest his head on a ceramic pillow that would bear the inscription "Don't talk among crowds, and come home early if you have nothing else to do." The advice was meant to penetrate dreams.

Teapots and pillows are only two examples of how pottery formed a regular part

陶
器

螳
螂

印
刷

of daily life in China. Pottery in the widest sense of the word includes everything from earthenware to stoneware and even porcelain. The word for pottery is *t'ao*, an ancient character that graphically depicts a kiln. Pottery in China passed through the usual stages of sun-dried and burned bricks, tiles, architectural ornaments, culinary utensils, funeral and sacrificial vases, and dishes.

Perhaps one of the most celebrated centers of modern pottery manufacture was at Yi-hsing-hsien in Chang-chou-fu. This is where the collectors found their teapots—often designed in fantastic forms, such as a dragon rising from a wave, a section of bamboo, or a gnarled trunk of pine. The body tints ranged from pale buff, red, and brown to chocolate. Different clays would be used on the same piece—embossed designs in red being contrasted with a fawn-colored background. Chinese potters had their own pet secret formulas for the glazes. Some added powdered precious stones, believing that would enhance the red color. Others might add the urine of a small boy to the mixture, reasoning that since it was the quintessence of *yang* or the male, and that red was also *yang*, the color would therefore be reinforced.

[See PORCELAIN and TEAPOTS.]

PRAYING MANTIS

Short on brains, long on stupidity,
the mantis seizes the cicada....
—Huang T'ing-chien (A.D. 1045-1105)

Depending on whether they are of the Taoist or the Buddhist persuasion, the Chinese will regard the praying mantis as either courageous ("heavenly horse") or just plain voracious ("insect killer"). Duke Chung of Ts'ai, in the T'ang Dynasty, was on his way to a hunt when he noticed a mantis with uplifted arms trying to stop his chariot.

"What manner of creature is this?" he asked an attendant.

"That, my lord, is a mantis," came the reply, "an insect that knows how to advance but not how to retreat."

Visibly impressed, the duke ordered a detour and thus won the admiration of all his warriors. The mighty mantis, feeling cheated of its evening meal, returned to his place among the bushes to await further developments.

PRINTING

Printing, like most good things, has its origins in magic, and in China as in Europe, was at first befriended by religion. Buddhist and Taoist monastic communities mass-produced charms and amulets from woodcuts as early as the seventh century A.D. These graven images were actually printed by stamping, as if they were oversized seals, but using the black ink devised in the Han instead of cinnabar red (vermilion).

The first books were religious and magical works, herbals, almanacs, calendars, dictionaries, and medical and astrological works. In short, they were practical, or at least intended to be so. The Buddhist classic *Diamond Sutra* is the earliest known printed book in the world; it was found in the caves of Tun-huang in 1907 by Sir Aurel Stein. It is a scroll sixteen feet long, containing one woodcut and a colophon that reads: "For Universal Free Distribution by Wang Chieh to Perpetuate the Memory of His Parents....May 11, 868."

In A.D. 932 a printed edition of the Classics was ordered by Prime Minister Feng Tao, the first mechanical copy made since thousands flocked to take rubbings of the Academy of Calligraphy's stone engravings, which were destroyed in A.D. 190. This

中國事物

BOOK SHOP. C. 1830.

set the imperial seal of approval on the process, and China burst into print. The ninth century saw the first gazette, and the tenth century the first newspaper, printed from wood blocks and displayed like a poster. Copperplate engraving was briefly tried, but was abandoned due to the unsuitability of Chinese inks and the expense of the metal itself. Playing cards and paper money were printed with wood blocks, and the paper money was quickly blamed for inflation.

Movable type (which was to appear in Europe four hundred years later) was invented in China around A.D. 1041, but abandoned entirely by A.D. 1400. Lovers of calligraphy thought it uncouth, while others pointed out (unnecessarily) that movable type was uneconomical in a language with a potentially infinite number of characters. Pi Sheng, the unlucky inventor, used wax to hold fired earthenware types in iron frames. Woodcuts were, by comparison, easy and cheap, and could be traced from the work of the best contemporary calligraphers. The Koreans later revived movable type and are universally credited with its invention.

The first books were printed on sheets that were glued together to form scrolls, in imitation of manuscripts, which in turn were bound in this manner. Books began to be bound in the modern manner (sewn between hard covers) during the Yuan Dynasty (A.D. 1279-1368), which also saw the publication of the first popular literature. By 1406 the imperial library boasted some three hundred thousand printed volumes and another six hundred thousand in manuscript.

Movable type got a second chance in China in the late seventeenth century, when the K'ang Hsi Emperor, at the instigation of the Jesuits, had a quarter of a million pieces of type engraved in copper. Official carelessness and cupidity caused the loss of this font, and metal type did not catch on in the Middle Kingdom until the 1850s, when an enterprising sort used it to print lottery tickets. One authority claims that until 1750 more books were printed in Chinese than in any other language on earth.

[See Ink, Seals, and Wood-block Prints.]

PUNS

Here is where spoken and written Chinese part company for good. Words like "pour" and "poor," "blew" and "blue," and "bare" and "bear," which are the exceptions in other languages, abound in Chinese. The word *i*, for instance, has sixty-nine separate meanings, including "barbarian," "soap," "doubt," "ant," "surplus," "city," and "hang." The tonal system adopted about A.D. 500 was an attempt to cope with this situation, but the Four Tones in modern use *(p'ing, sheng, ku, and chih)* relegate 156 meanings to *i* in the *chih* or falling tone—156 words that sound alike!

Bowing before the inevitable, the Chinese make use of this profusion of puns by punning symbolically. For example, the word for *litchi* (the fruit) sounds like the word for "many sons," so designs utilizing the *litchi* are common fertility motifs.

Intentional punning in Chinese can take on a Dickensian air. Characters in the novel *Hung Lou Meng (Dream of the Red Chamber)* are named things like "true matters concealed" or "pervading fragrance," which is a pun for "pushy." Chinese also pun onomatopoeically, where the sound is the sense, like *miao* for cat, *huo* for fire, and *ya* for duck.

[See Language.]

QUAIL

If cocks were nowhere to be found, and crickets were out of season, Chinese gamblers would inevitably quarrel over which quail were the fiercest. The Chinese carried their contestants around in a bag, which was hung from their girdles. They treated their quail with great consideration, if you allowed for their cramped living quarters. Before each match the quail were bathed very carefully. Then a little millet would be thrown on the ground, and the two adversaries would fight to the bitter end. The Chinese quail not only represent courage, due to their pugnacious character, but also poverty, on account of their ragged appearance.

QUEEN OF HEAVEN

For the Taoists the queen of heaven is somewhat analogous to the Buddhist goddess Kuan-Yin (the goddess of mercy), due to the fact that she traverses the sea, moves from the sun to the moon, and has a soft spot for the entreaties of humans in need.

The Queen of Heaven (T'ien Hou) is most popular among fishermen in her manifestation as goddess of the sea and mother of the North Star, guiding light to fishermen. Her devotees abstain from animal food on the third and twenty-seventh day of every month. Her feast day comes prior to the first day of the fishing season on the twenty-third of the third month. Offerings of meat are made, and incense and candles are burned. Shrines are dedicated to her along all Chinese waterways, and sacrifices are made before a new net is used for the first time. According to tradition fishing boats have an image of T'ien Hou, before which a lamp burns at all times.

QUOTATIONS OF CHAIRMAN MAO

It has been pointed out that many of Chairman Mao Tse-tung's quotations are basically common sense expressed in the form of simple proverbs. Modern Chinese who might have had trouble accepting common sense from traditional sources could

雙關語

鵪

天后

毛主席語錄

中
國
事
物

swallow it more easily if it came from the Great Herdsman himself. In less than three years after its publication in the late 1960s, 740 million copies of *Quotations of Chairman Mao* were issued—not to mention 96 million copies of his poetry, and 150 million copies of his *Selected Works*, along with 2 billion assorted pamphlets. That's pretty amazing, considering that it's almost impossible to find a copy of this little red book for sale anywhere today.

CHAIRMAN MAO AT A RALLY IN BEIJING IN 1965.

RATS

The rat is an emblem of timidity and meanness, and due to its food-hoarding abilities, a symbol of industry and prosperity. Rats are common in China and have played the same role in population control there that they have in Europe—through the transmission of various plagues. They are also popular food in Guangzhou, consumed both for health and as a hair restorative.

RATTAN

Fortunately there are fine rattan pieces among the array of Chinese furniture; otherwise Westerners could never hope to relax within the unmerciful confines of Chinese chairs, couches, and beds. Rattan, woven on a bamboo framework, has long been a favorite material for informal furniture, as well as for baskets and boxes. It is derived from one of the various climbing palms of the Calamus, which mainly grows in the Malay Peninsula. The furniture is lightweight, easily transportable, and relatively inexpensive.

RED EYEBROWS SOCIETY

In A.D. 9 a usurper, Wang Mang, seized the throne. He introduced radical reforms in land ownership, taxation, and commerce, which provoked much antagonism and a secret society, the Red Eyebrows. They were so called due to the makeup their members wore into battle. They arose in Shandong Province and played an important role in the uprising that overthrew Wang Mang in A.D. 23 and led to the founding of the Later Han Dynasty. However, when the Red Eyebrows continued with criminal activity after the overthrow, the new dynasty devised a simple plan to stop them. The imperial soldiers painted their eyebrows red, and confused and routed the real Red Eyebrows in battle.

RHINOCEROS HORN

The rhinoceros is not native to China, but as an exotic and impressive animal it was well known, especially since a live rhinoceros was always a welcome item when sent as a gift or tribute to the imperial court.

The horn of the rhinoceros, however, had a special value independent of the value of the animal itself. The horn was regarded as an antidote for poisons—a belief that seems to have begun in the fourth century, and spread from China to other parts

CEREMONIAL CUP CARVED OF RHINOCEROS HORN. EIGHTEENTH CENTURY.

鼠
籐
伏

紅
眉
會

犀
牛
角

中
國
事
物

of the world. The horns were often hollowed out to make medicinal cups, in imitation of older buffalo-horn cups, but many cups of rhinoceros horn were shaped much like any other Chinese cup.

Rhinoceros horn was also used as a precious substance, like mother-of-pearl, in ornamentation and jewelry, and high officials who could afford it sometimes wore belts decorated with plaques of the horn, which was as valued as jade or gold. Buddhist priests even used a sort of wand with curved tips as a kind of scepter when expounding scripture: These scepters were made of rhinoceros horn often decorated with other precious materials, or painted with exquisite designs.

The demand for rhinoceros horn was much greater than could be satisfied by animals sent as tribute or gift: A large trade grew up, and the near extinction of the rhinoceros in Indochina is due largely to this trade, which still persists, especially since the horn is also credited with aphrodisiac properties.

R I C E

Westerners tend to labor under the delusion that the Chinese eat nothing but rice and yet more rice, but Westerners should be forgiven, as they have been led astray by the Chinese language itself. There are about seven thousand different varieties of this grain, and the Chinese, while they do not name each and every one of these, distinguish among many kinds of rice: long-grain, short-grain, water-grown, upland, fragrant, sticky, red, ivory, brown, and dappled. They have numerous words as well for the rice crop in its various stages of ripeness, and a vocabulary concerned with the different methods of cooking rice.

The Chinese-language equivalent of "Hello, how are you?" is *"Ni ch'ih-kuo-fan ma?"* (Have you eaten rice?). To eat a meal is *ch'ih-fan* (to eat cooked rice); at a banquet, the last course served is a bowl of steamed rice, which one is expected to finish,

IRRIGATING AND WEEDING RICE PADDY. FROM THE *T'ien Kung K'ai Wu.*

down to the last grain. The children are warned that each grain left uneaten in the bowl will be a pockmark on the face of their future husband or wife, while the adults, who are aware of the enormous labor required to grow rice, show their respect without threats or cajoling. A sick man is referred to as one who "can't eat his rice." It is terribly unlucky to spill rice, and terribly rude to use only one hand when one's rice bowl is passed.

The worst insult a person can offer another is deliberately to spill his rice out on the ground. Losing one's job is spoken of as "breaking one's rice bowl." The Western custom of throwing rice at newly married couples would undoubtedly horrify the Chinese, although it is from them that we get both the rice and the notion that rice is a grain connected with fertility and felicity. At New Year's in some parts of China a bowl of rice is offered to the family ancestors; in other parts, popped rice, which is very like popcorn, is prepared as a holiday treat.

Chinese divide food into two groups: *fan* and *ts'ai*. *Fan* means cooked rice, but it can also mean the starchy part of the meal, be it millet or sorghum or noodles or bread. *Ts'ai* or *sung* are all the other foods served with *fan*: meat or vegetables or soy curd or birds' nests or whatever. Here, too, the Chinese sense of balance is exercised: A meal with too much *sung* is pretentious, and without rice one does not feel that one has eaten, but only the very poorest will make a meal solely of plain unadorned rice. The poor may sometimes make their rice go farther by cooking it as a sort of thickish soup, called by the Malay word *congee*, but even to this they will add, if they have it, a bit of fish or chicken.

Rice derives from an Indian wild grass called *newaree*. The Chinese have been cultivating this grain for over four thousand years. The classical Chinese term for agriculture is, in fact, synonymous with rice. The art of agriculture was originally taught to the Chinese by the legendary Emperor Shen Nung (2838-2698 B.C.), and it appears that very little has changed since he initiated the practice of "beating the spring ox." The fields are plowed, fertilized, and rice seedlings transplanted from their beds by hand. Irrigation is maintained during growing season by means of dikes or canals, which are drained when the rice is ready to be cut.

Rice spread throughout the East and kept going, arriving in Egypt about the fourth century B.C. By the fifteenth century rice was found all over Europe. English colonists in Charleston, South Carolina, were the first to cultivate rice successfully in the New World.

Today rice is the largest single crop in China. Because of China's vast population and demands on rice as an export item, the development of high-yielding, disease-resistant seeds has been of first priority. New China experimental research using radiation, lasers, hormones, and fast neutrons is being tried to develop new varieties of the seed.

ROSES

About to leave, yet by the lamplight she lingers—
Heartbroken, far from the vermilion door.
No need for the rouge-rain to cleanse fragrant cheeks:
Wait till the roses have faded,
he will come back.
                    —Chou Pang-yen (A.D. 1056-1121)

The Chinese were cultivating ornamental roses for centuries before this flower

中國事物

appeared in Western gardens. Modern roses are different from their forebears, of course, and the great bloom of hybridization occurred when Chinese roses were introduced into England toward the end of the eighteenth century. The most valuable innovation was the continuous blooming of the Chinese variety. The best-known species are the *Ch'iang Wei* (*Rosa multiflora*); the *Yueh Chi* (*Rosa chinensis*), better known as the Bengal rose; and the *Rosa rugosa*. Other singularly Chinese types were the "powdered-ball rose," the "lotus rose," and the hardy climber, the "Chinese rambler."

The Chinese would use dried rose petals to scent their tea as well as for culinary purposes, preparing a special sweet paste for flavoring certain dishes. A scented liquid, the "dew of roses," was also prepared from rose petals and enjoyed in the summertime as a cool drink.

SAGES

The sage, according to the Taoist philosopher Chuang Tzu, was one who tried to recreate the harmony of the *tao* of Nature within himself. The sage rejects the transitory values of society, and does not seek the honors or benefits pursued by men. Instead he pursues a life of balanced tranquillity, taking no action, and trying to imitate the rhythms of heaven and earth. The sage takes no action and is honored. "He is simple and plain and none in the world can compete with him in excellence." And again, "One who is in accord with the world is in harmony with men. To be in harmony with men means human happiness, and to be in harmony with Nature means the happiness of Nature."

Alongside the mystical qualities of quietistic life, Chuang Tzu's sage exhibited magical abilities, such as being able to mount the clouds and drive flying dragons, save men from disease, and bring a plentiful harvest. Because of these supernatural abilities the sages and men who lived lives of magic and contemplation soon began to ascend into heaven. Indeed, one of the goals of later Taoist sages was to attain immortality.

With the introduction of Buddhism into China, the notion of sagaciousness competed with the popular Buddhist tradition of monks looking for "rejection of the world" in their own quietistic mystical tradition. The two traditions became enmeshed in the popular imagination, and both borrowed each others' deified sages, putting them into enormously complex pantheons. The temples of China, both Buddhist and Taoist, were packed with the images and names of sages who had attained the status of *hsien*. But the two greatest sages of all China will always be Confucius and Lao Tzu.

[See THREE SAGES.]

SEAHORSES

Seahorses are most commonly found in Chinese art as a border pattern in paintings and on the backs of ancient bronze and tin mirrors. It is probable that this pattern was borrowed from the Greeks, for whom the seahorse played a large mythological role. Dried seahorse in Chinese pharmacies is a familiar sight. It is used to treat tumors and diseases of aging.

SEALS

Seals in China were never made with red wax or rings. The very earliest seals were uncovered among the treasures plowed up in An-yang, the capital of the Yin (Shang)

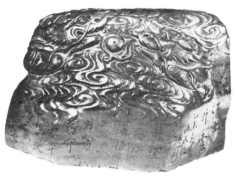 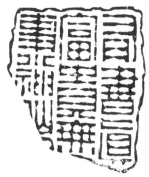

聖賢　砂石　海豹　秘密組織

CARVED STONE SEAL WITH ITS IMPRESSION MEANING "TO POSSESS LEARNING IS TRUE PROSPERITY, TO HAVE LEISURE IS TO BE LIKE A GOD."

Dynasty. This pair is between 3,000 and 4,000 years old, and their characters have not yet been deciphered. From the Yin to the Ch'in dynasties, about 1,500 years, a clay or metal seal was used to secure the string tying up the roll of bamboo strips that was the early Chinese book. Seals were also used on all correspondence and occasionally to secure packages.

More seals have been preserved from the Han Dynasty than from any other. Five chests with pairs of dragons lacquered on their lids yielded up 221 official seals and 1,070 personal seals engraved in a variety of scripts. Official seals measured about 2.4 centimeters square and gave one's official title. Personal seals are smaller, more eccentric in shape and script, and in addition to bearing one's personal name, can be used for artists' and writers' pseudonyms, dates, literary quotes, and the addresses of artists' studios.

From the first century B.C. to the sixth century A.D. silk and paper came to replace bamboo and wood strips as writing surfaces, and clay seals were slowly replaced by inked seals. From the sixth century on, red ink was made by mixing cinnabar with water or honey and later on with oil or wax, and these red seals were the only color printing known in China until the sixteenth century. The sixth century A.D. also saw the introduction of relief printing (a seal with red characters on a white background). Prior to this, all seals had been cut in intaglio (white characters on a red ground).

About the same time that artists in China began to sign their work, they also began to stamp it with seals that they had carved. This seal was supposed to authenticate an artist's work and was supposed to be destroyed after his death, but at times seals have been used to substantiate forgeries. Collectors' seals, used as sort of bookplates, but on paintings as well, began to appear in the Sung Dynasty, and from A.D. 1101 on, collectors began to collect seal prints, too.

Seals have been carved or cast of various substances, such as bronze, clay, pottery, ivory, wood, and jade, but most are incised in stones that bear names like transparent jelly stone, white hibiscus stone, pine green stone, and chicken blood stone.

SECRET SOCIETIES

China has been particularly fertile ground for the growth of secret societies. In the West we are most familiar with religious secret societies such as the Rosicrucians or Illuminati, or criminal groups like the Cosa Nostra, but in China secret societies were very often in the forefront of political change. The success of these secret societies

中
國
事
物

depended in large part on China's unique imperial monarchy, civil-service system, and rich religious symbolism.

The idea of imperial righteousness—that the monarch was the "Son of Heaven"—was closely connected with holistic beliefs about the universe. Natural calamities such as floods, or portents such as comets were held to indicate that the Emperor had failed in his duties and thereby lost his right to the throne. This belief when combined with the weather's resistance to political directives quite frequently led to popular rebellion.

The civil-service system, though it held sway for nearly fifteen hundred years, did not really reach into China's smaller villages. The market towns and farming villages held the lowest of bureaucratic offices, or yamen. Because they were unfettered by direct government control, they presented opportunities for subversion.

Like secret societies in most cultures, the Chinese drew on ritual to enforce the loyalty of their members. The particularly rich symbolism of Taoism and Buddhism (Confucianism being the philosophy of imperial regimes) provided meaningful rituals for secret societies.

The first recorded secret-society uprising—that of the Red Eyebrows—led to the overthrow of Wang Mang and the establishment of the Later Han Dynasty in A.D. 25. The later Han rulers were themselves victimized by secret societies such as the Copper Horses and the Iron Shins, which sprang from older states, clinging to their independence. These societies were associated with Taoist priests, who were frequently on bad terms with the government.

The unsettlement that followed the Han Dynasty produced a flowering of secret activity and produced three heroes of Chinese literature, Kuan Yu, Liu Pei, and Chang Fei, who swore a famous oath of blood brotherhood in a peach garden. They became heroes to later secret societies, and the "peach-garden oath" became a standard ritual.

The repression of Buddhism during the T'ang Dynasty (A.D. 618-906) led to many Buddhist secret societies. The most famous were the White Lotus or Red Turban rebels. They began as a meditative society in A.D. 376 (Ch'an-tao adopted the society's doctrine and transported it to Japan in 634) and were politicized during the T'ang era. Their greatest hour came in 1368 when a Buddhist monk drove the Mongols out of China, and Chu Yuan-Chang took the throne. The new dynasty took the name Ming (bright).

During the Ch'ing Dynasty (1644-1911) sects arose in bewildering numbers. The White Lotus were still around, changing their name to Incense-smelling Sect and White Yang Sect, to avoid suppression. The names of other sects indicated the colorful and symbolic nature of these groups. There were the Eight Dragons, the Nine Mansions, the Celestial Bamboo Sect, the Big Swords, the Small Daggers, the Yellow Beards, and many others.

In the nineteenth century these sects began more and more to aim their activities against foreigners and led ultimately to the Boxer Rebellion. The Boxers, or I Ho Chuan (which means the Fists of Righteous Harmony), gained their early reputation by massacring Western missionaries. The Boxers were believed to have supernatural powers, particularly the gift of invulnerability, and the Manchu court was quite afraid of their power. Their rituals involved prayer and incantation, during which the worshiper became possessed, while undergoing demonstrations of invulnerability.

In their violent attacks on foreigners the Boxers displayed the weakness that led to the disappearance of secret societies as a political force. They never produced a political program, which modern states require, but aimed only at government overthrow. Their effects therefore were not long-lasting.

[See Red Eyebrows Society and Triad Society.]

兜
椅

SEDAN CHAIR

Sedan chairs have been in use since ancient times in China, just as they were in the Middle East and in Europe through the Middle Ages. They are simultaneously a means of conveyance for the important and wealthy, and also fulfill numerous ritual functions.

The traditional Chinese sedan chair is constructed on a bamboo frame with bamboo carrying shafts. The passenger compartment is most often enclosed, or veiled to conceal the occupant from public view. The station, rank, or insignia of the chair's owner were frequently indicated by color, and markings on the outside, as well as by identical uniforms of the bearers, numbering from two to eight who carried the chair. Imperial family members were the only ones permitted to ride in yellow sedan chairs. The highest military honor, the *Pa-t'u-lu*, was awarded to Chinese generals in Ch'ing imperial times along with authorization to paint the props of their sedan chairs scarlet or purple.

The most common traditional use of sedan chairs by commoners was during the rituals of marriage and at funerals. Empty sedan chairs formed an important part of every funeral cortege in former times. Part of the Chinese marriage ceremony involves transportation of the bride in a completely sealed red sedan chair, with numerous feathered ornaments and carvings, from her parents' house to that of her bridegroom. The bridal chair is at the very end of the wedding procession, and the doors of the chair are opened by the bridesmaids only after the groom has asked to see his new wife.

Engraving of Chinese sedan chair used for carrying persons of rank.

中國事物

Until recent times, women did not only ride in sedan chairs on their weddings. The extreme seclusion in which upper-class women were kept required that they not be exposed to the public at any time. It was customary for unmarried girls, and even for the wives of gentlemen of means, to move about their daily routines completely enclosed in sedan chairs.

SEISMOLOGY

Systematic records have been kept of earthquakes in China from an early date. These records are the longest and most complete in existence for any geographical area.

Earthquakes were generally regarded as results of imbalance of *yang* and *yin*, the polar forces, within the earth. Ssu-ma Ch'ien records a statement attributed to Po-yang Fu: "When the *yang* is hidden and cannot come forth, or when the *yin* bars its way and it cannot rise up, then there is what we call an earthquake." As a result, it was thought that earthquakes, like other disasters, could be predicted astrologically.

The earliest known seismograph was produced in A.D. 132 by Chang Heng, who called it an "earthquake weathercock." It is described as a large bronze vessel about six feet in diameter. Around the outside of the vessel were eight dragon heads, each with a bronze ball in its mouth. Below each dragon was a toad with its mouth open, waiting to catch the ball. An earthquake was registered by the fall of one of the balls from a dragon's mouth into a toad's mouth; the direction the dragon and toad faced was the direction of the quake's epicenter.

Interest in these devices lasted well past the sixth century A.D., and seismographs were still being built at the beginning of the seventh century. The precise understanding of the mechanism sealed within the great bronze vessels does not seem to have lasted past the end of the T'ang Dynasty—that is, the beginning of the tenth century. Modern reconstructions of Chang Heng's seismograph suggest that there was a pendulum inside, and the tilting of the pendulum operated a mechanism that released a ball from the mouth of one of the dragons on the outside of the vessel.

Today China is still recognized as a world leader in earthquake technologies and predictions. Advanced research using animal sensitivity, radon gases, and astronomy, as well as thousands of trained field observers among the work force throughout the country, make China an important center in seismological research.

SEVEN EMOTIONS

A disciple asked Master Wang about the origin of evil. *The Record of Instructions* tells us that the master replied: "Joy, anger, grief, fear, love, hate, and desire are known as the Seven Emotions, and these seven are equally inherent in the human mind....When the Seven Feelings follow their natural course, they are all functions of intuitive knowledge and cannot be divided into good or evil."

SHADOW WALL

The Shadow Wall, sometimes referred to as a Shield Wall, is a nonfunctional ornamental structure. It was erected in front of official buildings in imperial China and protected the doorway from evil spirits and other noxious influences. On the side facing away from the building it was common to see an enormous red sun. It symbolized the *yang* principle and it reminded the officials entering the building to pursue purity and justice in their administration.

On the inner side of the wall, facing the doorway of the building, was depicted the mythical Beast of Greed (*T'ao-t'ieh*) as a representation of and warning against the vices of sensual self-indulgence, gluttony, and avarice. The Beast of Greed is shown with two large eyes, powerful mandibles from which curved tusks protrude, and a huge belly. It is said that the beast actually existed during the reign of Emperor Yao.

SHARKS' FINS

Sharks' fins are another texture food from Guangzhou cuisine. Traditionally, sharks' fins would form the third course of a wedding feast, which might have from eighteen to forty-six courses altogether. Sharks' fins are the dried, edible fins not only of sharks of various sorts but also of rays, skates, and swordfish. Caudal, pectoral, ventral, anal, and dorsal fins are sold in dried form; they come in several grades at different prices. The best fins are light in color and fairly thick and are often sold still attached to the base (comb fins). Sometimes the fins are boiled or steamed before drying, so that the skin and bones can be removed. What is left for sale is a gelatinous fringelike substance, varying in color from yellowish white (preferred) to a reddish brown.

The fins are used as the basis for a kind of bouillabaisse or seafood soup with crabmeat, onions, and roe, or are cooked as a casserole in an earthenware pot, or are used as a stuffing for duck. The fins are also good scrambled together with eggs, to which they add a texture of firm smoothness to the fluffiness of the eggs. To prepare the fins for cooking they must be cleaned and softened by soaking and boiling, and skinned and deboned, if necessary. Then the fins are boiled or steamed with water or stock and a little rice wine before being combined with other ingredients. Sharks fins are, in their roundabout way, extremely nourishing, and are popularly believed to have invigorating and aphrodisiacal qualities.

SHOES

In imperial China the "lily footed" women made their own silk or satin slippers, generally only three or four inches long. The heavily embroidered shoes were worn over the bandages that bound the feet. Some women with unbound feet made themselves look stylish by perching on pedestal shoes, which had a round wooden base fixed to the middle of the sole. When they walked on these, their gait resembled the mincing steps of their sisters with tiny feet.

The common people had to make do with what materials they had on hand. Once missionaries from the West were startled to find that their shipments of Bibles, so enthusiastically accepted by the local Chinese, had gone straight into saving their soles instead of their souls.

Silk, cotton, straw, and very little leather are commonly worn upon Chinese feet (when anything is worn at all; bare feet are still popular in country districts). After donning white silk or cotton stockings a Chinese man or a woman has a variety of shoes, clogs, sandals, and boots from which to choose.

Straw shoes—sandals for summer, closed-toe shoes that can be stuffed with cotton for winter—are popular, for though quickly worn out, they are easily made. Shoes of satin, silk, or cotton are most common. Occasionally they're graced with embroidery—a layer of cumulus clouds, a flight of butterflies, or the calligraphic sign for old age, which wished the wearer a long life.

Cloth shoes have soles of plastic or rubber. Chinese men will sometimes wear boots, especially during rainy times. Clogs with thick wooden soles that keep the wearer above the wet are popular then, too, with men and women both.

地震學

七情

影子牆

魚翅

鞋

中國事物

SHORT STORIES

The earliest Chinese stories we have are of the Han Dynasty, "written so vigorously," said Pearl Buck, "that to this day . . . . they run like galloping horses." Under Emperor Ming-ti (A.D. 57-75) of the Han, Buddhism was introduced into China, and the need to adapt and explain the *sutras* to an unlettered foreign audience produced new literary forms. By the Eastern Chin Dynasty (A.D. 317-420) a group of Buddhist hellfire preachers had captured the nation's interest by teaching the *sutras* through vivid stories of sulfurous gehennas and rosy paradises.

Whether to make sure that the stories would be clearly understood by all hearers, or as an effort to salvage the sonority of the *sutras'* polyphonic Sanskrit, Prince Tse Liang of Ching Ling proposed the Four Tone system in A.D. 489. This new music in the Chinese spoken language produced the unsurpassable T'ang poetry and an unworkable prose style called *pien-ti wen*, in which parallel sentences of four or six characters had to conform to a strict tonal pattern. *Pien-ti wen* passages were incorporated into the monkish and secular short stories to describe certain conventional subjects: war, or women, or an eloquent landscape.

By the year A.D. 756, when the eunuch Kao Li-shih comforted the Emperor Hsien Tsung after his abdication with popular stories, *pien-wen* (which originally meant illustrative text) were more often secular than sacred. In addition to the Buddhist *pien-wen*, people told each other ghost stories and detective stories, romances and adventures, tragedies and comedies. *Pien-wen* continued until the tenth century, by which time they had been almost completely supplanted in favor of *hua-pen* (prompt books). In the middle of this evolution the T'ang Dynasty produced stories of romantic love, mostly tragic, which to this day people discuss as if they were current gossip.

The new stories, *hua-pen*, were actually used as prompt books in the theater, as well as by puppeteers and shadow players. The new class of professional story-tellers that arose under Emperor Jen Tsung of the Sung Dynasty (A.D. 1023-32) used the *hua-pen* as *aides-mémoires* for their recitations, which often lasted a week or more. Poems, songs, and music were included at appropriate points in these narratives, and every day's episode had to end with a cliff-hanger. These story-telling techniques were transmitted through the short story whole into the early Chinese novel, just as some Western novels show traces of their beginnings in the popular journals. *Hua-pen* were written entirely in the vernacular.

The three great Ming novels, *San Kuo, Hsi Yu Chi*, and *Shui Hu Chuan*, were in fact based on story-tellers' narrations and *hua-pen*, and during the Ming Dynasty more than five major collections of *hua-pen* were made. A playwright named Feng Meng-lung gathered 120 stories from the Sung, Yuan, and Ming dynasties into three books: *Stories to Enlighten Men, Stories to Warn Men*, and *Stories to Awaken Men*. Ling Meng-tsu, who also wrote books on poetry and more than twenty operas, was responsible for the first and second collections of *Amazing Stories*, most of which he wrote. *Chin Ku Chi Kuan (Strange Stories Past and Present)* is a selection from these five books made by Pao Weng Lao-Jen. Each of these collections contains, for no presently understood reason, exactly forty stories.

[See NOVELS.]

SHUTTLECOCK

Shuttlecock, like kite flying, is a seasonal game among the Chinese. Like American football, shuttlecock is played late in the year, and like English soccer, the feet are used to keep the object in play. Europeans strike the shuttlecock with a battledore, an object similar to a Ping-Pong paddle, and it is considered a game mostly for girls. The more vigorous Chinese shuttlecock is played almost exclusively by men and boys.

The traditional shuttlecock was a ball made from eight to twenty layers of shark skin, topped by two outermost layers of snake skin, and crowned by three perfect duck feathers. Westerners may substitute a small cork ball and chicken feathers. The object of the game is to keep the shuttlecock in the air for as long as possible. Any number may play, standing in a rough circle; players who miss drop out. "Setting up" for a kick with the hand is permitted. Chinese kick with the inner side and the sole of the foot, both forward and backward. A good player can send the shuttlecock up twenty or thirty feet in the air and keep it going for hundreds of strokes.

SILK

The cunning Chinese, when asked by foreigners about the origin of silk, would casually reply that it was obtained from the fleeces of sheep, which on being sprinkled with water in the sunshine at certain seasons in the year would abound with fine threads. They managed to keep their secret until A.D. 300, when Roman Emperor Justinian enlisted the services of two Persian priests, who had lived in China for many years, to smuggle out some silk eggs in the hollow of their pilgrims' staffs. It was from these eggs that the West was supplied with silk for over twelve centuries when the overland trade with China fell off and silk from China became more and more rare.

Aristotle in his *History of Animals* describes "a certain great worm which has, as it were, horns, and differs from all others." This is the silkworm *Bombyx mori*. The silk first spun by the worm is called "floss" or "waste silk." The unraveling of the cocoon is the work of the filatures, done by hand and steam, and the resulting filaments of from four to six cocoons are united into a single thread. This then becomes the raw silk that is gathered into skeins.

Work was done on primitive looms by means of the weaver's fingers, but early in the history of weaving the Chinese invented the automatic draw loom. For plain

COLLECTING SILKWORMS. NINETEENTH CENTURY PAINTING ON RICE PAPER.

webs the weaver would use his feet, and through a system of treadles, lift the silk threads. This would free his hands to intersect the threads with the weft. What was left was the wonderful shimmering material that would adorn both the stately mandarin and European royalty.

After the Revolution of 1949 silk became less important to the Chinese, especially since the demand for luxury clothing dropped sharply. Recent developments in the export market, however, have revived silk production in China. It is now the main occupation and source of income for many communes in the South of China.

SILVERWORK

INTRICATELY WORKED SILVER VASE. NINETEENTH CENTURY.

The Chinese character for silver is composed of two elements: *ken* (obstinate) and *chin* (metal)—because silver is so difficult to come by in China. Although silver was mined in Yunnan, Jiangxi, Guizhou, and Sichuan, it was mainly imported from India. The finest silverwork produced in China was during the T'ang Dynasty. Ornamental spirals, frets, and key designs were common motifs, together with phoenixes, tigers, birds, demons, and other beasts.

During the T'ang Dynasty, Chinese silversmiths refined techniques that had been introduced to them from the Near East. Cups and bowls were decorated with tracings on the exterior. However, in order to conceal the reliefs on the interior, an inner bowl or lining was designed with an exact fit. It was almost impossible to detect the join. Not incidentally, this effect was also the beginning of the thermos as we know it today. Even if a cup were filled with hot liquid, it would remain cool to the touch. Silver scissors were popular export items, along with different types of cosmetic boxes. Hand mirrors were often covered in silver sheets. Among the most rare and interesting pieces are the globular incense burners that hang suspended, gimbal-fashion, on movable rings.

SLAVERY

Slavery was perhaps more moderate in China than it was in Western countries. A slave was forced into the role by economic factors, often in order to satisfy a family debt. He was Chinese, like his master. Master and slave accepted the idea that an abrupt reversal of fate was nothing more than the natural balance of life exerting itself. And in a country where gambling was so endemic that children bet on cricket fights, fortunes shifted quickly in fact as well as in theory.

If the slave was female, marriage would end her state of bondage, although there may have been no great difference between slavery and marriage in some cases. A contract would have been drawn up with the girl's family to retain their right of approval over the marriage and to prohibit her being sold into prostitution. If she bore a child to her master, by law she became a secondary wife. At death, sons would share equally in the estate, whether children of wives, concubines, or slaves.

The male slave did not have the same opportunity to escape by marriage, but he might work off the debt for which he was sold and even be set up in business by his owner. Although whipping and prostitution were sometimes part of slavery in China, on the whole the institution was much less dehumanizing than its Western equivalents.

SNAKES

The Chinese have a love-hate relationship with snakes. They love to eat them. Python steak is a great delicacy in southern China, and pythons can grow up to twenty feet. They hate snakes because the snake, unlike the omnipotent dragon, is said to represent all that's negative in the universe. In fact, all mental and physical ills are directly attributable to its malevolent influence. Pharmacologically speaking, the Chinese subscribe to the theory that like cures like. Therefore, snakes—and the more venomous the better—are avidly collected, their gall cut out, dried, powdered, or bottled, and used to cure everything from dandruff to dementia. During the T'ang Dynasty the imperial physician offered a remittance on all taxes to those who sent him two or three *chin-she* (golden serpents) per year. Most Chinese snakes are non-poisonous, although cobras are found in southern China.

SNUFF BOTTLES

Early Ch'ing references indicate that snuff was a "northern habit," basically centered in the imperial court. Its use didn't spread until the middle of the eighteenth century. The humid climate of China made snuff boxes impractical, so the Chinese adapted their *yao ying* (medicine bottles) with a cork top and a small spoon to contain snuff. A great deal of ingenuity in design made snuff bottles the new art form, actually an embodiment in miniature of the many varieties of China's fine arts. The bottles were beautiful to look at, reassuring to hold, and could easily be carried inside a sleeve. The most notorious snuff-bottle collector was Ho Shen, the Ch'ien-lung Emperor's chief adviser. He had a collection of over 2,390 bottles, and even so he specialized in only hardstone and amber bottles.

SOAP

Prior to being exposed to Western methods of soap production, the Chinese depended for their *fei tsao* on different kinds of soap trees. The most common source was the *Gymnocladus chinensis*, a leguminous shrub whose long pods contain a thick layer

銀器
奴隸
蛇
鼻煙壺
肥皂

中
國
事
物

of brown tallow. The pods would be cut up finely and ground into a paste with such perfumes as sandalwood, cloves, aloeswood, and musk. Occasional substitutes for soap were *ji-tzu* (animal sweetbread) and the oils of some plants.

SOAPSTONE

If the Chinese couldn't have jade, they would have it made. They tried virtually every kind of material as a substitute, but perhaps the most successful imitations were created from soapstone. It is especially deceptive in the form of carved grape clusters and other greenish fruits. The illusion cannot be sustained, however, because soapstone is notoriously soft. You can scratch it with a fingernail, or even break off a piece. And instead of the smoothness of jade, soapstone has a greasy feel to it.

Sometimes called French chalk, soapstone is a massive, amorphous variety of talc that is found all over the world. In China the best quality of soapstone is obtained near Fuzhou. It is also used in the manufacture of porcelain and chinaware, and in the making of certain toilet powders, tailor's chalk, and seals. From time to time an anonymous toiling artist might create a minor illusion of a masterpiece, but collectors are advised to heed a Chinese proverb when shopping for this breakable item: "The heart I can use, the head I can borrow." In other words, if you absolutely must have it now—now can wait.

SOYBEANS

What dairy products are to the West, soy products are to the East. The Chinese do not drink milk after infancy, and consider cheese and butter—which they call, unflatteringly, "cow oil," "milk cake," or "rotten milk"—disgusting. The first reaction of a Chinese to a well-aged Camembert or Brie might be comparable to a Westerners' first unsettling exposure to a hundred-year-old egg.

Soybeans in their natural state are not terribly digestible, but the technology for processing them follows Chinese history into the dim past. Liu Kan mentions *tou-fu* (bean curd) in the second century B.C., and the *Pen-ts'ao*, a Chinese herbal and materia medica published in the sixteenth century, contains a very complete recipe for making *tou-fu*. The French refer to *tou-fu* as *fromage de soya* (soy cheese), which sounds better than bean curd and is equally accurate.

Soy sauce (*chiang-yu*) is the next most common soybean product. It is made by fermenting soy flour and wheat or barley together with lactobacillus bacteria (cousins to the ones responsible for yogurt, sourdough starter, and summer sausages), salt, and yeast. The resultant sauce is horrendously nutritious and an excellent source of B vitamins. "Red cooked" Chinese dishes are those cooked in soy sauce, but "white cooked" dishes are often dipped in sauce when eaten.

Tou-fu is cooked and eaten many different ways, from fried to pickled. The whey left over from making *tou-fu* is used to produce soy milk, which provides a formula substitute for infants who are allergic to cows' milk. Bean paste or jam, sort of like Bovril, and called *miso* in Japanese, can be used as a flavoring in cooking or on its own as a sort of bouillon.

There is a genetic propensity among Chinese past infancy toward milk allergies. Due to a common enzyme deficiency, they cannot easily break down lactose. Historians point to the Chinese long-standing aversion to dairy foods as further proof of the antiquity of the noble soybean. If the Chinese had neither, they surmise, the Chinese diet would have been seriously unbalanced.

Soybean production has been encouraged in China today because it is a crop that can do well on agriculturally marginal land—the sides of roads and along ditchbanks. Furthermore, soybean products constitute a large proportion of the Chinese diet.

SPIRITS AND DEMONS

Until recently all Chinese believed the world to be populated with millions of *shen* and *kuei* who constantly interact with men. The *shen* are benevolent spirits, genies, gods, as well as the souls residing in living man. *Shen* protect men and intercede on the behalf of humans in a never-ending series of skirmishes with *kuei*.

Kuei depend on the living. They are ghosts, demons, goblins made of the dead who are not *shen*, and *kuei* must be maintained by their living relatives. *Kuei* are hideous and are often depicted as skeletons. *Kuei* are evil and lurk in dark places. They have no permanent resting place and have been locked out of the possibility of eternal bliss. They throw no shadows. Most *kuei* are considered malicious, deceitful, and harmful to men. They are responsible for all of the woes of mankind, especially plague, famine, and disease. Upon entering the human body they cause sickness, insanity, and death. There are *kuei* who come back seeking revenge against those who have wronged them in life, as well as those sent by gods to punish evildoers. They have been known to snatch away children. In short, whenever something bad happens, there's bound to be a *kuei* involved somewhere. Numerous charms, exorcisms, and religious practices such as burial furnishings exist for counteracting these malevolent spirits. Many of these techniques invoke the help of *shen*—and even more powerful gods.

[See AMULETS AND CHARMS and EXORCISM.]

SSU-MA CH'IEN

If for no other reason Ssu-ma Ch'ien would be remembered as the first biographer of Confucius and Lao Tzu. These are contained in the first real history of China, the *Shih Chi (Historical Record)*, completed about 91 B.C. Before the *Shih Chi*, so-called histories were mere jumbles of official documents, transcripts of speeches, and whatnot. Ssu-ma began with materials compiled by his father to write a comprehensive history of China from Chin Shih-Huang-Ti to about 101 B.C.; this project took Ssu-ma eighteen years to complete and ran to half a million characters.

At the age of ten Ssu-ma was able to read the Classics in archaic script. At twenty he left home and proceeded to wander all over China for the next fifteen years. In 110 B.C. his father, Ssu-ma Tan, died, and two years later Ssu-ma Ch'ien was appointed to his father's old post as *ta-shih-ling*, a sort of combination imperial secretary, librarian, historian, and astrologer. Using his father's notes he began work on the *Shih Chi*, taking time out in 104 B.C. to revise and reform the calendar.

In 99 B.C. Emperor Wu had Ssu-ma Ch'ien imprisoned, and the next year had him castrated. He was released, an understandably embittered man; in 96 B.C. he was once again appointed to an imperial post, which he did not pursue with any great eagerness. In his autobiography he admits quite freely that pride alone prevented his suicide. He was about fifty-five when he completed the *Shih Chi*; he died a few years later.

STONE CHIMES

Some stones can become musical instruments. When they are struck, they produce a musical note—the sound may be either bell-like or low and muffled. These sonorous stones are found in a few scattered parts of the earth, including Ethiopia, Venezuela,

滑石

大豆

妖魔鬼怪

司馬遷

石鐘

中
國
事
物

Sardinia, and China.

The Chinese may have played tuned stones (*ch'ing*) as long ago as 2300 B.C. A chant by a court musician of that era refers to the musical stone. Later, the Chinese formed an instrument, the *pien-ch'ing*, by gathering a set of tuned stones, in graduated sizes and thicknesses. The stones are cut in an L shape and the angled corner of the stone is pierced so that a string can be run through it. The stones are then suspended in two rows in a decorated wooden frame. There are usually sixteen stones.

Now stone chimes are used only in monasteries. The Heavenly Temple of Beijing contains an eighteenth-century set of stone chimes made of green nephrite. Confucius said, "A concert is complete when the large bell proclaims the commencement of the music and sonorous stone proclaims its close."

STONE RUBBINGS

For centuries stone rubbings were the accepted method for reproducing calligraphy. Impressions have been taken off stone or bronze very likely since the introduction of paper around A.D. 105. During the Sung Dynasty there was a fad for making rubbings of Han tomb inscriptions. A good grade of paper is dampened and pressed gently into the incisions with a stubbly brush. After one paper has dried, ink (either cinnabar red or soot black) is spread over the raised surfaces of the paper with a brush or dauber. Sometimes a very soft ink stick is rubbed over the paper in a process similar to the European crayon method. Archaeologists and historians use rubbings to help them decipher very faint inscriptions without harm to the often fragile originals. Paul Pelliot found many stone rubbings dating perhaps from A.D. 400-900 during his 1908 visit to the caves at Tun-huang.

STOVE BEDS

In northern China it is quite common to find beds built over stoves made of brick. The stove beds are called *k'ang*, and in wintertime a permanent fire is built in the stove to keep the house and the bed warm.

Until the introduction of electric blankets in the Western world, the only equivalent techniques for warming beds consisted of the low-efficiency hot-water bottle, and the heavy cast-iron bed warmers, which were filled with hot coals and run between sheets and covers to warm them before the bed was occupied.

STRINGED INSTRUMENTS

"The instrument of the holy Kings," as it is sometimes called, the seven-stringed *ch'in* is played now much as it was two thousand years ago. This zitherlike instrument was considered an essential part of the scholar's life, and thus holds a special place among Chinese stringed instruments. This does not mean that every scholar could play the *ch'in*—even though he might write pages of poetry extolling his own instrument. Wrote the Chin poet T'ao Ch'ien, who supposedly had a *ch'in* without strings: "I have acquired the deeper significance of the *ch'in*; why should I strive after the sound of the strings?"

The beauty of *ch'in* music lies not in the succession of notes making a melody, but in each note by itself. The same note may have different qualities, depending on the string it is played on, which finger pulls the string, and how the string is plucked. There are twenty-six different kinds of vibrato (ways of shaking the finger on a string to produce a quavering tone) and innumerable ornamentations. Like the Western violin or piano, the *ch'in* requires much practice to achieve technical skill in the fingers.

拓本　炕

弦樂器

CONFUCIUS PLAYING THE CH'IN. WOODCUT.

Written music for the *ch'in* is unusual because the characters do not refer to exact pitches. Instead, they tell which string to play; which finger of the right hand should play the note and whether to pull toward or away from the player; which finger of the left hand should touch the string, where, and how. This method, which apparently dates back nearly two thousand years, has resulted in more than two hundred special signs.

中
國
事
物

In ancient literature, the *ch'in* is usually associated with the *se*, a twenty-five-stringed zither. One ode in the *Book of Songs* says, "Happy union with wife and children is like the music of *ch'in* and *se*."

Although bigger than the *ch'in*, the *se* is simpler and probably older. The twenty-five strings are all the same length and thickness. Each string has its own movable bridge, a piece of wood that lifts the string off the body of the instrument. The strings are tuned by moving the bridge. Since the *se* is relatively large, it is placed on two trestles to be played.

Confucius, it is believed, played both the *se* and the *ch'in*. The *Book of Rites* has many references to the two instruments: A man is not to play them if his parents are sick; a student should not step over a *se* or *ch'in* belonging to his master; an official should always have both of them at hand.

Folk music makes frequent use of the *erh-hu*, the two-stringed violin, and the *yueh-ch'in*, the moon guitar. A four-stringed, pear-shaped lute, the *p'i-p'a*, became the dominant stringed instrument during the Sui and T'ang dynasties and was used extensively in ensembles. Players could accompany songs or play alone, drawing from a repertoire of descriptive solo pieces. One such piece, still popular, is "The Last Battle of Hsiang Yu," in which the player slides his finger along the string and taps the instrument to convey the course of the battle.

SUICIDE

If you received a gift from the Emperor of a long yellow-silk sash, you might consider it a most generous present even though you were supposed to employ it to strangle yourself. Your alternative in the matter, beheading or some more hideous capital punishment, would reflect against your family, while the obligatory suicide was without dishonor. Suicide was commonly undertaken by hanging, by diving into a well, or by indulging in an excess of opium. Insolvency would be cause enough, and a bride, oppressed by her new in-laws, might resort to it. Suicide was also employed as a means of saving "face."

If you had been offended by a neighbor, committing suicide on the front step of his house would be a remarkably effective form of retaliation. The officials would institute a very costly "investigation." Then too, he would be expected to pay the cost of your funeral, since you died on his premises. As if this weren't sufficient punishment, it was thought that the spirit of a suicide victim remained at the scene and did not rest until it could cause another person to lose his life in the same way. So widespread was this belief that the house where a suicide had occurred would often be considered uninhabitable. Your neighbor wouldn't even be able to sell it and move away from your restless spirit. It's hard to imagine a more thorough revenge.

SUNDIALS AND TIMEPIECES

The sundial in China probably developed from an astronomical instrument, the gnomon. The gnomon is used to measure the distance of heavenly bodies by measuring the length of a shadow cast by a vertical pole, while the sundial measures time by measuring the direction of a shadow cast by an inclined pole onto a regularly graduated surface.

The gnomon was developed in China by the fourth century B.C., and the sundial is mentioned by the first century B.C. The typically Chinese sundial is one in which the pole used to cast the shadow is vertical to the plate on which the shadow is cast; it is the plate itself that is tilted. When the plate is horizontal and the pole is tilted, the markings on the plate must vary so that the shadow will take the same time to move from, say, the mark for one o'clock to two o'clock that it takes to move from seven o'clock to eight o'clock. When the pole is vertical to the plate, and the plate is tilted, however, the markings can be equidistant.

The problem with measuring time directly from the sun is that it varies with the slight irregularities of the earth's orbit; thus, if you are trying to time some delicate process, you have to make corrections according to the time of year you are working. To get an unvarying measure of time, a mechanical device of some sort is needed.

There are records of standardized incense and oil lamps being used to measure various industrial and religious undertakings, like the length of an acid bath, or of a meditation period. These have the advantage that they can be used at night, but their disadvantage is that it can be hard to be sure you have standardized the rate of combustion.

The Chinese developed a special version of the clepsydra, or water clock, for use when very precise measurements of time were necessary. The Chinese clepsydra operates by letting water flow into a vessel at a standard rate. Inside the vessel is a float with an indicator on it, rather like the dipstick used to measure oil in an automobile. As the water level rises so does the float, and the time can be read off the scale of the indicator as it passes a pointer on the neck of the vessel.

There was another type of water clock in which the water flowing into a vessel was weighed: If the flow of water was regular, the increase in weight of the vessel would be regular, and short but delicate processes or events could be timed by referring to the readings on the balance arm.

The first mention of an inflow clepsydra dates from about A.D. 85, but archaeological evidence shows that such "clocks" existed between 75 and 201 B.C. They were used for official, ceremonial time-keeping until after 1900, although in daily life they had been replaced by Western-style clocks.

The Chinese were aware of all the adjustments needed to keep the water clocks accurate—not just maintaining a constant head of water in the inflow tank, but also regulating the temperature to keep the water at a constant viscosity (or at least to keep it from freezing)—and to control the rate of evaporation. Huan T'an, a court official who lived between 40 B.C. and A.D. 30, observed that one has to adjust such clocks "at dusk and at dawn, by day and by night, comparing them with the shadow of the sun and the divisions of the starry sky. In the end, one can get them to run correctly."

European timepieces were introduced in the late seventeenth century by Jesuits at the imperial court. The Emperor, as a patron of Western science, established a workshop within the Department of Public Works for the fabrication of clocks and watches. [See ASTRONOMICAL INSTRUMENTS and OBSERVATORIES.]

T'AI CHI CH'UAN

T'ai chi ch'uan (pronounced tie-gee-chwan) is a martial art deeply rooted in Taoist philosophy and practice. T'ai chi is a very ancient term that signifies the "absolute" or the "ultimate," and t'ai chi ch'uan, along with its sister art, shao-lin, are the oldest of the martial arts, going back about a thousand years. The father of t'ai chi was a Taoist monk named Chang San-feng (nicknamed "the Immortal"), who lived during the Sung Dynasty, about the twelfth century A.D.

Legend has it that Chang San-feng was awakened one morning by the sound of scuffling under his window. Looking out, he observed a crane engaged in mortal combat with a snake, and, from their thrusts and parries, he came up with the basic

自殺　日規計時　太極拳

中國事物

principle of *t'ai chi*, the balanced alternation of strength and yielding. (The battle, incidentally, lasted several days and ended in a draw.) Chang San-feng began to watch other wild animals, as well as the clouds, water, trees, and the wind, and synthesized these natural movements into a system of calisthenics and sparring.

In *t'ai chi* exercises, the *yang* and the *yin* energies are brought into perfect balance and harmony—a dynamic balance of strength and inner change. The monk Chang San-feng theorized that once perfect equilibrium was achieved, it would be possible to attain perfect health. *T'ai chi* not only promotes the balance of opposing forces, but also enhances the flow of *ch'i* (energy) throughout the body.

Practiced correctly, the hundred-odd forms that make up the ritual movement flow smoothly into one another, without interruption. Each motion is performed slowly, as if "swimming in air." For centuries *t'ai chi* was practiced only by Chinese nobility. Today, in New China, thousands perform the exercises daily in parks, as a form of exercise, and as preventive medicine.

TANGRAMS

In *The Eighth Book of Tan*, published in 1903, American puzzle expert Sam Loyd claims that the Chinese have been playing this puzzle game for over four thousand years, but he is probably wrong. First mention of the game appears in a Chinese book published in 1803. Tangrams swept Europe and America throughout the nineteenth century, ensnaring such notables as Lewis Carroll and Edgar Allan Poe. The seven puzzle pieces, or *tans*, became decorative motifs in nineteenth-century China, finding their way onto dishes, lacquer boxes, and inlaid tables.

Chinese folklore insists that tangrams were accidentally invented by an anonymous and clumsy gentleman who dropped a square tile onto the floor, where it broke into seven pieces. When he tried to assemble the pieces he instead found himself forming sailboats, roosters, and mountains. A tangram set may be any size, provided that its pieces can be rejoined to form a square. A seven-piece set contains at least sixteen thousand possible designs, using all of the pieces without overlapping any.

In China today tangrams are regarded as a children's game, but adult mathematicians sometimes use the *tans* to form geometric figures with a given number of sides (for instance, how many six-sided polygons can be devised?). Most people, however, just content themselves with making witty pictures of rabbits, windmills, dancers, and the like, or with duplicating a complex shape given in outline form in one of the tangram books. The game can be rendered yet more decorative by making the pieces different colors, or by combining several sets.

TAO

The original meaning of *tao* is to be found in the Chinese conception of the world as a living whole. The natural order of this world is *tao*. In the macrocosmic world it is expressed in the harmony and precision of the movements of the heavenly bodies. For everything in heaven there is precise correspondence on earth. There is therefore a *tao*, or order of Nature, manifested through the macrocosm and reflected upon the terrestrial reality of mountains, rivers, all of life, and consciousness.

Tao existed before the beginning of creation and was present in the Great Ultimate Principle from which *yin* and *yang* were formed, resulting in the generation of all things. The concept of an all-pervasive order of Nature that was at once immutable and always changing became important to every one of China's main religious and philosophical traditions.

The earliest Taoist work was the *Tao-te-ching* of Lao Tzu, which was closely followed by the more mystical writings of Chuang Tzu. These and other Taoist thinkers held that it was of vast importance to follow the "way" (*tao*) of Nature. For the Taoists, the *tao* encompassed all of the contradictions of Nature in a pattern that was not readily understandable, but the contemplation of which was one of the principal occupations of the sage.

[See GREAT ULTIMATE PRINCIPLE, PHILOSOPHERS, TAOISM, TAO-TE-CHING, and YIN AND YANG.]

THE "DIAGRAMS OF CHANGE" FROM THE NORTHERN SUNG DYNASTY ILLUSTRATES THE ACTION OF THE *tao*.

TAO-TE-CHING

Even his biographer knew very little about him. "Lao Tzu," complained Ssu-ma Ch'ien in his *Shih Chi (Historical Record*, 92 B.C.), "was a gentleman who lived in retirement from the world." He may have been born between 604 and 570 B.C. in the state of Ch'u in what is now Henan. His surname was Li, for the plum tree under which he was born. Comets or falling stars attended at his conception; his mother carried him in her womb for sixty-two, or seventy-two, or eighty-one years.

The infant Lao Tzu, if he ever existed, was incongruously capped at birth with the white hair of an old man. The words Lao Tzu may mean "old child," or "old philosopher," or simply "elder." There were a number of Taoist works extant in Ssu-ma Ch'ien's time with titles like *The Old Man* or *The Elder*, and it could easily be that the man was named after the book, instead of the more usual method.

七巧板

道

道德經

中國事物

From Ssu-ma Ch'ien we have an account of a meeting between Confucius and Lao Tzu in 517 B.C. at the imperial library of which Lao Tzu was a curator. Confucius had supposedly traveled to Luoyang to question his elder on the subject of ceremonies, and Lao Tzu is mentioned four times in the *Li Chi (Book of Rites)*. Old Li was remarkably rude to young K'ung. "The men about whom you talk are dead," he said, "and their bones are moldered to dust; only their words are left....Put away your proud air and many desires, your insinuating habit and wild will....this is all I have to tell you." Confucius was suitably impressed, and afterward told his students: "Today I have seen Lao Tzu, and can only compare him to the dragon."

At some point it became apparent to Lao Tzu that the Chou Dynasty was in decline, and resigning his post at the imperial library, he disappeared into oblivion. On his way out of the kingdom Lao Tzu had to pass through a barrier gate at Han Ku. There the gatekeeper, Kuan Yin, sensing his intentions, insisted on his writing a book before leaving. Lao Tzu is obligingly supposed to have written a book of about five thousand characters in two parts, the *Tao* and the *Te*.

The *Tao-te-ching* contains only the vaguest sort of history and not a single proper name. Over half of it is considerably older than the rest, and this is in rhymed verses. As a Taoist divinatory work it was spared the flames of Ch'in Shih-Huang-Ti. Like most very ancient books it was not so much written as compiled. Lao Tzu's students wrote down what they could remember of his sayings on slips of fragile bamboo.

The *Tao-te-ching* is shorter than the shortest gospel. Of the *Tao-te-ching*'s eighty-one brief chapters only one, the twentieth, is said to be slightly autobiographical. It was first translated into Latin by Jesuit missionaries and in that form arrived in London in 1788. Since then the *Tao-te-ching* has been translated into English alone more than thirty times.

TAOISM

By the second century B.C., the philosophy of Nature—Taoism—had penetrated the Chinese imagination and combined with various primitive shamanistic traditions into a popular religion. The Taoist church spread rapidly due to the pragmatic applications of the belief in a religion of Nature. Aside from the magic healing in charms, and thousands of mythological spirits and gods incorporated into organized Taoism, there was a serious tradition exploring the frontiers of science, especially in medicine and alchemy. All of this was done in search of an elixir of immortality, which the Taoists believed existed.

The Taoist religion, although based on the philosophy of the classical period, bears little resemblance to the teachings of its founding philosophers. Along with Buddhism and Confucianism, it serves more as a repository of Chinese beliefs and practices popular through the ages. The Taoists created and maintained elaborate mythologies and pantheons, as well as charms and magical traditions used by most Chinese until recent times. The Taoist church and tradition were so receptive that they could absorb every facet of popular Chinese belief through the centuries, and remain to this day fantastic amalgams of sometimes contradictory superstitions, myths, practices, and medical traditions.

[See PHILOSOPHERS; TAO, and TAO-TE-CHING.]

TAOIST SEX

China's revered physician Sun S'su-Mo (A.D. 581-682) explained, "If you can make love a hundred times without emission you can live a long life." The Taoists believed

道教　道教性學

LOVERS READING AN EROTIC BOOK. FROM THE K'ANG-HSI PERIOD.

the male life force was contained in a mixture of his breath and his *ching* (semen). Frequent ejaculations would rapidly deplete the man's *ching* and leave him susceptible to exhaustion and disease.

But if a man should avoid ejaculation, that did not mean he should abstain from sex. The balanced life required bringing together the feminine (*yin*) and masculine (*yang*) elements. The female life force was contained in the fluids lubricating her vagina. The more satisfaction the woman derived from making love, the more *yin* energy was made available to balance her lover's *yang* force.

中
國
事
物

The Taoist teachings recommend sexual union as often as three or four times a day, and Taoist sex manuals explained an endless variety of sexual techniques. Love positions had names such as "Leaping Wild Horses" and "Sky-soaring Butterfly." There were poetic descriptions of different styles of thrusting with the jade stalk; it could strike out to the left and right as a brave warrior trying to break up the enemy ranks, or move up and down as a wild horse bucking through a stream, or it might appear and disappear like a flock of seagulls on the waves.

The Taoist link between good health and lovemaking long into old age influenced the prescription of love as often as possible. Taoists recommend love affairs between older men and younger women, as well as between older women and younger men, claiming that the energy of the younger partner adds to the health of the older, while the younger lover gains a better understanding of love techniques from someone with experience.

TAXES

Taxation in China has been primarily dependent upon the systems of land ownership. Two views of land ownership have held sway in China's past. Throughout the imperial age Confucian theorists held that all land was subject to state ownership and that in an early "golden age" land had been worked by farming units of eight families. The opposing realist, or "legalist" view, first given credence under the government of Ch'in (221-207 B.C.), encouraged private ownership and use of land in the hopes of achieving a more prosperous agriculture. For this reason, land purchase and private holdings were legal during the early dynasties, and imperial revenues came from a property tax based on a percentage of the yield of the land. There was, in addition, a poll tax, usually paid in coin, levied in accordance with a person's age. There were periodic revolts against this system because it led to extremely unequal distributions of land and because powerful private landowners could become threats to the central government.

At the outset of the T'ang Empire (A.D. 618) the government undertook to give equal shares of land to all families. In return the families paid regular dues of grain and cloth and were liable to render twenty days' service annually. Later dynasties continually sought methods to raise revenues (though none were as important as land taxes). These included taxes on forest or lakeland produce, commercial property, and transportation vehicles. Taxes were sometimes declared on the monetary holdings of the rich, and during emergencies forced loans were demanded. In the Ch'ing period (1644-1911) tariffs were levied on all merchandise passing through some thirty points of control inside China.

Taxes in New China are once again based primarily on land taxes, although the growth of industry is creating new revenues. A progressive system of revenue sharing is the principal mechanism for redistributing resources among China's poorer provinces. There is no personal income tax in China.

TEA

Tea drinking began in China so long ago that its origins have become immersed in legend. The Chinese credit the discovery of the plant to Shen Nung, a mythical Emperor who reigned five millennia ago and who was known as the Divine Healer. One story says that Shen Nung was boiling water to drink when a few leaves fell in from an overhanging bush. From the wonderful aroma that arose from the infusion, Shen Nung discovered tea's value. He made a gift of the plant to his subjects, who first used it as a medicinal herb.

Most scholars believe that tea was in cultivation by A.D. 350. By the fifth century A.D., it was listed along with vinegar, noodles, and cabbage as an article of trade. By then, too, special groves of tea had been reserved for the Emperor. The poet Chang Meng-yan wrote that tea "superimposes the Six Passions/content and anger, sorrow and joy, like and dislike;/the taste for it spreads over the Nine Districts." Since the Nine Districts made up the entire kingdom of China at that time, tea was well on its way to becoming the national drink. About the eighth century, the Chinese adopted their current term for tea, *ch'a.* (When the Dutch first encountered tea, they heard the Amoy dialect word, pronounced *t'e,* and used that term, which passed into English.)

Although Lu Yu's classic *Book of Tea (Ch'a Ching)* was written during the eighth century, tea drinking did not come into its own until the Sung dynasty in the tenth century. In the thirteenth and fourteenth centuries the tea cult transferred to Japan, where it continues to flourish today. The tea of Lu Yu's time was made from pressed cakes of leaves. As to the manufacture of the cakes, Lu Yu writes tersely: "All there is to making tea is to pick it, steam it, pound it, shape it, dry it, tie it, and seal it." His description of the shapes of the leaves, however, are poetic: "Tea may shrink and crinkle like a Mongol's boots. Or it may look like the dewlap of a wild ox. . . . It can look like a mushroom in whirling flight just as clouds do when they float out from behind a mountain peak."

This remarkable plant that has exerted such influence on the world is a flowering shrub, *Camellia sinensis.* In the wild, the tea plant is more of a tree than a bush, reaching a height of some thirty feet. To simplify cultivation, however, the plants are pruned back to three to four feet. All the many varieties of tea come from the same plant. The differences in flavor arise from soil, climate, age of the leaf, time of harvest, and method of preparation. Tea grows best in tropical to subtropical climates. It is picked when it "flushes," or sends forth young, tender leaves. The leaves are harvested (plucked) by hand—in China, traditionally a woman's task. Once the leaves are harvested, they are processed in one of three ways that result in their becoming black, green, or oolong tea.

A century ago, China's annual exports of tea reached nearly 300 million pounds. Although India and Ceylon began to rival China in the tea trade, China's production before World War II was almost half the world total. The disruptions of war and the new priorities of the Communist Government caused output to drop drastically. The 447 million pounds of tea grown in 1972 were less than half the pre-World War II total. And China now contributes only 6 per cent of world tea exports. There is currently some evidence, however, that China is re-emphasizing tea cultivation.

TEAPOTS

Sharp mouth, big belly, ear
  placed rather high;
Proud and boastful ever barely
  escaping hunger and chill.
Too small to contain things
  of grandeur,
You make waves out of a few
  inches of water!
—Chang Hsieh (A.D. 1693-1765)

造瓶

中國事物

TEAPOT FACTORY SCENE WITH POTTERY WHEELS. FROM THE *T'ien Kung K'ai Wu.*

The Chinese consider the *I-hsing*-ware teapots to be absolutely the best for brewing tea. The *I-hsing*-ware pots are known for their ability to retain the taste, the color, and the aroma of tea leaves. Even in hot weather tea that is left overnight in an *I-hsing* pot will remain fresh. The pots are never washed. The old leaves are merely emptied, and the interior rinsed with cold water. Over a long period of use, the teapots will develop a rich patina that is highly prized by the connoisseur. The first recorded *I-hsing*-ware pots date back to the late Ming Dynasty. A strange monk was said to have appeared in the village one day, crying out: "Riches and honors for sale!..." The villagers laughed at him until he led them to a cave in the hills where they started to dig and discovered clay of five different colors that were brilliant as brocade. The teapots are made in a variety of shapes—from stylized objects of nature, like peaches or pomegranates, to more utilitarian models. According to Lu Yu, author of the classic *Book of Tea* (A.D. 804), *I-hsing*-ware cups are also the best suited for tea drinking. Being of a neutral shade, they effectively intensify and emphasize the color of the tea. He writes, "The first cup should have a haunting flavor, strange and lasting. There are those who allow it to continue simmering to nourish the elegance and retain the froth even through a first, second, and third cup. After the third cup, one should not drink more than a fourth or a fifth cup unless he is very thirsty...."

THEATER

Mei Lan-fang, one of the greatest Chinese opera singer-actors, was scheduled to open in Shanghai when the city fell to the Communists. Anxious ticket-holders did not dare to attend such a classic event as a Chinese opera, so for the first time in his career Mei Lan-fang performed to an almost empty house. The only people in the audience, applauding enthusiastically, were Mao Tse-tung himself, along with his top-ranking Party members.

Chinese classic theater—more accurately called "opera"—originated in Beijing, or *ching-hsi*, "the capital of theater." First historical references date back to the T'ang Dynasty, when there is mention of the "students of the Pear Garden," a conservatory established by Emperor Hsuan Tsu. Its dramatic form, which was crystallized in the nineteenth century under the Manchus, was that of a musical tragedy with comic interludes. Chinese actors, exclusively male, were singers who punctuated their dialogue with arias and recitatives. There are over five hundred plays in the repertoire of the Chinese theater, and these are either military or civilian in genre. Military plays featured loyal generals, generous emperors, and wise officials. Civilian plays focused on domestic joys and sorrows, home dramas with filial piety as the main theme, stories about unfaithful wives, and the effect of ghosts on people.

Makeup, masks, and costumes are a large part of the productions, and in China they are thoroughly standardized so that each role is readily identifiable. For example, a red costume expresses loyalty or a loyal subject, while a deeply lined face mask suggests a warrior or a general. Curiously, there are no sets. Drums, gongs, and cymbals supply the illusions of set and setting, the passage of time, and changing emotions. Once barred from theatrical production, women are now encouraged to participate, and since the end of Mao Tse-tung's regime, in 1976, many new and innovative themes have augmented the traditional in opera, drama, and dance.

THREE-CHARACTER CLASSIC

Until recently the *Three-character Classic* was the basic primer that was the literary fare of Chinese tots. In use for over 600 years, it contains the wisdom of the Middle

戲院

三字經

中
國
事
物

Kingdom—philosophy, biography, as well as common subjects—served up in lines of three characters each in a doggerel rhyme. The 560 different characters had to be memorized, although the meaning was usually lost on the budding scholars.

THREE MOST DESIRABLE OBJECTS

Advertising copywriters in China did not have to resort to jingles or come up with catchy slogans in order to sell their products. Instead it was considered sufficient inducement merely to extol the moral benefits of the merchandise. A common advertising approach was the *san to*, or the "Three Most Desirable Objects" (sons, money, and a long life). These were represented by the figures of a child, an official, and an old man accompanied by a stork. They were chiefly used in marketing remedies for anemia and debility.

THREE POWERS OF NATURE

According to the Taoists, the Three Powers of Nature or Three Spiritual Energies are heaven, *yang* (the male principle) and *yin* (the female). None of these has the power to bestow life in itself. It is only a union of the three that embodies the creative force. An infamous Chinese secret society, the Triads, adopted the Three Powers of Nature as their emblem.

THREE PURE ONES

This Taoist triad occupies three different heavens. Yu Huang, the Jade Ruler, lives on Jade Mountain, and is attended by various saints. Tao Chun controls the influences of *yin* and *yang*, and has heroes working for him. Lao Tzu lives among the immortals. Some Taoist iconoclasts suspect that Lao Tzu is actually behind the entire operation, and that the Three Pure Ones are really the personification of Lao Tzu transformed through a single breath into three individuals.

THREE SAGES

They are also the Three Friends—Buddha, Lao Tzu, and Confucius. These enlightened beings are supposed to have drawn their philosophies from the same source, and are frequently depicted in a symbolic attitude standing around a well. According to the *I Ching*, "The well is there for all. No one is forbidden to take water from it. No matter how many come, all find what they need....Wealth is inexhaustible; the more that people draw from him, the greater his wealth becomes."

TOBACCO

"Smoke weed" or *yen-ts'ao* was one of the evil gifts of the New World to the Old. Tobacco was introduced to China around A.D. 1620 via the Philippines. The people of Fujian were the first to pick up the habit. Now tobacco is grown all over the Middle Kingdom. Curiously, the Chinese take very little care in the cultivation and the curing of the weed. Much of it invariably loses its flavor and strength, and becomes moldy because it is not adequately protected from dampness.

The Chinese considered tobacco to be an antimalarial drug, and in order to insure this effect they mixed small amounts of arsenic in the leaves before curing them. However, they did recognize the negative effects of smoking. *Hao-fei sun-hsueh* refers to "wasting lungs and injuring blood." It was also said to result in *sun-jung* ("injuring the features"), since tobacco smoke would cause a chronic squint and make the skin appear sallow.

The most amazing Chinese innovation in tobacco was in their use of it for fishing. The flower stalks and leaves, laced with the usual mixture of arsenic, would be dropped into ponds and streams within green walnut shells. The fish would float up to the surface, stunned and ready for the picking.

In New China tobacco is a major industry. Many products are produced to meet a widespread domestic demand. Heavy cigarette smoking is common among the Chinese. One brand, Panda, incorporates foreign tobacco in its mixture. The cost and scarcity make Panda one of China's rare status items.

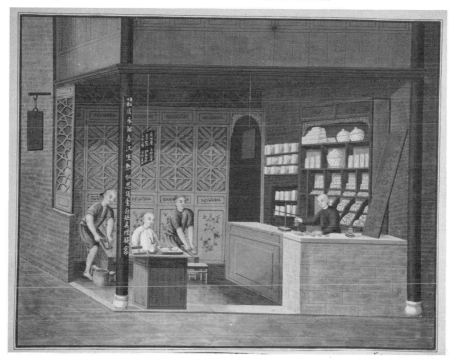

TOBACCO SHOP. C. 1830.

TORTOISE

The tortoise, along with the phoenix, the dragon, and the unicorn, is one of the four "spiritually endowed creatures" in the *Book of Rites*. The tortoise is an emblem of strength, longevity, and endurance. Sometimes called the "Black Warrior," the tortoise presides over the winter. To the Chinese the tortoise symbolizes the universe—in Buddhist temples tortoises are kept alive in tanks. It is considered very meritorious to feed them or to add to their numbers by purchasing more.

The tortoise is sometimes referred to as Wang-Po, or the creature who forgets the eight rules of right and wrong. The superstition is that the female tortoise is unchaste and mates only with snakes, or sometimes conceives by thought alone; therefore, the term *Wang-Po-tan* (turtle's egg) is equivalent to bastard.

TORTURE

Torture as official policy was inspired by a principle of criminal law that was conceived to be just—that a man should not be condemned until he confessed. To this end, the approved instruments of torture were coercive items. One antique device consisted of five bound sticks into which the suspect's fingers were inserted and then

中國事物

TORTURE VICTIM FORCED TO KNEEL ON CHAINS. C. 1900.

compressed. There was a similar gadget for squeezing the ankles. These instruments might be used on the witnesses as well as on the prisoner, in the interests of truth.

The most frequent form of punishment was the *canque*, a four-foot wooden square with a hole in the center worn like a portable version of the stocks. Other punishments escalated from beating with a bamboo cane to beheading. *Ling-che*, the ignominious lingering death, was reserved for crimes such as patricide and consisted of a drastic mutilation of the body prior to beheading.

Some of the elaborate devices had very graphic names such as "Frame of the Flowery Eyebrow" and "Monkey-Grasping Peach," when a man was suspended by one arm over a horizontal bar several feet above the ground with the other hand passed beneath the legs and both thumbs securely tied together under the knees.

During the Ming Dynasty, the Emperor required that every case involving capital punishment be presented to the Celestial Court before execution. This created a hardship for the outlying provinces: Just delivering the appeal required an arduous and time-consuming journey. In the meantime, the prisoner was placed with his head in a noose and his toes just reaching the ground. If he chose not to wait out the appeals process on his tiptoes, the Celestial Court would be advised that the prisoner had committed suicide.

[See CRIMINAL PUNISHMENT and FIVE PUNISHMENTS.]

TOYS

玩
具

樹

Smiley girley, losy boy,
S'posey makee buy my toy
Litee devilos make of clay,
Awful snakey clawly 'way,
Glate black spider, eyes all led,
Dlagons fit to scaree dead.
Dis de sortey plitty toy
Sell to little China-boy.
—Pidgin English Singsong, 1897

On a Chinese baby's first birthday it was customary to place him in the middle of an assortment of objects that represented different professions. The first object that the baby grabbed would supposedly predict what his career would be. In the meantime it was play, play, play. There is an early Ming scroll that depicts 100 little boys riding hobbyhorses, playing with puppets, feeding a phoenix, beating drums, and pulling each other's hair. Chinese toys encourage more than anything else the development of skill and dexterity—whether it's flying a kite, kicking a *ch'ien-tzu* football, or balancing a Diabolo. No wonder the Chinese excel in gymnastics and in Ping-Pong.

Yo-Yos are a Chinese invention that conquered the West in the eighteenth century. The American firm of Louis Marx copyrighted the name in the 1920s and quickly sold over 100 million of them. Chinese Yo-Yos were made of hardwood, lotus-seed pods, and conch shelltops.

Perhaps the most challenging toys in the world are Chinese puzzles. They epitomize oriental cunning, craftsmanship, patience, and confounded ingenuity. In the late eighteenth century beautifully lacquered black boxes containing Chinese puzzles began to perplex the West. Among other delights the boxes contained tangrams—a thin square of ivory cut into 7 pieces that can be arranged to form outlines of thousands of different objects, from fish and birds to men and windmills. Another box within the box appeared to be a solid ivory cube that was tipped over to reveal 10 irregular pieces. It would require hours to put back together again. Then there would be a ladder puzzle, and the inevitable ring puzzle. This last puzzle was invented 200 years before the birth of Christ by Hung Ming, and people are still trying to figure it out. The object is to remove 9 rings from a loop, a procedure involving 511 different maneuvers. This game is also known as "Detain Your Guests."

One of the most popular dolls in the West at the turn of the century was "Chinkee," a cute little Chinese baby with pink and green satin jacket and black trousers. It was a new kind of doll designed in America and mass-produced in China—stuffed with cork, with a supposedly unbreakable head. Its great success was followed by the appearance of the "Canton Kids," dolls that were modeled after two children in San Francisco's Chinatown.

[See JUMP ROPE, KITES, SHUTTLECOCK, and TANGRAMS.]

TREES

Although the Chinese have always admired the beauty of trees, they do like to keep warm in the winter, and there's nothing warmer than a bright wood fire. Consequently, there are few trees left standing, particularly in eastern China. Even the hills have disappeared through erosion.

中
國
·事
物

In 1957 China began a vast reforestation program. Chinese forests are composed of pine, larch, birch, poplar, and maple, and in the southernmost regions oak, laurel, and magnolia. Yet it will be many years before China recovers its forests. In the meantime, in New China, railroad ties and utility poles are made of concrete.
[See WORSHIP OF TREES.]

TRIAD SOCIETY

Although they participated in the Taiping revolt of 1850, the Triads are famous more for their secret signs and rituals than for their political activity. The punning nature of much of China's religious symbolism can be seen in the way Triads played word and number games with their leader's name, Hung. The top part of the Chinese character for the word Hung looks like 21. Because the numbers 4, 8, and 9 add up to 21, the number 489 was the highest rank attainable in Triad society.

The Triads apparently took an oath of blood brotherhood, and participated in rituals similar to those found in ancient Egypt, having to do with what befalls a man after death. These were mimed ordeals of death by fire and water, followed by a rebirth, and an otherworldly trip through guarded gateways to the "City of Willows," the haven of Hung heroes.

They supposedly got their start politically in 1674, but in the twentieth century the Triad activities have been decidedly more secular in nature. During the republic of Sun Yat-sen politicians and businessmen felt it necessary to join the Triads in order to make the proper contacts. As the Triads spread into graft and criminality, they also spread their geographic base to Chinese enclaves in Hong Kong, Southeast Asia, and the West Coast of California. In the 1940s and 1950s groups such as the Green Pangs, the Red Pangs, and the Triads were engaged in extortion, protection, narcotics, and prostitution throughout Asian cities. For the most part, however, groups such as the Triads survive as secret only in the ritual sense.

TWELVE ORNAMENTS

Among the earliest designs used to decorate textile fabrics in China were the "Twelve Ornaments." According to the *Shu Ching (Book of History)* they were referred to by Emperor Shun as being ancient even at the time when he made this declaration in 2000 B.C.: "I wish to see the emblematic figures of the ancients—the sun, the moon, the stars, the mountain, the dragon, and the flowery fowl, which are depicted *on the upper garment;* and the temple cup, the aquatic grass, the flames, the grains of rice, the hatchet, and the symbol of distinction, which are embroidered *on the lower garment.*" Only the Emperor could wear the complete set of twelve ornaments on his robes, while the nobles were restricted to certain symbols according to their rank.

TYPHOONS

South China is combined in a single monsoonal system with northern Australia and Southeast Asia. Monsoons are seasonal winds that blow for about six months from the northeast and six months from the southeast. The summer monsoons produce heavy rains, and are the birthplace of the numerous devastating typhoons that buffet the region. The typhoon is a severe tropical storm with hurricane-force winds of sixty-four knots or more.

While the annual monsoon system is essential to South China's agricultural well-being, the numerous typhoons arising within the system have proved devastating to life, property, and national economies throughout the region. Hardest hit are the coastal cities. Hong Kong is regularly battered by devastating typhoons killing hundreds each year. The strong winds turn any loose object into a dangerous missile, tear off rooftops, and collapse walls, while the rains erode foundations, resulting in collapsed buildings, broken levees, and widespread flooding.

While the southern coastal parts of China suffer from typhoons every summer, the greatest devastation usually takes place in nearby Vietnam or Japan. In 1881, a typhoon killed three hundred thousand people in Haiphong, Vietnam, just south of the Chinese border. The word "typhoon" has come down to us from the word *tai-feng* (big wind).

UMBRELLAS

UMBRELLA FACTORY AND STORE. C. 1830.

More than just a contraption to keep the rain off one's head, an umbrella in China is also a sunshade, a token of esteem, and an important Buddhist symbol.

The most common umbrella, found in all parts of China, has a bamboo handle, spring, and ribs, and is covered with oiled paper. It is known as a "kittysol" in the China trade, the word being a corruption of the Spanish and Portuguese *quitasol*. Its use in China goes back to the fourth century.

Silk umbrellas are even older. Often presented to a public official at a ceremony in his honor (upon leaving a district, for instance), they are symbols of dignity and respect for high rank. The presentation umbrella is usually made of fringed scarlet silk and embroidered in gilt with the names of the donors.

Once upon a time blue-green parasols of a certain type were reserved for the use of imperial princes. Some high officials admired them and began to use them, then women of the palace were permitted to carry them, until finally all the low-ranking officials and wealthy merchants were sporting them in the streets. Not even an imperial

中
國
事
物

edit was able to give the ruling family back its exclusive right to this popular fashion.

"The most important thing in life is to be buried well," says an old Chinese adage, and silk umbrellas frequently appear in abundance in funeral processions. A Victorian spectator once praised the many-colored umbrellas, inscribed with names of mourners and quotations from the classics, as "the handsomest part" of a Shanghai funeral.

UNICORN

The unicorn is one of the four great mythical animals of China. Like so many mythical beasts, it is a composite. It resembles a large stag, but has the body of a musk deer, the tail of an ox, the forehead of a wolf, and the hooves of a horse. It is colored yellow, red, blue, white, and black. It has a fleshy tipped horn extending from its forehead. It is the tamest and most virtuous of all living creatures, never eating flesh, the remains of another's meal, or even live grass. It drinks only pure water and walks without stepping on any living thing.

The unicorn is thought to be "the noblest form of animal creation, the emblem of perfect good." It lives a thousand years and appears to men only when a just ruler sits on the throne, or when a sage is about to be born. The unicorn appeared frequently during the time of the great legendary Emperors Yao and Shun, but the most famous unicorn in Chinese mythology is the one that appeared at Chiu-li before the birth of Confucius in 551 B.C. The animal carried a jade tablet, which it placed on the ground. The tablet was inscribed with the phrase, "Son of Choei-tsing-tse, King without scepter from the decadence of the Tcheou." Confucius' mother was surprised by the animal and tied a ribbon of silk to its horn to prove that the event occurred. In the year 481 B.C. a woodsman found an unknown animal and killed it. Confucius was summoned to tell what its name was. When he saw the dead unicorn, he wept, for the ribbon his mother had place on the horn seventy years earlier was still there.

Few unicorns have been sighted since the time of Confucius, except in the western Chinese regions inhabited by Tartars and Uighurs, where one or two cases were recorded during the reign of Genghis Khan. The unicorn is commonly used to symbolize good omens such as longevity, grandeur, illustrious offspring, and just government.

VESSELS

During the half-mythical period of the Hsia Dynasty (c. 2000 B.C.), nine bronze-tripod caldrons were presented to the great Emperor Yu. They represented the united provinces of the empire. Bronze vessels have gone largely unchanged in form throughout Chinese history, even up to modern times. While some have a certain grace in their appearance, the majority are heavy-looking, and somewhat imbalanced in their proportions. It is as though craftsmen have been careful to preserve the original rituals, to measure the exact swelling of the body, the profile of the neck, the flare of the mouth, the spread of the tripods, and to reproduce each line of decoration and design.

The bronze caldron (*ting*) in China was a vessel that contained the cooked offerings in the temple of the ancestors and at banquets. The head of the family served food from the *ting* into the bowls of his guests. It is one of two hexagrams in the *I Ching* that represents man-made objects. (The caldron is used in the service of the divine; the other object, the well, serves mankind.) While the well relates to the social foundation of life, the *ting* refers to the cultural superstructure. The *ting* is the image of nourishment. The *ting* is the enduring ritual that is China.

獨
角
獸

器
物

麒
麟

THE MYTHICAL UNICORN. FROM *Researches into Chinese Superstition* BY HENRI DORÉ.

中國事物

VISITING CARDS

Made from slips of vermilion paper eight inches high and three inches wide, these social greeting cards are still employed. No one knows how long they have been in use, although a major change occurred when the government was headed by the famous eunuch Lui Chin around A.D. 1500. Prior to that year visiting cards were always white, but from then on white was reserved for people in recent mourning, and the cards became more colorful.

The cards would normally be folded once, but four, eight, or more folds would indicate the rank of the visitor in imperial days. They might have the name stamped in the corner, or a personally written greeting. More elaborate cards would have a design. Bats, a symbol of happiness because both words have the same sound in Chinese, often decorate the cards.

The Western business card serves a similar purpose, except the bright visiting cards are not cut to wallet size and have a more casual social connotation.

WATER BUFFALO

The Chinese water buffalo is the same useful, powerful, sluggish, and unwieldy animal that exists in all the warm countries of Asia, and that was introduced into Greece, Egypt, and southern India in the Middle Ages.

Although it is dangerous to approach, as it has a natural repugnance to strangers, it is thoroughly docile with its masters, and appears to be perfectly controlled by little boys whose chief task it is to drive them to and fro from the fields, and to guide them when pulling the harness and plow. That is such a common sight, in fact, that the image of a boy sitting on a water buffalo's back, playing a flute, enters into most Chinese descriptions of rural life.

 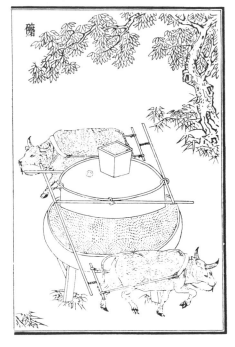

EXAMPLES OF MILLING GRAIN USING WATER BUFFALO AND WATERWHEEL. FROM THE *T'ien Kung K'ai Wu.*

The body of the water buffalo is scarcely covered with hair. Each horn is neatly semicircular and bends downward, while the head is tilted up so as almost to bring the nose horizontal. This peculiar carriage enables the animal to submerge its entire body and head under the surface of water in pools and ponds, in which it delights in lying, to cool itself off or to escape its usual consortium of gnats. It is not unusual to see submerged herds of water buffalo with only the tips of their noses showing in this manner.

The water buffalo, or ox, is the Chinese symbol for spring and agriculture. It also represents the principles of life and of truth in action. In the twelfth century, Chinese Zen master Kuo-an drew pictures of ten water buffalo, basing them on earlier Taoist bulls. Searching for the bull, discovering its footprints, perceiving the bull, catching the bull, taming the bull, riding the bull, transcending the bull, transcending both the bull and the self, reaching the source, and emerging into the world—these are the ten steps leading to perfect enlightenment.

Although the milk of the common cow is sweeter than that of the buffalo, the buffalo's milk is richer. Also, beef tea is credited in the Chinese Materia Medica with great strengthening powers owing to the muscular character of the beast.

WATER CHESTNUT

Three chestnuts for morning, four at night;
What is right today is wrong tomorrow.
　　—Ch'iao Chi (A.D. 1280-1345)

These lines allude to the tale from the *Chuang tzu* in which Master Tsu, the keeper of monkeys, tricks his herd into obedience by promising them four chestnuts in the morning and three in the afternoon, when what they are demanding is three chestnuts in the morning and four in the afternoon.

The water chestnut, or *Castanea vulgaris*, grows in several different varieties throughout the Middle Kingdom. It is a common article of diet, and is most frequently cooked with chicken. Since it is difficult to digest, Chinese doctors do not recommend it to sick people or to those suffering from dementia. The chestnut was one of the few fruits that was considered to be appropriate as a gift to the Son of Heaven. Ancient Chinese would also present chestnuts to women as a means of introduction.

WATER-SPOUTING BOWL

The water-spouting vessel is a sort of pan or bowl that, when rubbed, sends jets of water into the air at its four quarters. When the vessel is rubbed rhythmically it vibrates rather like a bell, or a wet crystal goblet whose rim is rubbed by a finger. It is said that an experienced and skillful operator can send a jet as high as three feet into the air.

It has been hypothesized that the walls of the vessel are under some sort of strain that generates a peculiarly intense set of standing waves on the surface of the water— but no bowls of this sort have yet been examined thoroughly enough for this to be anything more than a speculation.

WATERWHEEL

The earliest reference to the use of waterwheels in China (in an essay by Huan Tan in A.D. 20) indicate that the Chinese used water power not only for pounding grain, as was done in the West, but also for the much more sophisticated task of blowing metallurgical bellows. The waterwheels used were probably vertical in design, but

拜帖　水牛　荸薺　噴水碗　水車

中國事物

most Chinese waterwheels being used today are horizontal. The metallurgical water-wheel (*shui-tui*) was used to drive a series of trip-hammers, which in turn activated the bellows. The system was probably derived from the agricultural device called a spoon-tilt hammer, which later developed into a bucket wheel.

A thirteenth-century text called the *Nung Shu (Book of Agriculture)* depicts a variety of medieval Chinese waterwheels. While the majority were used for agriculture, several were employed for metallurgical blowing, and some even for the operation of machinery used to spin silk.

WEIGHTS AND MEASURES

The standardization of weights and measures was a part of the legalist-inspired program of standardization during the Ch'in Dynasty. Though the Ch'in lasted only fourteen years, from 221 B.C. to 207 B.C., this program of standardization had a lasting effect.

Among other things, the decimalization of weights and measures was begun during the Ch'in, and gradually extended to all measures of volume, weight, and length. The decimalization of weights and measures was made fully official in A.D. 992, but nonstandard, nondecimal usages persisted into the Ming Dynasty, which began in 1368.

The earliest measures were, like English measures, based on the size of various parts of the human body. Naturally, this could not survive the decimalization of measures, and various objects were used as standards throughout Chinese history, with the rather odd result that the standard foot, for example, continued to increase over the three thousand years it was in use. One of the most interesting standards was the millet seed, which was used both as a measure of length and as a measure of volume—as well as a standard weight.

WHEELBARROW

The first wheelbarrow was invented during the Three Kingdom period in China. The invention is accredited to a military hero named Chu-ko Liang, captain-general of the state of Shu (in Sichuan), who introduced what was called a "wooden ox" in A.D. 232. It took over a thousand years for the device to reach Europe.

The wheelbarrow made it possible for one person to carry a much heavier load than even two could carry if it were suspended between them on a stretcher or litter. The wheelbarrow's introduction effectively doubled the efficiency of much heavy agricultural and construction work.

WHITE TIGER

The tiger represents the West, and the white tiger rules the Western Quadrant. It is the mixture of blue dragon and white tiger that is often used to indicate the action of heaven and earth mingling. For the alchemists, the white tiger is also a chemical synonym for mercury when it is extracted from cinnabar.

The tiger is also an emblem of ferocity and strength. It is a common military symbol and was used to decorate the parapets of forts as well as the tunics of imperial generals. There were several periods in ancient China when soldiers were entirely garbed in the skins of tigers—including the tail.

It is said that the tiger lives a thousand years. At the age of five hundred his color changes to white. The tiger is the sacred beast who watches over the hidden treasures of the god of wealth and guards entrances to Taoist temples. The tiger is considered to be a demon-expelling creature, and his image is a powerful charm—often embroidered onto the slippers and hats of children to protect them.

WINE

Technically, Chinese wine is not really wine but either beer, if it is made from fermented grains, or spirits, if it is distilled. Grape wine is a relative newcomer to China, having been introduced there in the second century B.C. from Iran by traveler Chang Ch'ien. The art of distilling may have been practiced as early as the T'ang Dynasty (A.D. 618-906), perhaps introduced by those conquerors from the Northwest. But liquor fermented from grains (which we shall call "rice wine," since everyone else does) is probably the most ancient of alcoholic beverages. Between the Chou Dynasty and the end of the Mongol reign lie about twenty-four hundred years, during which records show that prohibition laws against the manufacture, sale, and consumption of wine were enacted and then repealed—forty-one times!

The earliest brew was probably made from millet, which may have been the first grain widely cultivated in China. This beverage, called *chiu,* preceded tea as a popular accompaniment to meals. All drinks made from fermented grains were called, with great impartiality, *chiu,* and when distilled liquors invaded they too were assimilated under the term *chiu.* The three main sorts of Chinese wines are distinguished as "white" *chiu,* "yellow" *chiu,* and "burning" *chiu,* which is, of course, spirits.

There is a story, taken from the classic *The Country's Policy* that tells how Yi Te, chef to Emperor Yu, accidentally invented *chiu* thirty-five hundred years ago. A crock of forgotten rice fermented, and the court, upon tasting it, threw a party that left everyone totally incapacitated the next day. Emperor Yu decided to avoid repetition of this incident by instituting three rules for wine drinkers: Wine must be served in tiny cups instead of soup bowls like the first time; one must eat while drinking; one must indulge in some mild form of physical or mental exercise while drinking.

Before Western customs began to invade the East, the Chinese imbibed alcohol only in conjunction with food, and developed along the way a cuisine based on the hors d'oeuvre—"dot hearts" or *tien hsin,* known by its southern equivalent, *dim sum.* Chinese look down on solitary drinkers, and have devised innumerable number games, finger games, and word games to play while companionably convivial. Poets especially are reckoned to be fond of drink, and there was even a school of writers whose wine-praising work earned them the title of "Drunken Dragons." Of these the poet Li Po is the best known, who dead drunk fell out of a boat and drowned one night while trying to embrace the moon's reflection in a lotus pond. Confucius, as usual, had the last word on the subject: "There is no limit to drinking wine, but one mustn't get drunk."

Wine is used in Chinese marriage ceremonies and figures prominently in Chinese cuisine, where it is used, like ginger, to neutralize the strong odors of meats and fish. Medicinal wines are made by the addition of herbs and other odd things. There is ginseng wine, which is ginseng root soaked in the strongest distilled spirits, and there is Cantonese snake wine, green and virulent, made from snakes pickled in spirits and taken as a tonic in the fall. *Kaoliang,* or *sanshu,* is made in the North by triple-distilling sorghum wine, and is sometimes flavored with rose petals. The Chinese make liquor brandies, as well, out of quince, plums, oranges, and pears.

Rice wine, called "white" or "yellow," starts out almost colorless and just a little thicker than water. Good wines age as well, thickening and becoming a darker yellow. Because Chinese consider cold drinks bad for the digestion, rice wine is

中國事物

米漂流長

WASHING THE FERMENTED RICE AS A PROCESS IN WINE MAKING. FROM THE *T'ien Kung K'ai Wu.*

紫
藤
鍋

always served hot, in very small cups. The wine is normally gulped; a common forfeit in guessing games is to drink a cup of wine at a swallow. The alcohol in rice wine is extremely volatile; it will frequently stimulate the drinker's nose on the way to stimulating his palate. Heat plus volatility hasten the wine's effects, but interestingly, the intoxication that so quickly arrives seems to depart with equal rapidity.

The ancients had five terms for the various states of drunkenness: giddy, not confused although drunk, belligerent, merry, and hung over. To these moderns add the phrase "getting red in the face" for getting tipsy, a phrase that has a basis in fact, as the peoples of eastern Asia have a genetic tendency to blush more easily than other peoples, especially after drinking alcohol.

WISTERIA

Thin mists—thick clouds—sad all day long.
The gold animal spurts incense from its head.
—Li Ch'ing-chao (A.D. c. 1084-c. 1151)

The *Tsu-teng* (purple vine) (*Wisteria chinensis*) is perhaps the most artistically decorative of all Chinese flowering vines. It can grow up to a hundred feet high, and has been growing in stature in the Celestial Kingdom since its introduction over five hundred years ago. The Chinese venerate such ancient specimens with their twisted trunks, still bearing long-drooping clusters of pear-shaped, lilac-colored fragrant flowers. The *Tsu-teng* is usually found on trelliswork in gardens, forming long-covered walks, or trained picturesquely on walls and arbors. It is not uncommon during the flowering season for visiting poets and artists to be gripped suddenly by masses of wisteria, in the aromatic clutch of inspiration.

WOK

The *wok* is an efficient all-purpose metal cooking vessel that is used in every household in China. Its origins are obscure, although there is an early reference to a *wok*-repair shop in the city of Hangzhou in the Sung Dynasty. The *wok* has two handles and is shaped like a shallow half sphere. By pouring a small amount of oil or fat into it, it can be used as an economic deep fryer. Water can be poured into it, and rice, soup, or noodle dishes prepared. As the sides of the *wok* slope outward, it is possible to fit two or three latticed bamboo trays above the boiling water and to cook in steam under the lid.

It only takes minutes to cook a meal. Chinese cooks spend most of their time slicing and chopping the meat and vegetables *before* they begin cooking. Chinese cuisine is not so much distinguishable as being Chinese except for the unique way that foodstuffs are prepared beforehand and for the way they are mixed together.

There is a popular Chinese tale that blends the ingredients of *haute cuisine* and love. Chang O was the most beautiful woman in the Middle Kingdom before she became the moon goddess. A high court official was madly in love with her. While her husband was away at war, he kept wooing her. Finally, Chang O invited him to an evening of dinner, music, and wine games. Because he was so distinguished, instead of preparing a dinner of nine or seventeen dishes, Chang O served the full thirty-four. Each dish was brought in by a different serving girl—each more beautiful than the other. At the end of her feast her satiated admirer begged to know Chang O's secret. To his amazement, he learned that each of the thirty-four dishes was

中國事物

chicken. More to the point, each of the beautiful maidens was none other than Chang O herself.

WOLF

To all early sheepherders the wolf is a symbol of literal rapaciousness. In Beijing, it was at one time customary to draw large white rings on house walls, to scare wolves away. Two varieties of wolf, including the large gray wolf, are native to China's northern steppes.

WOOD-BLOCK PRINTS

The Chinese have been obsessed with developing printed images from the earliest times. During the Han Dynasty, so many scholars would come to the gates of the imperial library to get at the engraved tablets of the *Six Classics* in order to make copies, that their carts created the world's first traffic jam. The most famous early illustrated wood-block print dates to A.D. 868, being the seventeen-foot-long *Diamond Sutra*. It was dedicated "For Universal Free Distribution by Wang Chieh to Perpetuate the Memory of His Parents." Wood-block prints are dated as early as A.D. 757. Chinese printers made black ink of burned wood or lacquer mixed with glue and formed into a paste or brick, soluble in water. Cinnabar red was their second most popular color, and it is still used today on seals and calendars. Wood was usually pear or jujube. It was squared off into blocks, planed, and sized with rice and flour paste. The image drawn or cut on paper was pasted face down to the wet surface and carved by the form cutter.

After the Mongol invasion, in addition to accompanying religious classics graphically, woodcuts were used to illustrate volumes on medicine, botany, agriculture, poetry, and literature. *Beautiful Women Who from Dynasty to Dynasty Overturned Empires* was a big hit in its illustrated, unexpurgated edition. The unique

MODERN WOOD-BLOCK PRINT FROM THE LIAONING PROVINCE ENTITLED "SUNRISE AT THE REFINERY."

ability of Chinese woodcuts to narrate and express human problems in active situations helped make them viable folk art. The popular *Nien Hua*, or New Year's prints, would pinpoint what the people longed for the most: happiness, riches, peace, many children, justice, or health. These themes would be depicted either symbolically or through allegorical motifs, such as the phoenix, dragon, tiger, bat, carp, peach, and pomegranate.

[See INK, PIGMENTS AND DYES, PRINTING, and SEALS.]

WORSHIP OF ANTIQUITY

The worship of antiquity in China is deeply rooted in the ancestor cult. Just as there were founding, or ultimate, ancestors in the Chinese family, whose names were inscribed on tablets kept in the house, the heroes and great men of mythological and historical times often found themselves deified and worshiped along with the Nature gods of the older, more primitive religion.

P'an Ku and the Five Emperors are the original deified mythical characters, but sages and Emperors were accorded the status of immortals and gods down to the nineteenth century. All of the great philosophers, alchemists, generals, and folk heroes can be found in the highly organized pantheons of Taoism and Buddhism.

The practices of paying homage to the past and totemizing historical figures are derived from the belief in a "Golden Age" of perfection in which the rules of Nature were established. Thus, we have the imperial system ordained by a "mandate of heaven" in ancient times. The philosophy of Confucius did much to perpetuate the respect for antiquity and reverence for the things established in "those times."

Gradually the legitimacy of ideas and practices became associated with their age. Confucius himself became deified within a few hundred years of his death. The practice of ascribing some new idea, discovery, or invention to a fabricated mythical character became common. The authorship of most Chinese classical works is in doubt because the real writer often gave his work legitimacy by claiming it to be the newly found classic of a respected or known character long dead.

The worship of antiquity served primarily to preserve the status quo of many Chinese institutions to an extent unknown in other parts of the world. The authority of the ancients was so important until this century that little could be said or done in China without finding some precedent in the life, words, or writings of an ancient authority.

WORSHIP OF HEAVEN AND EARTH

Heaven and earth (*T'ien-Ti*) have traditionally been revered and sacrificed to in dozens of different forms. Heaven and earth are at once philosophical concepts, as well as popular representations of the prime forces of Nature. In the *I Ching*, it is written that "When heaven and earth exert their influences, all things are transformed and vivified." Heaven and earth together are therefore symbols of regeneration, of the New Year, of spring. The *Book of Rites* claims: "When in the first month of the vernal season, the celestial breath descends and the terrestrial breath ascends, heaven and earth unite harmoniously, and the vegetable kingdom is revived and set in motion." Heaven and earth are also represented by the eternal duality principle, *yin* and *yang*.

The worship of heaven and earth permeated all of Chinese culture. Incense was burned before the image of *T'ien-Ti* by most Chinese families in their homes on the first and the fifteenth of each month. The offering was made in a small niche near the

狼
木刻畫
崇拜古人
崇拜天地

中
國
事
物

northern door of the house to a paper or wooden image of "Father Heaven and Mother Earth." The ritual required a person to bow six times a day.

[See YIN AND YANG.]

WORSHIP OF MOUNTAINS AND RIVERS

While every mountain and waterway in China is associated with numerous historical personalities, spirits, and genies, there is a tradition elevating the Four Great Rivers and the Five Sacred Peaks of China and paying them special tribute beyond that accorded to local divinities.

The Four Great Rivers are the Yangtze River, also called the expansive source; the Yellow River—the wondrous source; the Huai River—the perpetual source; the Chi River—the pure source. Together the four are called *Ssu-tu*: Four Great Rivers That Flow into the Sea. While the rivers have all changed course since they were first worshiped, and no longer all flow into the sea, they were extremely important to Chinese agricultural development, and had to be appeased in times of flood.

While it is easy to understand the importance of rivers to an agricultural society, the origins of worshiping the Five Sacred Peaks is more mysterious. Four of the Five Sacred Peaks once marked the ancient "Chinese Empire" of legend. The fifth was added to indicate centrality, with the others standing for each of the four directions. The five are: North—Heng Shan of Shaanxi; South: Heng Shan of Henan; East: T'ai Shan of Shandong; West: Hua Shan of Shaanxi; Center: Sung Shan of Henan.

The practice of worshiping the mountains is traced back to the legendary Emperor Yao, who made a circuit of the Five Sacred Peaks in 2346 B.C. in order to sacrifice to Shang Ti—the Supreme Being. The practice was continued by later Emperors and in A.D. 396 the first temples to the gods of the high peaks were erected.

WORSHIP OF NATURE

Most of the elements of popular Chinese religions, as well as many of the driving concepts of Chinese philosophy, are based on a primitive prehistoric religion of Nature in which the natural surroundings became deified by an early agricultural society. The many gods and goddesses in the Taoist and Buddhist pantheons are often representations of natural phenomena, abstract renderings of processes and objects in Nature that man interacts with and depends on.

With the political development of China during the Shang and later Chou dynasties, these elements became formalized, and the worship of heaven and earth became institutionalized by imperial decree. The science of geomancy—*feng-shui*—developed and was used to interpret the will of earth gods, along with that of astrology, to interpret the will of heaven. Chinese sensitivity to the natural environment culminated in the philosophical evolution of concepts like the *tao* (the way of Nature), and the philosophy of adjusting human behavior to the rhythms of a more sublime natural order. While the Taoist religion moved away from its original purity, the tradition of reverence for Nature continued to have a major impact on Chinese life, and has exercised influence even on the most contemporary events in China.

[See GEOMANCY and TAO.]

WORSHIP OF STONES

The use of sacred stones to protect certain places from malignant influences has been traced back to the Warring States period (480-222 B.C.). Stones bearing the inscription "This Stone from Mount T'ai dares to oppose" were often used to mark sharp

崇拜山川　崇拜自然　崇拜石頭

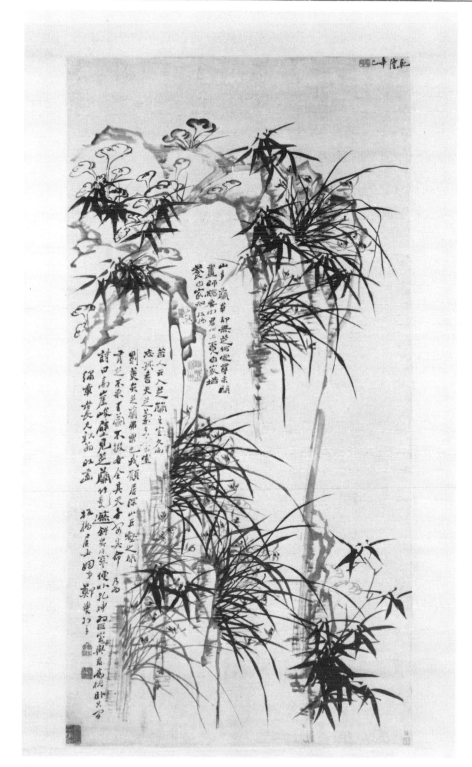

A BLENDING OF ROCKS, BAMBOO, PHILOSOPHY, AND THE FUNGUS OF IMMORTALITY.

中
國
事
物

turns in roadways and off bridges. These places are thought to be particularly vulnerable to the influence of demons. The inscription is most efficacious if the stone is actually from T'ai Shan—the eastern and most sacred of the Five Sacred Peaks of China.

There is a related custom of conferring honors on stones and other inanimate objects, thus investing them with titles equal to those of dukes and other high officials. *T'ai-hu* rocks, those much-valued stones with eccentric shapes, are highly prized in China. To find such a stone is the greatest fortune, and usually they are passed down through the family for many generations.

WORSHIP OF SUN AND MOON

The *Book of Rites* contains instructions for sacrificing to the sun and the moon, but the practice of worshiping both extends farther back into archaic Chinese agricultural rites.

The sun god, T'ai-Yang Shen, rules the day and is composed of fire. His greatest feast is on the nineteenth day of the third month. Of equal importance, and closely associated with T'ai-Yang Shen, is T'ai Yin, the moon goddess—in charge of the months, good harvests, and ruler of the tides. The moon is worshiped at the time of the Harvest Festival in the middle of the eighth month.

Inscriptions worshiping and beseeching both the sun and the moon used to be commonly sold in shops. Recitations of the prayers on the scraps of paper were meant to preserve the health of the devotee while protecting his future incarnations. The sun god was also prayed to when special favors were sought—such as luck in examinations.

WORSHIP OF TREES

Trees have always been imbued with sacred powers. Old trees are thought to have stored up more vital energy (*ch'i*) and are often the objects of worship. They are decorated, and on certain days incense may be burned to them and firecrackers set off. Religious shrines to local deities are often built in the fork, or by the roots of an old tree. The larger and broader a tree, the more powerful the spirit or god residing there.

Almost every type of bush or tree known in China has been invested with certain powers and effects. The most revered is the peach tree. Symbolizing immortality, the peach is associated with sagacity and magical power. Ornaments and branches are fashioned from peach wood in the hopes of attaining longevity, and children wear peach-wood amulets to give them long life. The pomegranate is also highly praised—for it is the emblem of fertility. The jujube, bamboo, willow, and plum all have special powers, and references to them are common in pictorial and verbal rituals.

WORSHIP OF THE WIND

According to some accounts, the wind is due to compression and expansion; it is the respiration of *yin* and *yang*. According to other traditions the constellation *Chi* is a stellar master of the wind. Roasted meats are often offered to the stars of Sagittarius to appease the wind.

The most popular representation of wind worship is Feng Po, an old man with a white beard. He carries a bag of winds, which he controls by tightening or loosening his grip over its mouth. Occasionally he is in the company of a wheel, which he rotates with a fan. Feng Po is a member of the First Celestial Ministry and is called the Earl of Wind.

WU SHU

All of the Chinese martial arts are close cousins, descended, if one is prepared to believe tradition, from an art that emerged sometime during the Ming Dynasty (c. A.D. 1400). A woman warrior, already an expert fighter with the long pole, invented this early, original martial art. Her teacher was a white crane who snapped her pole in two with an easy graceful turning wing the first time they met.

Since the Ming Dynasty different teachers and students have tended to favor different techniques, and various schools or styles of Chinese martial arts have developed. *Wu shu*, which means "war arts," is the term used in New China for all the martial arts in modern use, including the ones we know in the West as *t'ai chi ch'uan*, *shao-lin* boxing, and White-Crane and Praying-Mantis *kung fu*.* Other *wu shu* styles in common practice in China are *hsing yi*, *ti-t'ang*, *t'ung pi* and *chin nei*.

Hsing yi is called "five-element boxing" because it combines the characteristic movements of five animals: tiger, monkey, eagle, horse, and bear. *Ti-t'ang* involves tumbling skills and may be compared to *aikido*. *T'ung pi* is a limited version of *hsing yi*, and somewhat akin to Western stand-up boxing. *Chin nei* is mostly holds and escapes, similar to *jujitsu* or wrestling.

In addition to the original long pole, *wu shu* weapons styles teach the use of such exotica as the Double Hooks, the Spear, the Rope Dart, and the Nine-section (Double) Whip. But the pre-eminent *wu shu* weapon is the sword. A synonym for *wu shu* is "swordmanship without intent to cut." The Chinese people call the sword itself "the mother of weapons" and know some sixteen methods for her use. About four are in common practice today: single sword, double sword, long-tasseled sword, and short-tasseled sword. According to the All-China Sports Federation, the sophisticated and highly stylized weapons used in *wu shu* styles are derived from the crude but lethal arms the peasantry devised from farm implements.

Wu shu is the national sport of New China, where office workers gather by the thousands in the early mornings to practice the slow grace of *t'ai chi ch'uan* in the parks and squares. *Wu shu* as a competitive sport is judged on five points: leaping, balance, stance, footwork, and tumbling.

The New Chinese insist that *wu shu* is not "military" but a folk art and part of the Chinese cultural tradition. They practice it because it's part of their heritage and because it promotes health; they disapprove of the old-fashioned "hardening practices" for the hands of punching sand, beans, or stones because they eventually make it impossible for a person to work.

[See PA KUA and T'AI CHI CH'UAN.]

---

*In Chinese *kung fu* merely means "proficiency" and could just as correctly be applied to calligraphy or cooking.

YANGTZE RIVER

The Yangtze, which the Chinese call Chang Jiang (Long River) or even Blue River, is China's longest, and the world's fourth longest river. The river flows 3,434 miles from its source in West China down to the East China Sea, and traverses twelve provinces, including the Autonomous Region of Tibet.

Nearly half of the crops grown in all China are produced in the Yangtze basin, including up to 70 per cent of all the rice. The cities of Shanghai, Nanjing, Wuhan, Jung-Ching, and Chengdu are all located in the Yangtze Basin.

崇拜日月

崇拜樹木

崇拜風　武術　揚子江

中國事物

For the first 1,600 miles of its course, the Yangtze moves through the mountainous country of western China and the Tibetan highlands, often flowing for hundreds of miles in deep, inaccessible gorges. Emerging from the mountains near Yibin, the river widens and flows through the most agriculturally fertile part of the country. Much of Chinese sericulture is centered in this part of Sichuan Province. After leaving Sichuan, the river enters a mountainous region characterized by three dramatic gorges with towering limestone cliffs rising as much as 2,000 feet above water. While tumbling through these Shangsia gorges, the river reaches depths of 500 to 600 feet, making it the world's deepest river.

The Yangtze exits the gorges onto a wide plain covered with a complex system of tributaries and lakes. At the end of the Liang-tzu Plain, the river becomes a slowly meandering .5-mile-wide giant, often looping around itself. This area is known as the rice bowl of China. After entering the North China Plain, the Yangtze reaches widths between 3,000 and 6,000 feet and maintains a depth of 100 feet. Before entering the sea, the Yangtze divides into two arms, one of which is 6 miles wide, the other 15. Between them lies an island of 300 square miles that has been formed over the past 1,000 years by alluvium deposited by the river. The long estuary feeding into the sea is in places 50 miles wide.

The Yangtze Delta area contains over 1,700 miles of built-up and dammed banks

ROOFTOPS OVERLOOKING THE YANGTZE RIVER. C. 1905.

because of an annual water-level fluctuation of as much as 65 feet. Throughout history the Yangtze has overflowed to a catastrophic extent nearly once every 50 years. In 1931 a disastrous flood destroyed dams and dikes in 23 places, flooding over 35,000 square miles of land and leaving 40 million people homeless. The city of Wuhan remained submerged beneath 6 feet of water for 4 months.

The Yangtze is one of China's main transportation arteries. It is navigable by large ships for up to 700 miles from the sea, and is linked to other major rivers by a system of canals. The Yangtze contains 500 varieties of fish, of which 30 are economically important. The river is capable of generating 217 million kilowatts of electricity, less than half of which is currently being produced.

YAO

Yao was the first of the three legendary rulers Yao, Shun, and Yu, who followed Huang Ti, the "Yellow Emperor." Born with the surname Chi, Yao ascended the throne at the age of 16 in the year 2357 B.C. and ruled peacefully for 90 years, dying at the age of 115. He was the patron of the astronomers Hsi and Huo, who observed the rising and setting of the sun, the cycles of the moon, and planetary revolutions. Yao compiled a calendar consisting of 360 days and dividing the year into 4 seasons in order to help the people cultivate their land. He is considered an ancient model of wisdom and virtue, and has been accorded divine status in both Taoist and Buddhist traditions.

YARROW

The yarrow is a perennial herb that is native to the Northern temperate regions of China. Several species are cultivated for their flat-topped clusters of flowers, and for their scented foliage. The most common variety is the *Achillia millefolium*, or the milfoil, which has been used in China since the dawn of the *I Ching* as a tool for divination.

YELLOW RIVER

China's second longest river flows 3,011 miles from the Tibetan highlands to the Yellow Sea. Over 120 million inhabitants reside in the Yellow River Basin, many of them in major cities such as Baotou, Xian, Taiyuan, Luoyang, Zhengzhou, Kaifeng, and Jinan. Archaeological excavations indicate that Chinese civilization originated in the Huang Ho or Yellow River Basin, the middle and lower sections of which have always been essential to China's rice economy.

The Huang Ho is the muddiest river in the world. It carries an average of 57 pounds of silt per cubic yard of water down to the sea, where it is deposited in a 160-mile long delta. So much silt is carried down that the coastline has been known to gain as much as 12 miles of land extending into the sea in 3 years. The silt comes from upstream, where the river traverses several hundred miles of a highly friable loessbed.

Over the past 4,000 years the Huang Ho's course has fluctuated immensely, resulting in the nickname "ungovernable." The mouth of the river has moved by as much as 500 miles in this time. Until 602 B.C. it flowed through the northern city of Tientsin, but then shifted southward into the Shandong Peninsula—hundreds of miles away. The river has occupied its present bed since 1854. It is connected to China's other major waterways by the Grand Canal, which runs 1,100 miles from Beijing in the North to Hangzhou in the South, but itself is only navigable for about 100 miles of its lower reaches.

中國事物

YIN AND YANG

Yin and *yang* are the negative and the positive forces in the universe. They are the principle of duality, the eternal opposites contained in the Great Ultimate Principle (*t'ai chi*). The words for *yin* and *yang* have been found on Chinese artifacts dating back to the eighth century B.C. By the time of Confucius they were firmly implanted in the Chinese conception of the world as being a single entity with two aspects permeating everything. They are fundamental to an understanding of Chinese astrology, divination, religion, and science.

Yin and *yang* are fully explained in commentaries on the *I Ching*. They are at the roots of Nature and of material reality. Some of the attributes of the principles are as follows:

YIN	YANG
Negative	Positive
Shadow	Sun
Earth	Heaven
Passive	Active
Dark	Light
Female	Male
Quiescence	Vigor
Even Numbers	Odd Numbers
Absorption	Penetration
Duality	Monality
Valleys	Mountains
Cold	Heat
Water	Fire

Yin and *yang*, as can be seen, affect every aspect of nature as well as of human activity. It is through their constant interaction that change takes place and that the order of the universe expresses itself. *Yin* and *yang*, it has been said, "are the exhalation and inhalation of the universe."

They are represented in a number of symbolic ways. The most important is the *t'ai chi* symbol. They are also written as solid and broken lines: *yang* ——— and *yin* — —. These lines were combined into eight groups of three known as trigrams. The eight possible combinations of the trigrams, when combined with each other, yield the Sixty-four Hexagrams of the *I Ching*.

In Chinese philosophy, *yin* and *yang* are infused in the most elementary processes of nature, and therefore of life. Neo-Confucianist philosopher Chu Hsi (A.D. 1130-1200) wrote: "There is no other event in the universe except *yin* and *yang* succeeding each other in an unceasing cycle. This is called change." Modern philosopher R.L. Wing, in a commentary on the *Book of Changes* wrote: "From the oscillating dichotomy in the cosmos (negative *yin* and positive *yang*), all of that which exists is being produced. This constant changing is the interplay in the cosmos that creates life, while life, in turn, generates the creative energy that manifests the cosmos. *Yin* and *yang* represent the negative and positive dualism existing within all things, from the protons and electrons of the atoms to the conscious and subconscious of the human psyche. This duality is a profound fundamental in both ancient Chinese and modern scientific thought."

陰
陽

P'an Ku could be considered the Chinese Adam. He was the first being brought into existence from the cosmos. His function was to set the universe in order. He is shown here holding the "egg of chaos," actually the *t'ai chi* symbol containing *yin* and *yang*, the two opposites of the universe. P'an Ku hatched from the "egg of chaos" and grew at a rate of six feet daily for 18,000 years until he filled all of the space between heaven and earth. When he died he gave birth to the details of the world. His eyes transmuted into the sun and the moon, his head became the mountains, and his breath the wind and clouds. From his voice came the sounds of thunder, while his blood and skin were transformed into the rivers flowing over the earth. His beard formed the stars and his hairs formed the plants and trees; his teeth and bones became minerals and from his marrow came precious stones and pearls.

Further Reading

ANCIENT CHINA by John Hay. Walck, New York 1974. (*paper*)

THE ARCHAEOLOGY OF ANCIENT CHINA by Kwang-chih Chang. Yale University Press, New Haven 1977. (*paper*)

THE ARTS OF CHINA by Michael Sullivan. University of California Press, Berkeley 1977. (*paper*)

CHINA TODAY AND HER ANCIENT TREASURES by Joan Lebold Cohen. H. N. Abrams, New York 1974.

CHINA AT WORK: AN ILLUSTRATED RECORD OF THE PRIMITIVE INDUSTRIES OF CHINA'S MASSES . . . by Rudolf P. Hommell. MIT Press, Cambridge 1970. (*paper*)

CHINESE CHILDHOOD by Marguerite Fawdry. Barron's, New York 1977.

CHINESE FLOWER ARRANGEMENT by H. L. Li. D. Van Nostrand, New York 1959.

THE CHINESE GARDEN; HISTORY, ART AND ARCHITECTURE by Maggie Keswick. Rizzoli, New York 1978.

CHINESE MEDICINAL HERBS by Shih-chen Li. Georgetown Press, San Francisco 1973.

CHINESE MYTHOLOGY by Anthony Christie. Paul Hamlyn, Feltham, Middlesex 1968.

THE CONFUCIAN PERSUASION, Arthur F. Wright, ed. Stanford University Press, Palo Alto 1960.

COOKING IN CHINA by Emily Hahn. Time-Life Books, New York 1968.

CRAFTS OF CHINA by Michael Carter. Doubleday, Garden City, N.Y. 1977.

DREAM OF THE RED CHAMBER by Hsueh-ch'in Ts'ao. Doubleday (Anchor), New York. (*paper*)

ENCYCLOPEDIA OF CHINA TODAY by Frederic Kaplan and Stephen Andors. Harper and Row, New York 1979.

THE FACE OF CHINA AS SEEN BY PHOTOGRAPHERS AND TRAVELERS, 1860-1912. Aperture, Millerton, N.Y. 1978. (*paper*)

AN HISTORICAL ATLAS OF CHINA by Albert Herrmann. Aldine, Chicago 1966.

A HISTORY OF CHINA by Wolfram Eberhard. University of California Press, Berkeley 1977. (*paper*)

THE I CHING WORKBOOK by R.L. Wing. Doubleday, Garden City, N.Y. 1979.

THE MIND OF CHINA by Ben-Ami Scharfstein. Dell, New York 1975. (*paper*)

NAGEL TRAVEL GUIDE TO CHINA. Hippocrene Books, New York 1978.

OUTLINES OF CHINESE SYMBOLISM AND ART MOTIFS by C. A. S. Williams. Dover, New York 1976. (*paper*)

THE SHORTER SCIENCE AND CIVILIZATION IN CHINA; AN ABRIDGEMENT OF JOSEPH NEEDHAM'S ORIGINAL TEXT by Colin A. Ronan. Cambridge University Press, London 1978.

A SOURCE BOOK IN CHINESE PHILOSOPHY by Wing-tsit Chan. Princeton University Press, Princeton 1963. (*paper*)

SOURCES OF CHINESE TRADITION, by William T. De Barey, ed. Columbia University Press, New York 1960. (*2 v. paper*)

SPEAKING OF CHINESE (*a description and cultural history of the complex and fascinating language that unites over 800,000,000 people*) by Raymond Chang. W.W. Norton, New York 1978.

SUNFLOWER SPLENDOR: THREE THOUSAND YEARS OF CHINESE POETRY, by Wu-chi Liu and Irving Yucheng Lo, eds. Indiana University Press, Bloomington 1975.

TAO: THE EASTERN PHILOSOPHY OF TIME AND CHANGE by Philip S. Rawson and Laszlo Legeza. Avon, New York 1973.

THE TIMES ATLAS OF CHINA. Quadrangle/The New York Times Books Co., New York 1974.

TRADITIONAL CHINESE STORIES; THEMES AND VARIATIONS, by Y. W. Ma and Joseph S. M. Lau, eds. Columbia University Press, New York 1978. (*paper*)